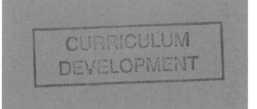

DEVELOPING SUBJECT KNOWLEDGE

PRIMARY ENGLISH

IAN EYRES

Paul Chapman Publishing Ltd
A SAGE Publications Company
6 Bonhill Street
London EC2A 4PU

SAGE Publications Inc
2455 Teller Road
Thousand Oaks, California 91320

SAGE Publications India Pvt Ltd
32, M-Block Market
Greater Kailash - I
New Delhi 110 048

British Library Cataloguing in Publication data

A catalogue record for this book is available from the British Library

ISBN 0 7619 7115 7
ISBN 0 7619 7116 5 (pbk)

Library of Congress catalog card number available

Typeset by Pantek Arts Ltd
Production by Bill Antrobus, Rosemary Campbell and Susie Home
Printed and bound by Cromwell Press, Trowbridge, Wiltshire

Contents

Non - fiction genre.

Preface

The purpose of the Developing Subject Knowledge Series is to provide authoritative distance learning materials on the national requirements for teaching the primary curriculum and achieving Qualified Teacher Status. The series includes key study and audit texts to enable trainees to develop subject knowledge in the three core National Curriculum subjects of English, mathematics and science up to the standard required for achieving QTS as part of an initial teacher training course. Contributors to this series are all primary practitioners who also work in initial teacher training and have experience of preparing materials for distance learning.

Each book in the series draws on material that will be relevant for all trainees following primary ITT courses in higher education institutions, employment based routes, and graduate study routes. Teachers who completed their training before 1997 will also find these texts useful for updating their knowledge. The series will be of interest to an international audience concerned with primary schooling.

Primary English is a comprehensive and essential guide to the structure of English. It draws on the reader's own knowledge and understanding of English as the basis for analysis of texts at word, sentence and whole-text level. The book develops the reader's understanding of the linguistic and literary knowledge required by the National Curriculum at Key Stages 1 and 2 and by the National Literacy Strategy. Key concepts such as Standard English, approaches to grammar, genre, clause structure and the role of phonics in reading are addressed in an interactive way which develops the reader's skills as an active analyst of English, leading to a far deeper understanding than the do's and don'ts of traditional grammar. An in-depth self-assessment activity is included with the text.

Hilary Burgess

Series Editor

Companion books in this series are:

Primary Mathematics by Heather Cooke.

Primary Science by Jane Devereux.

Copyright Acknowledgements

The editors and the publishers wish to thank the following for permission to reprint copyright material.

P. 50 From the DfEE *National Literacy Strategy Training Modules* 4 YR and Y1. Crown copyright.

P. 113 From *3 positive reasons to vote for Susan Kramer*, Liberal Democrat Candidate for Mayor.

P 122 From *The Mouse and His Child*, Russell Hoban, Faber & Faber, 2000. Permission applied for.

p. 141 From *Daddy fell into the pond* by Alfred Noyes, reprinted by permission of The Society of Authors as the Literary Representative of the Estate of Alfred Noyes.

p. 142 From *Sea Fever* by John Masefield, reprinted by permission of The Society of Authors as the Literary Representative of the Estate of John Masefield

p. 144 From *Cargoes* by John Masefield, reprinted by permission of The Society of Authors as the Literary Representative of the Estate of John Masefield.

p. 144 *Haiku* reprinted from *Voices* edited by Geoffrey Summerfield, 1968, Penguin Books. Permission applied for.

p. 148 from *Anthem for Doomed Youth* by Wilfred Owen, reprinted with permission of the Trustee of the Wilfred Owen Estate.

p. 149 *Word* by Stephen Spender, reprinted from *Collected Poems* by Stephen Spender, Faber & Faber Ltd.

p. 149–50 *Mushrooms* by Sylvia Plath, reprinted from *The Colossus* by Sylvia Plath, Faber & Faber.

p. 150 (b) from *Winter Ocean* by John Updike, from *Telephone Poles* and other poems by John Updike. Permission applied for.

p. 150 (c) from *Silver* by Walter de la Mare, from *The Complete Poems of Walter de la Mare*. Reprinted by permission of The Literary Trustees of Walter de la Mare, and the Society of Authors as their representative.

p. 150 (d) from *The Highwayman* by Alfred Noyes, reprinted by permission of The Society of Authors as the Literary Representative of the Estate of Alfred Noyes.

p. 153 Riddle 68 from *The Earliest English Poems*, translated by Michael Alexander (Penguin Classics 1966, Third revised edition 1991) copyright © Michael Alexander, 1966, 1977, 1991.

p. 154 *November Night* by Adelaide Crapsey from *Verse* by Adelaide Crapsey © 1922 by Algernon S Crapsey and renewed 1950 by the Adelaide Crapsey Foundation. Permission applied for.

p. 154 From *On the Ning Nang Nong* by Spike Milligan taken from *I Like This Poem* edited by Kaye Webb (Puffin, 1979) reprinted by permission of Spike Milligan Productions Ltd.

p. 155 *Mid-term break* by Seamus Heaney from *Death of a Naturalist* (1966) Faber & Faber Ltd.

p. 156 *Sonnet* by Mathew Festenstein, reprinted from *Does it Have to Rhyme* ? Sandy Brownjohn, 1980, Hodder & Stoughton Educational. Permission applied for.

p. 173 *ygUDuh* is reprinted from *Complete Poems 1904–1962* by E.E. Cummings, edited by George J. Firmage, by permission of W.W. Norton & Company. Copyright © 1991 by the trustees for the E.E. Cummings Trust and George James Firmage.

Every effort has been made to trace the copyright-holders but if any have been inadvertently overlooked the publishers will be pleased to make the necessary arrangements at the first opportunity.

Acknowledgements

My thanks go to Eve Bearne, Nikki Gamble, Frances Smith and Anne Storey, who made substantial contributions to the text level chapters, and additionally to Frances for contributions to Chapters 1 and 7 and the final assessment, to Nikki for her work on the history of spelling and to Eve for wise counsel throughout the project (often during brief encounters). I am grateful also to Jill Bourne, Liz Grugeon and Claire Richards for their invaluable comments and advice on the typescript. Naturally, responsibility for all errors, omissions and infelicities remains mine.

I should also like to thank Hilary Burgess, Sue Dutton, Jane Devereux and Lavina Porter for essential practical and moral support, June Down for days and days of typing and Hilary, Isobel, Alison and Rosalind for their forbearance and understanding.

Introduction

Your knowledge of English

If you can read this you know a lot about English. You may not think you do, and you may well be reading this book for the very reason that you feel you don't know enough. You might even think that your own English *is not good enough*. Whether you feel like this or not, you obviously want to know more about the English language, so let's start by looking at the kinds of things you know already.

Using your language knowledge	Activity 0.1

Read the following text. What language knowledge do you need to have in order to be able to understand it? Think about:

▷ how you decipher the printed words

▷ how you make sense of sentences

▷ what you know about the 'ingredients' of a story

▷ what you notice about the vocabulary used

▷ how the text makes you use the 'world' knowledge you already have.

> *I first started to act at the age of three. We were a very poor family and it was my mother's idea to have me help out with her many outstanding bills. She wrote the script and directed the action. The cue to begin my performance was a ring at the front door. Grasping my small hand, my mother rushed down the three flights of stairs from our small flat and hid behind the front door as I opened it. The unsuspecting third member of the cast – the rent collector – was standing there as I delivered my first lines: 'Mummy's out.' I said, and slammed the door in his face.*
>
> From *What's it all about?* Michael Caine

Reflection

How is it that you are able to translate some small black marks on a sheet of paper into comprehension and amusement? Obviously a lot is going on.

1. You can recognise individual **letters**. You know all the possible **speech sounds** the letters can represent and know how to put these together into words. Some of the **words** you recognise by sight. You also notice that the **spelling** is correct (or at least you would notice if it wasn't). You know all the **words**, including some which are made from smaller units (e.g. *unsuspecting*). You know that some words carry more than just a straightforward meaning – you will know the convention in this kind of story that the character called the rent collector is more than likely to be an adversary.

2. You recognise that all the **sentences** are correctly formed (or again, at least you would know if they weren't). What you know about **word**

order tells you that *The unsuspecting third member of the cast* and *the rent collector* are the same person. It also tells you that in the sentence that begins *grasping my hand*, it is the author's mother who is doing the grasping, while your knowledge of **pronouns** tells you that the same person wrote the script. A lot of your understanding at this level depends on your ability to recognise words' membership of classes like **noun** and **verb**. Your recognition of the **inflexions** of **tense** is the means by which you know that the story happened in the past.

3. You probably recognise that the **text** follows the conventional pattern of **story**. **Characters** are introduced and the **setting** is sketched in. A **problem** is stated (or at least implied) and a **resolution** reached. How far were you into the text before you realised that it was a story; what were the clues that told you this? You also recognise the **vocabulary** of the theatre (*script, cue, performance* etc.) and your knowledge of the wider world helps you recognise the **irony** of portraying this episode in such grandiose terms. Your knowledge about the author himself will probably influence the way in which you understand the story too. Finally, you recognise that the whole story is written in a kind of language which is known as **Standard English** and you would immediately be able to spot any words or structures which broke the rules of that variety.

You may not have known any of the terminology used in the last three paragraphs, but that doesn't stop you using all this language knowledge, any more than not knowing the anatomical names for the bones in your fingers would stop you from playing the piano.[1] Any user of English knows *implicitly* a bewildering array of rules about all aspects of language. You know how to speak 'correct' English in a way which matches the demands of any context. You notice whenever people use English which is 'incorrect' or inappropriate. So why do you need a book like this?

You may well feel confident of your ability to discuss and explain some of the knowledge indicated in paragraphs 1, 2 and 3 – you have **explicit knowledge** of the sounds associated with letters, for example, and can talk about that knowledge. On the other hand, much of what you know will be in the form of **implicit knowledge**. The next activity will help give you an idea as to how much of your own language knowledge is explicit.

Activity 0.2

1 This section includes a lot of grammatical terminology. The point of it is to illustrate how much you know, even if you don't know what everything is called. Please don't think you have to learn all these words now – all will be explained in due course.

Do you agree that each of these samples of English is in some way incorrect? Can you say *why* each one is incorrect?

1. *He know.*

2. *My father happy.*

3. *Helen and Julia are playing together. Helen is digging and Julia was climbing.*

4. *We are going to swim, dance and athletics.*

5. *This traditional English woodworking tool is called a bnock.*

6. A story begins 'Once upon a time there were three fluffy squirrels...' and ends '..."Take him away officer; Prendergast is the killer."'

Reflection

I would be very surprised if you found any of these completely acceptable, although you could probably guess at the meaning of most of them and also find ways of 'correcting' most of them. But how many of your answers can you explain? How much of the terminology in the following explanations is familiar to you?

1. In Standard English this should be *He knows*. The final *–s* is an **inflexion** needed to mark the **verb** as **third person singular**, **present tense**.

2. This sentence needs a **verb**. You might expect *My father **is** happy*.

3. The verb *was climbing* is in the **past tense** when the rest of the verbs are in the **present tense**.

4. You might say again that the sentence is missing a verb e.g. *do athletics*. Alternatively, you might say that the end of the sentence is a list of words functioning as verbs and *athletics* does not fit the pattern because it is a **noun**.

5. *Bnock* would break the rule of English **phonology** which says that initial /b/ can only be followed by /l/, /r/ or a vowel.[2]

6. The start of this story belongs to the **genre** *Children's story*, while the ending belongs to the genre *Whodunnit*. In this case it is possible that the author intends to use the features of more than one genre, but you will probably agree that you have expectations about how a story beginning 'Once upon a time' is likely to end.

You probably found that you could make explicit your objection to some of these sentences but not all of them. One of the things which makes language study so interesting is that it is the study of ourselves. To discover the rules of the language that we use, we can examine and reflect on our own language behaviour (and language is just that: an extremely complex form of behaviour). As you work through this book, for each topic you will need to think about your own linguistic knowledge and judgements before seeing how that aspect of grammar is conventionally described and explained. In other words, the aim is to help you turn your implicit knowledge into explicit knowledge.

How is this knowledge useful?

You are probably reading this book because at some point in the near or distant future you intend to put the knowledge it contains to use in a primary classroom. If that is the case, then you are entitled to ask how it will be of practical use to you.

There will be elements of subject knowledge which you will want or need to teach explicitly. You will be able to help children develop their writing by looking at different ways of structuring information within a

2   Of course, English is able to accomodate words from other languages (*loan words*) which break these rules, though just as often speakers make adjustments to fit an English pattern. So, for example, some English speakers will pronounce the place name *Brno* as in the original Czech, but many will pronounce a vowel after the 'B' since English does not usually allow this string of three consonants.

text, for example, or you might draw a child's attention to a word's internal structure in order to help them spell it. The Framework of the National Literacy Strategy[3] sets out objectives which can only be taught effectively if they are fully understood by the teacher.

As a teacher of English your overarching objective is to ensure that children use language as effectively as possible. Armed with a sound knowledge of English, teachers are able to understand a child's current stage of language and literacy development and offer appropriate explanations and tasks. It may seem frustrating, for example, when a young child cannot 'hear' all the letters in a word in order to spell it; with a good understanding of how the sound system of English works teachers understand why the child finds the task difficult and also know which aspects of a word to concentrate their teaching on. To a layperson a child's story may simply seem boring or repetitive; a teacher should be able not only to identify the less successful features of the text (maybe restricted vocabulary or over-reliance on a single type of sentence structure) but also to make the child aware of vocabulary and structures which are more sophisticated whilst still within their personal range. One way of doing this is to expose the child to texts which will model these attributes; good subject knowledge enables teachers to identify texts which will support their teaching. A teacher who is sensitive to the forms of language used by children will also be aware of the potential for difference between a child's own language and the language of instruction and therefore the potential for misunderstanding. S/he will, therefore, when teaching, use language structures which are accessible and at the same time conducive to the development of the child's language repertoire.

Through understanding the language of children, the language of texts and the language of the classroom, teachers are able to plan, teach and make assessments more effectively.

Levels of language

If you look back to the discussion of activity 0.1 on page vii, you will notice that it has been organised into three paragraphs according to the size of the language unit referred to. Paragraph 1 deals with words and smaller units. We can call this area of study **word level**. Paragraph 2 is concerned with sentences and the units through which they are structured. This area we can call **sentence level**. Paragraph 3 is concerned with ways of organising whole texts. This area of study is called **text level**. The structure of this book owes much to this classification, with a chapter dedicated to each of word and sentence level and three linked chapters on text level matters.

The three levels correspond loosely to the distinctions made by linguists[4] between **phonology** and **morphology** (word level), **syntax** (sentence level) and **textual studies** (text level). If you are familiar with the workings of the National Literacy Strategy then you will recognise word, sentence and text level as the three organising categories of its Framework. Examining the language one level at a time makes the job of analysis and description simpler, though, of course, in practice elements of each level always occur together.

3   An approach to teaching literacy adopted in 1998 by almost all English primary schools.

4   In this book the term 'linguist' is used in the sense of 'one who studies language' – an academic whose field is linguistics (i.e. the study of language). Linguist is a near synonym of grammarian.

The structure of this book

The first chapter deals with some basic information about language, language study and the English language which will provide a foundation for the detailed study in Chapters 2, 3, 4, 5 and 6. The final chapter draws on material from the preceding chapters to discuss some of the differences between speech and written language and to look a little deeper into the processes of reading and writing.

The order of Chapters 2–6 is a little problematic, for the very reason that although separating levels helps us to see things more clearly by focusing on a chosen theme, explanations are usually impossible without reference to other levels. So, for example, study of an aspect of sentence structure may involve reference to inflexions (word level) or how repeated use of that structure promotes cohesion (text level). In the writing of this book I felt the need to reverse the direction of these chapters more than once, before finally settling on the present order of *word, sentence, text*. The order inevitably means (as any order would) that in the earlier chapters I sometimes need to refer to elements of language which are not properly explained until later. Often this won't matter because the knowledge you already have will see you through. If there is a reference to 'nouns', for example in Chapter 2, then the definition you learnt at school ('the name of a thing') will enable you to understand the point; you won't need to know all the detailed information in the definition on page 75. Throughout the book you will find page references in the margin for any terminology which is not explained within that section of the text. If you are having trouble following an explanation it might help you to go back to pages referred to. If you are working through the book from beginning to end it should not usually be necessary for you to skip forward. If, however, you are using the book for reference or revision then you might well find all the references helpful.

The order of Chapters 2–4 might appear to imply a view that language users begin with the smallest units and work by combining them into ever larger chunks until they finally arrive at a meaningful whole. Such a view is, of course, untenable – when we speak, listen, read or write we operate at all levels simultaneously. Unfortunately, although the human mind is capable of working at all levels at once, books simply aren't.

Using this book

Each chapter of this book contains activities which explore your implicit language knowledge and help you assess the current level of your explicit knowledge. Through reflection and further activities you will then be able to make essential areas of linguistic knowledge explicit. Most activities are discussed fully in the following reflection but in some cases it will be useful for you to compare your responses with 'correct' ones. Where this is the case the activity is marked with a symbol (✔) and you will find the answers on pages 193–204.

You may decide, on the basis of your answers to activities 0.1 and 0.2, that your knowledge of language at one or more levels is sufficient to allow you to skip one or more of Chapters 2–6. If you decide on this course I would advise you to at least skim through the chapter(s) in case elements unfamiliar to you are included. There will probably be some detail which is new to you, and, perhaps more importantly, some of the explanations will probably not be quite what you expect. Be prepared also to return to particular sections after doing the final assessment activity.

In this section we have seen that:

▶ As proficient users of English we have an extensive implicit knowledge of its rules and patterns.

▶ We can increase our understanding of how English works by making our implicit knowledge explicit.

▶ Language can be studied at word, sentence and text levels.

1. Understanding language

This chapter explores some issues of general importance to the study of English.

> **In this chapter we shall see:**
>
> ▸ that language is used for a variety of **purposes**;
>
> ▸ how purpose, information content and factors relating to the audience shape spoken and written **texts**;
>
> ▸ that **grammar** is a term with a number of meanings;
>
> ▸ that there is a difference between **knowing** a language and **knowing about** a language;
>
> ▸ that children's language can illustrate how simple **grammatical rules** work;
>
> ▸ some of the factors involved in language **variation**;
>
> ▸ what is meant by the term **Standard English**.

What is language?

The English language is a subject most of its speakers feel comfortable with at some level, and one on which many feel qualified to express strong views. Behind these views (however strongly held) is the premise that we know what language is. This section begins by asking you to explore what the word 'language' means to you. If you can discuss the following points with friends and family then so much the better.

Using your language knowledge   Activity 1.1

Answer these questions on your own or discuss them with a group:

What is the difference between 'language' and 'a language?'

What is the difference between 'good' and 'bad' language?

What does it mean to 'speak the same language'?

Even if you speak only English, do you speak 'the same language all the time'?

What is language for? (How many different reasons can you think of for using language?)

Do you ever speak with somebody who speaks a 'different English' from you? What (if any) problems does that cause?

Where does language reside – in books? In brains? Somewhere else?

Reflection

I expect you found that this discussion raised many issues that were not easy to resolve. For example:

▶ What uses do you make of language beyond the most obvious one of conveying information from person to person?

▶ What counts as 'English'? To what extent do you speak the same language as Ally McBeal, Ali G, Rab C.Nesbit or E. Nesbit? What criteria do you use to decide?

▶ What counts as 'good English'? Is 'bad' English language that lacks clarity, language that gives offence or simply language that differs from the Standard variety?

▶ How do written and spoken language differ? Some languages are not written and others are no longer spoken – is either kind in any sense 'incomplete'?

This chapter will help you to understand some of the basic features of language in order to underpin your understanding of how English works in practice. Sometimes you may feel the need to question your current views, but the important thing is always to try to understand *why* you hold a particular belief about language or about how it works.

Functions of language

Let us begin by addressing the most basic question of all – what is language for?

Activity 1.2	Exploring your own language

Think about your own use of language – written, spoken, read and heard. You have probably done some of the following things:

telling children to hurry up
listening to the weather forecast
filling in a form
chatting to friends
writing a shopping list
reading a novel/biography/poem . . .
phoning the local cinema
sending an email to a friend.

Make a list of some 'language events' you have been involved in over the last few days.

When you have a list of 10–20 items, try and put them into groups according to their purpose (e.g. 'reading a novel' and 'listening to a radio play' might both be examples of language being used for entertainment, or you may have examples of giving instructions or 'getting what you want').

Reflection

Some of your examples, whether they be written or spoken, will have the function of gaining or giving ideas or information, some will be just for yourself, expressing feelings, recording events, acting as reminders, while some will be for others. Some may have very little information content (How are you? Fine, thanks, and you?) but have the important function of relating to friends, family or neighbours. Some examples may serve to control (or attempt to control) the behaviour of others, perhaps enabling you to get what you want.

Even the very youngest child begins to exercise some of these functions. When babies first cry they may simply be expressing the discomfort they feel at being hungry or alone. As any parent knows, however, sooner or later (usually sooner) they learn that the cry is a means for getting their needs met.

The linguist Michael Halliday (whose work has had a significant influence on how English is taught in schools) identified six main ways in which language was used by his own young child. His list comprised:

▶ using language to obtain something

▶ controlling the behaviour of others

▶ interacting with others

▶ expressing personal feelings

▶ finding out

▶ using language for imaginative purposes.[5]

Interestingly, he found that the function of giving information develops at a later stage than the functions listed above.

All these functions are, of course, evident in adult use. Some of them relate more to content, ideas and information, and the real world; in Halliday's terms these highlight **ideational**[6] meaning. Others are more concerned with the language user's interactions with others and with the establishment and maintenance of relations with other people; they tend to emphasise **interpersonal** meaning.

Exploring your own language   Activity 1.3

Go back to your list of language acts in activity 1.2. How are interpersonal and ideational meaning combined in each? Are there any which are purely interpersonal or purely ideational?

Reflection

Purely interpersonal acts would include things like greetings, while reading a bank statement would be a purely ideational activity (though you might say that in some cases the bank had the interpersonal aim of changing your behaviour!). Most language acts would, however, fall

5   Halliday, M. A. K. (1975) *Learning How to Mean*, London Edward Arnold.

6   Halliday M. A. K. (1985) *An Introduction to Functional Grammar*, London, Edward Arnold.

---

somewhere in between. Even when we write a note to cancel the milk we choose a style appropriate to the recipient; in a similar way, teachers and lecturers marking students' work have to perform a balancing act between conveying accurate information and paying heed to interpersonal factors affecting motivation.

If you think about what you actually say or write in each context you will find sometimes that particular words and structures are associated with particular purposes. Obvious examples of this are special words used only for greetings (e.g. 'Hello'), the language of 'finding out' being full of question structures and commands being used to control the behaviour of others. In Chapter 4 you will see how the purpose of a piece of writing can be an important factor in its structure and in the writer's choice of words. In this sense, language functions are the foundation of written *genres*.

You will also see (in Chapter 3) that the term 'function' is applied to lower level units (words, phrases) as well as to whole texts and utterances.

In this section we have seen that:

▶ Using language has many functions; far more than just transmitting and receiving information.

▶ Using language may convey meaning in terms of information or interpersonal meaning; usually it conveys both.

▶ Both the purpose and content of a piece of writing or speech can influence its structure.

Grammar: the rules of language

If you were asked what the meaningful units of language were called you would probably say 'words'. Look at the words in the following sentences:

Bill hit Bob

Bob hit Bill

Do the words mean the same thing in each sentence? Do the two sentences mean the same thing? Obviously the answer to the first question is 'yes' and the second 'no'. It follows then that the order in which the words occur has a bearing on the meaning of a sentence. The fact that we can interpret the two sentences correctly shows that we know something about word order which allows us to access that meaning. Knowing a language means more than knowing the words of a language; we need also to know how to put words together in a way which is both predictable and meaningful. The rules which govern how elements of language are put together are known as the **grammar** of the language.

Although this definition appears straightforward the term is used with a range of related but distinct meanings.

Traditional grammar

The origins of traditional grammar teaching lie in the application of the forms of Latin grammar to English. A combination of the facts that English is grammatically quite different from Latin and that only the most formal and literary varieties of English were chosen for study meant that for most students traditional grammar was a pursuit with little or no relevance to their own use of English. Do you say:

It was me

or

It was I?

The traditional grammarian would be in no doubt, since the correct form in Latin would be the latter, even though most speakers would say the former and probably find the form 'It was I' affected and artificial.

Traditional grammars usually have a view on what is 'correct' usage and in this they represent a kind of **prescriptive grammar**.

Prescriptive grammar

As its name suggests, this form of grammar prescribes what it is permissible to say or write. Like traditional grammars, prescriptive grammars assume that there is a model of 'correct' English and their rules preclude the use of other (e.g. regional) forms. In fact, the rules of prescriptive grammars tend on the whole to *pro*scribe 'incorrect' forms. You quite probably learnt at least some prescriptive rules of grammar when you were at school; for example, the rule which requires:

John and I went...

in preference to:

Me and John went...

Prescriptive grammars do not have to be based on archaic or artificial language forms. Nowadays they are usually based on **Standard English**,[7] a variety familiar to most speakers. There is, however, still an assumption that one variety is superior to all others, a notion we shall look at a little more closely later in this chapter.

Descriptive grammar

This kind of grammar starts from the facts of a sample of language (maybe all the sentences of a variety such as 'Standard English' or 'Liverpool English') and tries to account for them by means of a comprehensive set of rules. A descriptive approach may be taken to any variety of a language, including regional and social dialects and the developing language of young children.

A descriptive grammar of Standard English would have much in common with a prescriptive grammar in terms of its rules, but there would be

7   Standard English is examined in detail a little later in this chapter. For now a working definition of Standard English as 'the language of Radio 4 news' or even 'the language of this book' will be adequate.

important differences. Whereas a prescriptive grammar would describe a word or structure as 'correct' or 'incorrect', a descriptive grammar makes no such value judgements, simply stating whether a form belongs to the variety or not. The goal of descriptive grammars is to account for as much of the language variety as possible, whilst the tendency of prescriptive grammars is to concentrate on areas of the language which are in some way contentious and where a ruling is felt to be necessary. In practice a descriptive grammar may be used in a prescriptive way; for example, in foreign language textbooks.

Grammar and the speaker

At the beginning of this section I said that grammar was something which speakers of a language need to know. There are actually two distinct kinds of grammatical knowledge. First there is *implicit knowledge*. This enables us, without reflection, to form sentences which our fellow speakers recognise as grammatical (i.e. which conform to the rules of our grammar). It also allows us to identify 'sentences' which are not grammatical. In addition to our implicit knowledge, we may also have an *explicit knowledge*. If so, then when we hear an ungrammatical sentence we are able to describe the 'errors' and state which rules have been broken, probably with the use of technical terminology. The first kind of knowledge is acquired in the natural process of learning to speak; the second kind implies explicit teaching.

Activity 1.4	Using your implicit language knowledge

Which of the following sentences do you consider to be 'correct'? Explain your reasons; how much grammatical terminology do you need to use?

(a) John and I went to the shops.

(b) Me and John went to the shops.

(c) He came back with sweets for Helen and me.

(d) He came back with sweets for Helen and I.

Reflection

(a) and (c) are the 'correct' Standard English. If you could state that much then you have an implicit knowledge of (at least this part of) Standard English.

You may be able to explain your judgement by checking what the sentence sounds like without the 'extra' word.

(a) I went to the shops.

(b) *Me[8] went to the shops.

(c) He came back with sweets for me.

(d) *He came back with sweets for I.

8 In this and later examples I use the convention of marking ungrammatical items with a star*.

It is now immediately obvious that the starred sentences are not 'grammatical'.

Notice that *word* is a technical term which helps you talk about language (all such terminology is known as *metalanguage*). You don't need to know the word *word* in order to speak and your use of it would be evidence of some explicit language knowledge. If you knew that the extra word was called a *noun* or that *pronouns* functioning as *subjects* have different forms from those functioning as objects then your explicit knowledge is all the greater.

As implicit language knowledge is the foundation upon which more explicit linguistic awareness is built, many of the activities in this book will ask you to use your own implicit language knowledge (sometimes known as **linguistic intuition**) as a first stage of examining aspects of English grammar. I hope you will be able to shed any preconceptions of grammar that involve rote learning of rules and see yourself rather as an active investigator of the forms of language, with your own linguistic knowledge and intuition being your richest source of evidence. This brings me to another meaning of the word grammar.

Grammar as psychological structures

All our definitions of the term grammar have so far referred to written descriptions of language patterns. However, the term can be applied to those structures within the mind of a speaker which allow the formation and recognition of acceptable sentences. Some forms of descriptive grammar have the description of these psychological rules as their goal and the term 'grammar' is often used ambiguously to refer to both the rules in the speaker's mind and the same rules written down. There is plenty of evidence that these psychological grammars are real; how else can the consistency of language forms be explained? It also seems to be the case that our personal grammars are far more complex than any 'explicit' grammar yet written. Every speaker has to learn the forms of their native language anew and one consequence of this is that the grammars of no two speakers will be exactly alike. We each have a personal grammar.

Using your implicit language knowledge	Activity 1.5

Which of these sentences do you consider to be 'correct'? Can you explain why you find certain sentences unacceptable? Are there any you are uncertain about? Can you explain why? Are there any which you might say yourself, even if you consider them to be incorrect? Which kind of grammatical knowledge are you applying when you judge these sentences?

My aunt has measles.   *Eat this with a left-handed bus.*

If I'd have known that he'd still be alive.   *This is the world we live in.*

From whom is that letter?

I didn't do nothing.

My aunt bucket measles.

Who is that letter from?

That's the man who I saw yesterday.

He climbed out of the window.

He got off of the bus.

When you have done this activity for yourself, ask a friend to do it and share your conclusions – do you agree in every case?

Reflection

The list includes some sentences which most speakers of English would be happy with. One sentence is definitely grammatical but makes no sense, while one clearly does not follow the basic rules of sentence structure. At least one follows a pattern used in many non-Standard varieties and so is grammatical within that variety. Others you might feel are condemned by prescriptive grammar even though you feel comfortable saying them. Remember in such cases that usage changes over time and that even if you remember rules about 'who' and 'whom' and about prepositions at the end of sentences, the fact that almost everybody says *Who is it from?* is an important consideration.

You probably found that if you did this activity with a friend, even if you feel you speak the same variety of English, you did not agree on every point. This illustrates the fact that we all develop our own individual form of English (and explains why so many disputes arise over 'correctness').

In this section we have seen that:

- Traditional and prescriptive grammars are principally concerned with supporting a particular (Standard) variety of the language.

- Descriptive grammar tries to view language objectively and to explain all its forms and often the judgements of native speakers too.

- All speakers possess their own grammar and employ grammatical rules automatically.

- For every utterance which you know implicitly to be grammatical there is an underlying linguistic structure which is susceptible to analysis and description.

Child language: developing rules

The language of children is fascinating to study in its own right, but it is also able to teach us two important lessons about mature language:

- Language is rule governed.

- Communication does not depend on speakers sharing identical grammars.

One-word utterances – starting to speak

If you have children of your own, or have known a young child very well, try to remember their very first words.

▶ What were they?

▶ What kinds of words were they?

▶ How did you or their parents help them to communicate and learn?

If you don't have children, try to discuss this with someone who has.

Reflection

If you have had children of your own, you will remember some of their early speech. First words are often of the Mama or Dada kind and tend to be 'content' words such as the names of objects or actions or important adjectives like 'big'. An interesting feature of early vocabulary development is the way children often overextend the references of words. 'Doggy', for example, may be used to refer to any four-legged creature. As children become more experienced, they find that they have to distinguish by size and other properties as well as 'leggedness' to understand, say, 'elephant', 'cow' or 'mouse'.

For a time children utter only one word at a time, but their intonation, expressions, gestures and the context all combine to create richer meanings. For example, the single word 'Daddy' might mean:

That's my daddy'

'Where is daddy?'

'I'm very angry with you, Daddy'

'I want some more milk'

'Come here, Daddy'

You can probably think of many other possible meanings. The role of context in communicating through speech (even among adults) should not be underestimated; the lack of a supporting context is one of the significant differences between speech and writing and something which young children often find difficult to understand. With young speakers, adults go to great lengths to understand what they are saying and often give considerable support to their developing language.

Two-word utterances – early syntax

Most children go through a stage where they mostly speak in two-word 'sentences' like 'more milk' and 'Mummy gone'. It is possible to describe this stage in terms of some very simple grammatical rules.

The following is a set of words which might be used by a child at the two-word stage. Use your knowledge of children's language to suggest some possible combinations – are there any combinations which, in your opinion, would not be possible?

milk	shoes	car	Daddy	more	hat
eat	down	off	on	up	ball
biscuit	gone				

Reflection

It would not be possible to make sentences which are well-formed in terms of mature grammatical rules. However, you probably came up with recognisable immature structures such as:

Car gone

More biscuit

Hat on

Shoes off

You would probably also feel that strings like:

Car biscuit

Eat off

Off up

are not acceptable.

One possible analysis of this data leads to the development of what has been called a 'pivot grammar'. In this model, all words are members of either an 'open class' consisting mostly of the kind of words used at the one-word stage or of a smaller 'pivot' class of words which give additional information.[9] The pivot class is relatively 'closed' as it admits new members only rarely whilst the open class is able to grow rapidly.

The words above would probably break down as follows

pivot	open
down	milk
up	shoes
off	ball
gone	biscuit
eat	hat
on	car
more	Daddy

9   The terms 'pivot' and 'open' originate in: Braine, M. A. S., 'The autogeny of ontogeny English phrase structure: The first phase' in *Language* 1963, 39, 1–13. Later work showed the principle to be problematic, but this form of grammar serves us well as a simple example of how grammatical rules operate.

A grammatical rule:

$$S = \begin{Bmatrix} P + O \\ O + P \end{Bmatrix}$$

allows for Sentences to consist of a Pivot and an Open word in any order.

The rule also excludes sentences like:

eat gone (P+P)

and

ball hat (O+O)

We have then a fully functioning grammar to account for acceptable and unacceptable sentences at this stage of development.

Pivot grammar offers a simple example of how language operates by applying rules to classes of words. In Chapter 3 you will see examples of more complex rules of adult grammars which nonetheless work according to the same principles.

Overgeneralisation – more evidence for rule-making

Developing word structures give further evidence that children are not simply mimicking the language they hear around them but making their own rules. In English, most verbs form their past tense by adding '-ed'. A few common verbs like run/ran, bring/brought, sing/sang have irregular past tense forms and children seem to have no difficulty in learning these at an early stage. However, at a time when these forms seem well established something interesting happens; children who had been saying 'I ran' and 'I brought' start to say 'I runned' and 'I bringed'. It seems that when they have learnt sufficient regular forms to enable them to deduce the 'add -ed' rule they apply it to all verbs. Only later do they learn to limit its application to a particular set of verbs.

Developing to maturity

Children continue to develop the complexity of their sentence structure and begin to link clauses, especially with 'and'. The development of an understanding of jokes shows a growing understanding of the richness of word meanings and can be related to an understanding of devices like metaphors.

Throughout this process of developing spoken language, children are active makers of meaning, trying to make sense of the language that surrounds them, searching for rules and order.

We must not forget that as well as learning how to structure what they say, children are also learning the social rules which help them match their remarks to different contexts.

Standard English

We have just seen how young children employ a non-Standard version of English as they develop towards more mature language forms. As a reader of this book you are obviously a competent user of **Standard English**, though you may use another variety too.

Varieties of language

The notion of 'the English language' is quite a complex one. Is there only one 'correct' form of English? Or is English the sum of all the ways of speaking and writing used within 'the English speaking world?' It is a very rare person who speaks only one kind of English.

Non-Standard varieties

Non-Standard forms usually reveal the regional or social origins of a speaker. Regional varieties of English are often known as **dialects**. They may be characterised by certain grammatical patterns (e.g. *He do.*) or by particular words (e.g. some forms of Scottish English have *greet* (to cry), *forkie* (earwig) and *breeks* (trousers)). Members of different social classes similarly use distinctive words and grammatical forms, though it is interesting to note that usually only those employed by 'lower' social classes are considered to be non-Standard. (Linguists often also refer to social varieties as *dialects*.) Sometimes speakers choose to distance themselves from the constraints (and social implications) of Standard English by adopting highly informal language forms.

Variation according to context: register

The discussion so far has been of variation which occurs because of differences between speakers' social and geographical origins. Whatever variety we habitually speak, Standard or non-Standard, we also make changes in the way we use grammar and vocabulary according to the context in which we find ourselves. We might leave home in the morning with a hurried *bye* but begin the working day with *Good morning*.

Think about how you would use language

(a)   to book a trip to Disneyland over the telephone

(b)   to tell a nine-year-old that you are taking them to Disneyland.

How would your language differ?

Reflection

Your language with the child is likely to include words (*great, wow*) and structures (*Guess what, What do you think?*) which you would be unlikely to use in your exchange with the travel agent, where you would use a more measured style, beginning with 'complete' questions and tentative statements. (*I'm interested in booking... . Can you tell me what's available please?*) You would be likely to use words (*departure, accommodation*) you would not contemplate using with the child.

The more formal the context, the more formal our language becomes. Each context is associated with a particular language **register**. This term can also be used to apply to special language varieties which are used in very specific contexts; legal English and the language of sailing are two examples of specific registers.

Accent

It is important to make clear the distinction between a language **variety** (or **dialect**) and an **accent**. Accent involves features of pronunciation only. You may feel that a sentence like

'E's got 'is 'at on 'is 'ead.

is an example of non-Standard English, but it is only non-Standard in terms of its pronunciation. Its words follow the patterns of Standard English. Many people (probably the majority) speak Standard English with a non-Standard accent. Non-Standard varieties differ from Standard because of differences of vocabulary and rules of grammar (though usually, they are spoken with a distinctive accent as well).

Being able to judge whether another speaker shares our language variety is another aspect of our linguistic intuition.

Which of these sentences do you consider to be Standard English and which non-Standard? Explain your judgements.

I stowed the bent fender in the   He's frit.
trunk of the car.

He's gotten down from his horse.   *I didn't eat nothing.*

I wouldn't do that if I was single.   *I wouldn't do that if I was you.*

Do you want that I should do that?   *He ate nowt.*

I demand that he do as I say.   *He do go on sometimes.*

Reflection

This task probably seemed easy at first; you could just tell which sentences did not 'feel right'. You can justify many of your decisions on grounds of vocabulary and word structure (*nowt, frit*) and others by reference to grammar (*He do go on*). There are probably some sentences you are not sure of. Is 'If I was single' wrong? Is 'fender' non-Standard?

Is there more than one Standard English? Some of these sentences would be more acceptable in the USA than they are in the UK, for example.

How then do you and the people you know define Standard English?

Activity 1.10	Investigating language use

Jot down your own ideas about what counts as Standard English. Then try to get the views of your friends and family. Are there any common threads in the responses you get? Is Standard English seen as the same as good English by most people, for example? Is it seen as the English of certain people and not others?

Reflection

You may get definitions such as 'good English', 'grammatical English', 'posh English' and 'speaking properly'. We all have a general idea of what is meant by the term, but a little reflection tells us that some of these definitions are questionable or at least incomplete.

There are two ways of defining Standard English. The first involves describing features which make it different from non-Standard varieties. (Theoretically it could be defined by listing all its rules and vocabulary, but in practice linguists are a very long way from being able to do this.) These features would include the inclusion and exclusion of particular words (standard dictionaries do this for us) and particular rules of grammar and word structure (publishers have style manuals partly for this purpose). So we can say that:

He never run down the snicket 'cause he was frit.

is non-Standard because:

▶ it uses a non-Standard word (snicket)

▶ it uses non-Standard past tense forms (run, frit)

▶ it uses a non-Standard grammatical structure ('he never' rather than 'he didn't').

The second way of defining Standard English is by reference to those who speak and write it or the context in which it is spoken or written. Gone are the days when the touchstone of Standard English is that variety spoken by members of the Royal Family ('the Queen's English') but you can probably identify certain groups that you would associate with the use of Standard English (newsreaders, teachers, telephone operators, politicians perhaps).

The National Literacy Strategy chooses to base its definition on formal features (a few of which are explicitly stated), context and purpose and the contrast with non-Standard varieties.

Using your language knowledge   Activity 1.11

The following is the definition of Standard English applied to education in English state schools. How far do you find it useful? Would it help you distinguish Standard from non-Standard varieties? Would it help a non-native speaker?

the language of public communication, distinguished from other forms of English by its vocabulary and by rules and conventions of grammar, spelling and punctuation. [It] contrasts with dialect, or archaic forms or those pertaining to other forms of English, such as American/Australian English.

Reflection

You would probably agree that this goes some way to defining the Standard form but has problems at the level of detail. Is all public communication conducted in Standard English? Which vocabulary items are non-Standard? It also, interestingly, dismisses US English as non-Standard. Because of its lack of precision it seems to be a definition for people who already know what Standard English is.

This fits well with a situation where most 'educated' people, whilst being unable to offer a satisfactory definition, nonetheless behave as if they know exactly what the term refers to.

Is Standard English better than other varieties?

The fact that Standard English is hard to define does not, of course, mean that there is no such thing, or that learning to speak and write it does not have its advantages. There has been much controversy over assertions that different varieties (including Standard English) are of 'equal value', much of this debate in the context of education. It will be useful here, therefore, to examine the claim on linguistic, communicative, social and educational grounds.

Linguistic arguments

Each variety of English has its own full set of rules and vocabulary. All speakers develop their language use to meet their own purposes fully. There is no linguistic reason why 'nothing' is better than 'nowt', 'frit' better than 'frightened' or 'snicket' better than 'alley' any more than 'mouton' is a better word than 'sheep'. All these words work perfectly well for different people in different places.

Sometimes non-Standard grammar is dismissed as 'illogical', with the case of double negatives (e.g. *I didn't do nothing* 'really means' *I did do something*) often used as evidence. But are double negatives inherently wrong? In French the position is reversed:

Standard French

Je	*ne*	*fais*	*rien.*
I	not	do	nothing.

Non-Standard French

Je	*fais*	*rien.*
I	do	nothing.

The fact is that languages are not logical systems. Structures are often discontinuous and repetitive and we usually rely on context, shared understandings and an agreement to use the same structures in order to support communication. This is not to say that 'I didn't do nothing' does not sometimes lead to misunderstanding (especially in writing), but the misunderstanding is more likely to be due to the fact that the listener (or reader) is using a different variety from the speaker (or writer), than to any inherent weakness in the grammar itself.

One tenable linguistic argument for the superiority of the Standard form rests in the sheer size of its vocabulary, though it is also true that this vocabulary is accessible to non-Standard speakers should they require it and that for most of the time Standard speakers only use a small core of the huge vocabulary which is listed in a large dictionary.

Communicative arguments

It is obviously easier to communicate with people who speak the same variety, though the case can be overstated. There may be subtle differences between two apparently identical varieties, whilst the effect of apparently large differences can be minimal once accommodated to by the listener. The fact that 'natural' language is rarely unambiguous is illustrated well by the case of legal English, whose convoluted forms are designed to avoid ambiguity at all costs. However, in the area of writing, where clarity is not supported by gesture, facial expression, intonation, context and so on, agreeing on a single variety has obvious value in at least reducing the scope for misunderstanding. How often do you say something that you would not write? Writing is overwhelmingly done in Standard English.

Social arguments

Standard English is generally accepted as the language of power and prestige. Not to be able to write, speak and understand Standard English is to be disadvantaged and disempowered. Standard English is the language of the educationally, the politically and the financially advantaged. It is certainly the case that there are contexts in which people are judged by the way they speak and write (e.g. when applying for jobs). Effective users of English do not necessarily speak Standard English all the time but they do so when appropriate and the power to judge when it is appropriate is itself an important sociolinguistic skill.

Educational arguments

For the social and communicative reasons already advanced it is clearly important that children learn Standard English at school. Beyond a certain level the development of literacy and the development of spoken forms go hand in hand, and written English is almost exclusively Standard English. This is not to say that non-Standard varieties should be suppressed or discouraged within schools. Children's home language is very important to them personally – to tell a child their language is 'wrong' is to set up a conflict between home and school which school may well lose. Most non-Standard varieties differ from Standard English in relatively minor ways and it is perfectly possible to build the development of written and Standard English on the foundation of a child's home language.

In everyday usage, non-Standard varieties are often known as **dialects**. To a linguist the term dialect refers to the language variety of a particular social or regional group which can be defined by its grammar and vocabulary. Thus Standard English is one among many English dialects: the one which happens to enjoy the highest social and political prestige. However, even in the linguistic literature the term dialect is regularly used to refer to non-Standard, often regionally defined varieties.

Redundancy

The sentence 'I didn't do nothing' does illustrate one feature of language very nicely: that of **redundancy**. If we say something twice in a sentence then one of the instances is unnecessary in terms of information. Note that this judgement is not one of value. The French example demonstrates how a construction containing redundancy can be considered 'good' use of language. Consider the following sentence (which is a real example and an answer to the question 'who (out of a man and a woman) cut your hair?'):

'I don't know *her* name, but *she* was a woman.'

The question is answered twice (in the underlined words) before the explicit statement of the answer.

A sentence like this is perfectly acceptable and it would seem odd if we were to try to avoid redundancy of this kind. Another example is found in

English spelling. The presence of 'u' after the letter 'q' is (with the exception of a few loan words) absolutely predictable. If the decision were taken to replace 'qu' with 'q' (and write *qen*, *qiet* etc.) there would be no loss of information and no confusion. The 'u' is redundant, but English is happy to accommodate it. There are very many examples of redundancy in the grammar of Standard English at all levels. Natural languages do not function like computer languages, where each piece of information is expressed explicitly and once only. Language has evolved to suit its various purposes and does not need to be maximally economical or efficient. It simply has to follow the conventional patterns that speakers expect.

This may have seemed like a lengthy digression, but it is made because the question of redundancy will occur more than once in the chapters which follow.

In this section we have seen that:

- Standard English is one of a number of varieties of English, each of which has its own rules and vocabulary.

- Variation may be due to social and regional factors (dialect) or governed by context (register).

- Varieties overlap considerably and the differences between Standard and non-Standard varieties can be exaggerated.

- There are social and educational advantages resulting from mastery of Standard English.

- Learning to read and write is largely a matter of learning to read and write Standard English.

- Suppressing non-Standard varieties does not in itself foster the development of Standard varieties.

- Redundancy is a normal feature of natural languages and occurs in Standard and non-Standard varieties alike.

2. Understanding English at word level

This chapter is concerned with the word and units of analysis smaller than the word.

Several systems of written and spoken language come together at word level and this chapter, therefore, has a number of distinct but linked sections.

In this chapter we shall see:

▷ how **words** carry meanings of different kinds;

▷ how the sounds of English are formed and how they work together as a system known as English **phonology**;

▷ how phonology is represented by the English **alphabetic writing system** and why this is not such a straightforward process as it might appear;

▷ how English spelling is (despite appearances and popular opinion) consistent and systematic in ways which may not be immediately obvious;

▷ how English **spelling** reflects not only the sounds of the language but some aspects of **grammar**, **regional variation** and **history**;

▷ how words can be constructed from smaller meaningful and grammatical units according to the rules of **morphology**

It is at this level that the power of language to represent meaning (the semantic level of language) with a small stock of speech sounds (the **phonological** level) is most easily visible.

Words

In Chapter 1, the example of pivot grammar showed how we can view grammar as a set of rules for arranging basic units. Within this model, words play the part of the basic building blocks of language. In fact the status of the word as a fundamental unit has not gone unchallenged, with some linguists arguing that the rules of both word and sentence structure operate on smaller meaningful units. It is certainly the case that in speech the concept of 'word' is more problematic than in writing – there is nothing in spoken language which corresponds to the spaces which demarcate words in writing, for example.

This is not to say, however, that there is no such thing as a spoken word and you will see later in this chapter how some morphological processes can only be explained by reference to words.

Words and meaning

One of the most powerful properties of the human mind is the ability to use **symbols** to represent and comprehend the world. Using symbols enables us to think outside an immediate context, and to imagine how things might be. Words are the symbols at the heart of the complex symbolic system we call language, and as such they are capable of representing the whole range of abstract and concrete concepts accessible to human thought. Words are identifiable strings of speech sounds which carry meaning and which can be put together in a way which makes new meanings.

Aside from a few onomatopoeias (e.g. splash) and semi-onomatopoeias (murmur, stutter) the form of words is arbitrary; there is no inescapable link between the particular sound of a word and the thing it refers to. The sound 'dog', for example, does not represent a domestic quadruped except in as far as the speakers of English agree that it does. Speakers of French agree to use the word *chien* and speakers of Swahili *mbwa*. The process by which words represent meanings is called **reference**.

Onomatopoeia p. 146

The foregoing suggests a perfect symmetry between a set of mental concepts and a set of words to represent them. This is not, however, the case. First of all, some word sounds refer to more than one thing. The sound of the word spelt *so* can also represent an act of needlework (*sew*) or the planting of seeds (*sow*). Words which sound the same but have different meanings are called **homophones**. Conversely there are **synonyms**: words which sound different but refer to the same thing.

Activity 2.1	Using your language knowledge

How many words can you think of which mean *animal*? Do they all mean exactly the same thing?

Reflection

Your list probably includes most of *creature, beast, brute, critter, being. Critter* differs from the others in register and/or dialect, but the remaining four (plus the original word *animal*) could be ranked according to the degree to which they convey a positive view of the concept *animal*.

Register p. 12
Dialect p. 12

positive				**negative**
creature	*animal*	*being*	*beast*	*brute*

You may not agree with this ranking but you probably agree that such ranking is possible and it is possible because words carry a second kind of meaning known as connotative meaning. **Connotative** meanings are concerned with the **associations** words carry.

Reference and connotation

Referential meaning is as close as we come to an objective representation of a concept. If anybody talks about a *house*, listeners are likely to agree that a certain type of building of a certain size with a certain purpose is the intended meaning. (There will be some dispute about marginal cases, even with a word like this, but the agreement will be overwhelming.) On the other hand, some words are more likely to carry connotations for the speaker and listener. If someone tells you 'It was like being at school' you may interpret this as meaning the event referred to was stimulating, exciting and fun, led by knowledgeable and caring people; it may alternatively mean that participants were treated in a disrespectful and authoritarian way as they endured hours of boredom. It depends on your personal experience of school. Advertisers and politicians make great use of connotative meaning. The phrase *the white heat of technology* skilfully used the implied meanings of *purity* and *intensity* (*white*), *energy* (*heat*) and advances which make life easier (*technology*). *Technology* (in 1964 at least) implied a clean application of scientific knowledge which *engineering* and *industry* (which for many would evoke grease, big spanners and boiler suits) would not. The word *new* and its near synonyms *young, fresh, original, novel, innovative, latest* seem to have nothing but positive connotations; when they want to tell us about something *old* advertisers usually prefer terms like *pre-owned, traditional* and *classic*.

Using your implicit language knowledge   Activity 2.2

What connotations do the following words have for you? Do you think all speakers of English would agree with you? Do some words have both positive and negative connotations?

work	*survival*	*controlled*	*sofa*
management	*rain*	*storm*	*bread*

Reflection

Your response to this will have been a personal one. Is *survival* about triumph over adversity, for example, or about grimly getting by? Is *management* something you do to keep your life in order, or something frustrating that is done to you? Is *bread* an essential form of nourishment or the most boring form of food you know? Maybe *sofa* is the only word here which has positive connotations for everybody.

Register and dialect

Another non-referential aspect of meaning is provided by the effect of **register** and **dialect**. Whether a speaker says *telephone*, '*phone*, *blower* or *dog* (*and bone*) the reference is to the same object (or class of objects). However, the choice of word conveys additional information about the speaker and the constraints of the context.

Semantic features

The study of meaning is called **semantics**. One way of understanding how meaning operates within words is to try to analyse the meaning into simpler semantic components. For example, the word *girl* contains elements meaning *human*, *female*, *young*. We can represent this as

Girl ➤   +human
                   +female
                   +young

Each of these is a **semantic component**. Componential analysis deals quite neatly with the question of **antonyms**. English has many pairs of words which we consider to be 'opposites'.

man ~ woman
wet ~ dry
wide ~ narrow
dog ~ bitch

Antonyms are words which differ by a single feature; the antonym of girl is not something which is

     – human
     – female
     – young

(an old male animal?)

but something which is

     + human
     – female
     + young

(a boy)

or possibly something which is

     + human
     + female
     – young

(a woman)

Componential analysis can also account for near synonyms. The sentences

He walked aimlessly and clumsily along.

and

He shambled along.

mean more or less the same thing. We can analyse the meaning of the verb *shamble* then as

     + walk
     + aimless
     + clumsy

Writing can often be made more precise and effective if we find ways to use words which are semantically richer. The art of the poet often rests on the ability to compress meaning into few words, for example. On the other hand, clarity sometimes depends on disentangling components which might be less well expressed when 'packaged' in a single word.

Content words and grammatical words

Having just looked at the possibility of words being semantically rich I want now to consider words which appear to carry no information at all.

Consider the words in bold type in these sentences:

*I am going **to** eat it.*
***In** going there she admitted defeat.*
*Sheila ate **some** beans*

What do they add to the meaning of each sentence? They are there because they make the grammar of the sentence work. Grammatical words like this are often described as the glue or mortar which holds the meaning-rich **content words** or **lexical words** together.[10]

In this section we have seen that:

▶ Words are visible or audible **symbols** which carry meaning.

▶ Meaning may be **referential** or **connotative**.

▶ The meaning of some words may be analysed in terms of **semantic components**.

▶ Some words carry only **grammatical meaning**.

Analysing words

In both speech and writing, words can be broken down into smaller units. Consider the following ways of analysing the word 'brotherhoods':

(a)   b/r/o/t/h/e/r/h/o/o/d/s

(b)   b/r/o/th/er/h/oo/d/s

(c)   bro/ther/hoods

(d)   brother/hood/s

In example (a) the written word is simply broken down into its component **letters**. Example (b) attempts to show how the word can be broken down into distinct **speech sounds**, while in example (c) the word is broken into **syllables**. In isolation, none of these units carries a meaning of its own; the presence of the letter 'b' in the words *brotherhood* and *by*, for example, implies no common element of meaning, whilst the syllable *hood* has a different meaning from the same syllable used as a word in its own right (to mean 'a covering for the head').

Phonemes p. 36

10 *Content word* is probably a better term as the word *lexical* is also used to refer to words in general: the **lexis** of the language.

Example (d), on the other hand, breaks the word into the smallest elements which convey meaning. These elements are known as **morphemes**.

Word level study is often subdivided into:

▶ The level of whole words and smaller meaningful units known as the **morphological level**.

▶ The level of speech sounds, known as the **phonological level**. In writing the analogous level, based on individual letters, is known as the **graphological level**.

We will look at the morphological level in some detail at the end of this chapter but before that it will be useful to examine first the sound system of English and then the way in which our alphabetic writing system operates.

Phonology

This section examines the **phonology** of English – its sound system. It then goes on to describe how our alphabetic writing system makes use of it in representing the language for readers.

Just like the term 'grammar', the term 'phonology' is applied both to the internal rules of the system and to the means of describing it. The phonology of English can be described in terms of a set of units (usually **phonemes**) and the rules for putting them together to form larger units such as syllables and words. Phoneme is a term with a more complex meaning than is usually assumed, so until we arrive at a working definition for the term I will refer rather to sound **segments**, even though the notion that the stream of language can be cut into recognisable segments is itself not without problems.

Phonemes p. 36

Basing an outline of English phonology on readers' own language is a more or less impossible thing to do. English pronunciation varies very noticeably from country to country and from region to region. It also varies from individual to individual. Faced with the choice between offering numerous alternative activities and annotating each activity according to possible variations I intend to take a third course by basing all activities on a single accent. This will be the kind of pronunciation known as Received Pronunciation (RP), the accent usually associated with the speech of members of the 'highest' social classes. The origins of RP lie in the south east of England, but RP speakers can come from any part of Britain and very many people from the south east do not speak RP. It may be that you think of this accent as 'BBC English'. Although RP may well not be your own accent, many of its features will probably coincide broadly with your own usage, and where they do not then you are probably aware of the difference, thanks to your contact with RP speakers and with the broadcast media.[11]

11 This illustrates nicely one of the benefits of a Standard form of language. It is well known to almost all speakers of the language.

Accent p. 13

Notation

As you will be aware, one of the more obvious features of English spelling is that it does not represent the sounds of the language consistently. Consequently, it is much easier to use an alternative transcription system when discussing the sound of words. Many such systems exist. The system adopted here is based on the one used in National Literacy Strategy training materials for teachers. In terms of describing the phonology of English this system has many shortcomings, but it has been chosen for its chief advantage which is that it is relatively easy to read and learn.

Consonants

p	*as in*	pip
t	*as in*	tip
k	*as in*	cat, kit
b	*as in*	bat
d	*as in*	dad
g	*as in*	gate
f	*as in*	face, phase
s	*as in*	sun, centre
s^h	*as in*	ship, station
v	*as in*	vase
z	*as in*	zebra, result
z^h	*as in*	pleasure, badinage
c^h	*as in*	church, witch
j	*as in*	jump, gym, ridge
m	*as in*	mouse, climb
n	*as in*	nice
n^g	*as in*	hanging
l	*as in*	lamp, table
r	*as in*	run, train
w	*as in*	wing, swing
y	*as in*	yacht
t^h	*as in*	think
d^h	*as in*	these, bother
h	*as in*	hat
2 (glottal stop)	*as in some pronunciations of*	water [wau2ə], hot [ho2]
w^h (voiceless w)	*as in some pronunciations of*	whip [w^{h}ip], when [w^{h}en]

The symbols s^h, c^h, n^g etc. are used in preference to sh, ch, ng etc. in order to emphasise that each represents a **single sound**, rather than the two which the spelling might imply. In conventional spelling pairs of letters which represent a single sound (ch, oa etc.) are known as **digraphs**; three-letter combinations are **trigraphs**. Sometimes the term **grapheme** is used to refer to groups of letters which together represent a single speech sound.

Vowels

i	*as in*	p<u>i</u>t
e	*as in*	p<u>e</u>t
a	*as in*	p<u>a</u>t
u	*as in*	c<u>u</u>p
ə	*as in*	lett<u>er</u>
o	*as in*	p<u>o</u>t
o^o	*as in*	l<u>oo</u>k
e^e	*as in*	k<u>ee</u>p
a^r	*as in*	c<u>ar</u>t
u^e	*as in*	m<u>oo</u>n
o^r	*as in*	th<u>or</u>n
u^r	*as in*	ch<u>ur</u>ch
a^e	*as in*	p<u>ai</u>n
o^e	*as in*	b<u>oa</u>t
i^e	*as in*	m<u>i</u>ne
o^w	*as in*	c<u>ow</u>
oⁱ	*as in*	b<u>oy</u>
e^{ar}	*as in*	f<u>ear</u>
a^{ir}	*as in*	p<u>air</u>
u^{re}	*as in*	c<u>ure</u>

Again u^{re}, a^{ir} etc. are used to indicate a single sound.

Activity 2.3 Using your implicit language knowledge

The transcription system above was designed to represent Received Pronunciation. Work through all the symbols to make sure you recognise the sound each one represents. Then think about how well the system represents your own English. Do you have the same number of sounds? In terms of scope for variation, is there a difference between vowels and consonants?

Reflection

Even if you are an RP speaker you will be familiar with some non-RP features, the most commonly cited being the use of /a/ in words like *bath* and *castle*, where you would use /a^r/. This is a difference of **distribution**. Northern varieties do have both /a/ and /a^r/, but /a^r/ is found in fewer words than in RP. On the whole, variation in vowel quality is more common than consonantal variation and many accents will have slightly different vowel pronunciations, which nonetheless correspond to the RP vowel set in terms of distribution. If you speak a variety in which the [r] in such words as *bird* and *feather* is sounded you may well feel the symbol a^r is inappropriate for words like bath and castle, where no [r] sound is present. (And, incidentally, where the conventional spelling does reflect the sound pattern accurately – a point to which we shall return.) Although an RP transcription system has been adopted, this does not imply that other accents are somehow 'variants' of RP or that the pronunciations being described are somehow 'correct'. In fact, if you do have a non-Standard accent the ability to compare Standard and non-Standard forms may at times heighten your understanding.

You will have noticed the use of slashes and square brackets around words and sounds in the above paragraph. This follows the convention that phoneme symbols occur between slashes and square brackets enclose sound segments. At this point the distinction will probably seem arcane, but the difference is a real one, as you will see.

Phonemes p. 36

Making speech sounds

This section goes into some technical detail, with the intention of helping you observe carefully the way in which you (and others) pronounce the sounds of English. This is partly necessary because our perceptions are often quite strongly influenced by our familiarity with written forms. It is not, of course, expected that you will commit all this detail to memory.

Speech sounds are produced by action upon a controlled stream of air coming from the lungs, through the throat, mouth and nasal cavity. An important organ of speech is the **larynx** or voice box, which contains the **vocal cords**. These can be stretched tight as air passes through them to produce a range of clearly audible sounds, known as the **voice**. Although voice is very important to speech it is not always present.

You are probably familiar with the terms **vowel** and **consonant**. Broadly speaking, vowels are produced when the voice and airflow have a relatively clear passage through the mouth, whilst most consonants are accompanied by some kind of obstruction.

Consonants

The consonant sounds of English can be grouped according to their manner of production, as follows.

Stops

Say the words *paper* and *baboon* aloud. What do you notice if you place your hand close in front of your mouth when you say them? You should feel each word being delivered as a series of pulses rather than as a continuous flow of breath. At the start and in the middle of each word the lips are completely closed for a moment before allowing the breath to explode outwards. You can probably also see the link between these movements and the sounds written as 'p' and 'b'. These sounds are examples of **plosive** consonants or **stops**. The flow of air is completely interrupted for a moment and then allowed to burst out. These two sounds are both formed by making a closure at the lips. The lips, however, are not the only parts capable of stopping the flow of air.

Plosive consonants are formed by completely stopping the airflow at any point on its journey between the lungs and the outside world. Work your way through the alphabet and investigate which other consonants can also be classed as plosives. Where is the closure made in each case?

Reflection

Remember that plosives involve both a closure (implied by the word 'stop') and a release (implied by the term 'plosive'). You may have found some consonants which involve closure without release (e.g. [m], [n]), but also found that the sounds [d], [t], [k] and [g] are plosives. (There is some sense in adding the sounds [ch] and [j] to your list, but we shall see later that they are examples of a more complex phenomenon.) The four sounds [t], [d], [k] and [g] all use the tongue to stop the airstream either at the front or the back of the mouth.

An additional stop consonant is the glottal stop (found in the pronunciation of e.g. *'butter'* [bu?ə] found in parts of London, Glasgow and many places in between (and also, if you listen carefully, by RP speakers before many words spelt with an initial vowel). It is formed by complete closure at the vocal cords.

Language varieties pp. 12–14

Fricatives

You now have some experience of investigating how we make particular English sounds, so we'll begin our examination of another major group of consonants with an investigation.

12 Two other fricatives often heard in English speech are the 'll' often found in Welsh places names (e.g. Llangollen) and the 'ch' in Scottish varieties (e.g. 'loch') – the former sound sometimes appears in English as the so-called 'lateral s', while the latter sound is found in some English regional varieties.

Try to describe how the sound s^h is made. Describe what is happening to the airstream and exactly where the sound is formed. It might help you to feel how your mouth moves to this sound from a 'rest' position.

Reflection

[s^h] is a sound made at the front of the mouth. You probably noticed a noisy rushing of air somewhere in the region of the tooth ridge. (You may also have rounded your lips at the same time.) The front of the tongue rises towards the roof of the mouth to a point where the airstream is so constricted that friction occurs. Sounds like this are known as **fricatives**. Unlike [p], [t] etc., these are sounds which may be continued for as long as you have the breath to sustain them. In most varieties of English all the fricatives are formed towards the front of the mouth and include the sounds [f], [v], [s], [z], as well as [s^h], [z^h], [t^h] and [d^h].[12]

Investigate the fricatives in these words:

　sing, thing, zip, fin, that, vine, shout, leisure.

Try to pinpoint the exact place in which the constriction occurs – are there any which are formed in exactly the same place?

Reflection

The precise way in which consonants are formed will vary according to the variety of English you speak, so you might find that you don't agree with all the details which follow. If this is the case it is a useful exercise to try and describe exactly what you are doing and compare your own pronunciation with that of other people who live in your area. (If a teacher's pronunciation differs significantly from that of the children in a class then it is vital that the teacher understands and is sensitive to those differences.)

Language varieties pp. 12–14

You should have found that these consonants are articulated in four different places. |f| and |v| are formed by the lower lip approaching the upper teeth. Behind these come the two consonants represented in spelling by 'th', [th] and [dh], which are formed between the tip of the tongue and the top teeth. [s], [sh], [z] and [zh] are formed between the tooth ridge at the front of the mouth and the front of the tongue. For [sh], the tip of the tongue is placed down behind the bottom teeth, leaving the wider blade of the tongue to make the constriction. For [s] the constriction is narrower and made by the tip of the tongue. If you observed very carefully you may have spotted some more subtle differences too.

The sound [h] can also be considered a fricative – the friction is produced within the larynx by air passing between the vocal cords.

Affricates

Investigate the consonants in the words *church* and *judge*. In what way do they resemble fricatives and plosives? In what way are they different?

Reflection

In the consonants [c^h] and [j] there is complete closure at the start of their articulation and friction on release. In effect we have a plosive immediately followed by a fricative formed in the same place. [c^h] consists of [t] followed by [s^h], while [j] consists of [d] followed by [z^h]. Sounds like this are known as **affricates**. Although each is composed of two segments, both of which are identifiable as distinct English speech sounds, most speakers intuitively feel that they are individual sounds in their own right.

Voice

We have seen how the place and manner of articulation (so far fricative, affricate or plosive) can be used to describe a consonant. However, you will also have noticed by now that these kinds of consonant tend to come in pairs, with the members of each pair sharing a single place and manner of articulation.

plosives	fricatives	affricates
p–b	f–v	c^h–j
t–d	t^h–d^h	
k–g	s^h–z^h	
	s–z	
	h	

The difference between the members of each pair is quite difficult to identify, but can be shown to depend on the use of the voice. To pronounce the first of each pair (p, t, k etc.) the vocal cords stop vibrating for a moment. In the others, voicing continues.

The concept of **voicing** versus **voicelessness** is the third feature used by phoneticians to identify consonants. Compare your pronunciation of *pin* and *bin*, for example. Try saying the two words with your fingers resting lightly on your larynx to see if you can feel a later start to the vibrations in the first word. In the same way, compare *bland* (all voiced) and *plant* (unvoiced at the beginning and end). You might notice with *plant* a different, more breathy quality to the [l] sound too.

Nasals

Activity 2.8   Observing sounds and articulation

13 In most southern varieties 'ng' represents a single sound. In some northern varieties it represents two sounds, the second being [g] (or sometimes [k]). In these varieties the first of the two sounds is not the same sound as the [n] in 'night' but the same as at the end of RP *song*.

Investigate the consonants [m], [n], and [n^g].[13]

Is there closure – if so where? Is it in a place used by other consonants?

Is there voicing – when you hum (i.e. pronounce a very prolonged [m] sound) can you feel vibrations when you touch your larynx? Can you feel them anywhere else?

Can you feel vibrations by touching any other part of your throat or face?

Reflection

These consonants are known as **nasals** and are formed in a similar way to the stops, by making a complete closure somewhere in the mouth. [m],[n] and [n^g] are articulated in the same places as [p], [t], [k] respectively.

In this case, however, the air is allowed to flow outwards via the nose (you may have felt vibration here). There is a kind of valve at the back of the mouth which can be opened to allow air through the nose. When vibrating air passes through it resonates within the nasal cavity. In English the nasal consonants are always voiced.

You now understand how the following consonants are produced:

plosives	fricatives	affricates	nasal
p–b	f–v	c^h–j	m
t–d	t^h–d^h		n
k–g	s^h–z^h		n^g
	s–z		
	h		

In this section we have seen that:

▸ **Speech sounds** are formed by using parts of the mouth and throat to modify the flow of air from the lungs.

▸ Most **consonants** are formed by closing or constricting the air flow in some way.

▸ The **voice** is used for some consonants, but not all.

▸ Consonants can be described in terms of **place** and **manner of articulation** and **voicing**.

Before looking at the few remaining members of the consonant set it will be useful to look at vowels.

Vowels

Vowels are speech sounds which can be pronounced at length (or even sung) with the mouth (relatively) wide open. English vowels are always voiced and the differences we hear between them arise from the different shapes that the oral cavity is able to adopt because of the mobility of the jaw, lips and tongue.

Compared with many other languages, English has a large set of vowels (by most accounts about 20 distinctive ones). It will be useful to begin by investigating the formation of two contrasting examples.

Observing sounds and articulation   Activity 2.9

Note: This activity will work better if you exaggerate the vowels somewhat – [a^r] as for the 'ah' requested by the doctor looking down your throat, [e^e] as for 'cheese' when you have your photograph taken.

Practise saying in isolation the vowel sounds [a^r] and [e^e].

As you pronounce [a^r], open your mouth wider by lowering your jaw. How widely can you open it before the sound ceases to be recognisable as an [a^r]?

Now try doing the same with [e^e]. What difference do you notice between the behaviour of the two vowels?

Repeat the two vowel sounds alternately and continuously – [a^{r}e^{e}a^{r}e^{e}a^{r}e^e] – whilst keeping your jaw as still as possible. Note what your tongue is doing.

Finally, try to locate the exact position your tongue adopts for each vowel.

Reflection

The difference in the ways these two sounds are formed is focused on the height of the tongue in the mouth. In many varieties of English, for [e^e] the tongue is as high as it can go without causing friction – in fact you may even have heard a little turbulence, especially if you tried the exercise without using your voice. By contrast, the [a^r] sound is formed by holding the tongue very low in the mouth (which is why doctors ask you to say 'aaah' when they want to see down your throat).

Another dimension: front or back?

Of course, there are other vowels to be found between these extreme positions of height (you might like to investigate where some of them fall before doing the next activity), but height is not the only feature which differentiates vowels.

Activity 2.10	*Observing sounds and articulation*

This activity is similar to the last one, as it involves comparing two vowels, [e^e] (as in *feet*) and [u^e] (as in *boot*). This time certain Northern pronunciations of the [u^e] sound will work best, or even the 'ooooooooooo' sound usually identified with ghosts!

First experiment with what happens to the u^e sound if you try lowering your jaw as you say it.

Again, try repeating the vowels alternately [u^{e}e^{e}u^{e}e^{e}u^{e}e^{e}u^{e}e^e]. How does your tongue move?

Can you feel anything else happening? Use a mirror to watch your mouth as you do this. Do you see any differences?

Reflection

In most varieties these two vowels are articulated very high. You should have felt your tongue moving back to form the [uᵉ] sound and arching forward again for [eᵉ]. You should also have noticed that while [eᵉ] is formed with the lips spread wide (this is why we are told to 'say cheese' to simulate a smile) for [uᵉ] they are rounded to form a kind of extension to the mouth.

Vowels: key features

Phoneticians identify vowels according to the position of the highest point of the tongue along the two dimensions high–low and front–back. A third feature is whether the lips are rounded. These vowels are three of the five simple long vowels (the other two being /iʳ/ and /aʷ/ , which can be plotted on a diagram, as follows:

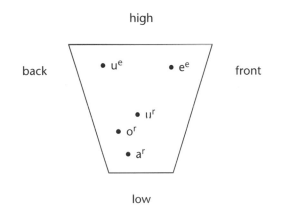

Figure 2.1 English long vowels

Long and short vowels

To the phonetician the terms *long* and *short* refer purely to the length of time for which a vowel is pronounced. RP has 7 simple short vowels. Six of them are to be found in the words *pit, pet, pat, pot, putt* and *put*. The seventh is found only in unstressed syllables, such as the final syllable of *litter*. As we shall see, this short central (sometimes called 'neutral') vowel plays an interesting role in the sound pattern of English. It is usually known as *schwa*, a shortened form of the name given to it by Hindu grammarians over two thousand years ago, and represented by the symbol [ə] (see Figure 2.2 on page 34).

Figures 2.1 and 2.2 may suggest a pairing of long and short vowels since several pairs – eᵉ and i, for example – are articulated in approximately the same place.

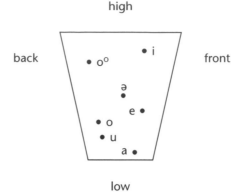

Figure 2.2 Engish short vowels

Pure vowels

All the vowels we have looked at so far are what can be called **pure vowels**. Of course, when we are talking our tongue is never static, it moves constantly between one position and the next. However, when articulating a pure vowel the tongue tends to linger for a short while in one particular place. Pure vowels account for only about half of the English vowel stock.

Diphthongs

If the pure vowels can be thought of as points on a map of the mouth then diphthongs are journeys.

English diphthongs are of three kinds:

▶ rising to the front, ending in the position for *eᵉ*

▶ rising to the back, ending near the position for *oᵒ*

▶ moving to the centre, ending near the position for *ə*.

The vowel in each of the following words is a diphthong:

> *plain   boat   might   loud   boil   fear   pair   cure*

Activity 2.11 | *Observing sounds and articulation*

Investigate the sounds of the vowels in these words:

> *pay   roe   my   cow   boy   fear   pair   cure*

Can you feel where each begins and ends? Can you group them according to where they end? Can you link this final position to how the word is spelt?

Reflection

The vowels in *pay, my, boy* end in [e^e].

The vowels in *cow, roe* end in [u^e].

The vowels in *fear, pair, cure* end in [ə].

One particular transcription system reflects the start and finish points of the diphthongs as follows:

> ei, ai, oi (pay, my, boy)
> au, əu (cow, roe)
> iə, ɛə, uə (fear, pair, cure)

Links with spelling are not very consistent, though the 'centering' diphthongs are often spelt with an 'r'.[14]

In fact, for many speakers of English, especially in the south of England and the USA, many of the 'pure' vowels resemble diphthongs. Many speakers will, for example, pronounce the vowel in 'cat' with a glide to the centre [kaət].

When young children are 'sounding out' words they often 'hear' the component parts of diphthongs and offer spellings like:

boyold (*boiled*)

and

fliying (*flying*)

In this section we have seen that:

▶ **Vowels** are speech sounds produced by modifying the sound produced by the voice without obstructing the flow of air from the lungs.

▶ Differences between vowels are achieved by the adoption of different positions by the **lips** and **tongue**.

▶ English phonology includes **long vowels**, **short vowels** and **diphthongs**.

More consonants

Understanding how vowels are formed makes it easier to understand the last four consonants, [y], [w], [l] and [r].

Semivowels

w and **y** are **semivowels**. They are articulated in exactly the same way as [u^e] and [e^e] respectively, differing from the vowels in that their duration is shorter and that they occur only between or before vowels.

14 In some accents this is pronounced as [r]. Even in RP there is an interesting link between [r] and [ə] in, for example, 'Peter [r] is here', 'The sofa [r] is comfortable'.

Observe your pronunciation of the following words. Do you pronounce the rhyming pairs identically? Do you articulate [y] or [w] in some and not others? How far is your perception of the segments coloured by your knowledge of spelling?

doing–screwing
playing–neighing
going–snowing
ploughing–rowing (quarrelling)
buyer–higher

Reflection

It would be unusual to pronounce the rhyming vowel elements differently to match the spellings and you probably at least entertained the possibility that your pronunciation included [y] or [w] in each case. This should illustrate how similar in articulation [y] is to [e^e] and [w] is to [u^e].

Liquids

l and **r** work in the same way as the vowels and semivowels, by modifying the way a sound resonates. With /l/, the tongue touches the roof of the mouth, as for [t], but a wide space is left at each side for the air to pass through freely. /r/ is articulated in a similar place to /s^h/ and /z^h/[15] but not so closely as to produce friction. It is also accompanied by a kind of lip rounding using the lips and top teeth. /r/ is a consonant which has a number of regional variants, ranging from taps and trills with the tip of the tongue to a sound in the throat similar to the French /r/ sound.

In this section we have seen that:

▶ Some consonants resemble vowels in their articulation.

▶ We recognise them as consonants because of their short duration and their position within words.

Phonemes

You now know how all the major sounds of English are articulated and more importantly you have developed the skills to listen carefully to hear exactly how the sounds of your own speech are formed. You have also begun to consider the difference between the 'raw' sounds of the language and its **phonemes**. The term phoneme represents an abstraction, with each phoneme symbol referring to a set of sounds which we somehow recognise as belonging to the same entity.

15 This is why the first part of 'train' sounds a lot like the first part of 'chain' in many people's pronunciation.

Listen carefully to the [t] sound in each of these words – are they all 'the same'?

top   *stop*   *pot*

Reflection

The [t] in *stop* comes closest to the articulation described above. It differs, however, from the [t] in *top*, which is followed by a slight breathy sound (something like an [h] and known as aspiration). Compared with this, the sound in *stop* sounds a little closer to a [d] (and interestingly [d] does not occur in this position – there are no words like /*sdop/). You may pronounce the [t] in *pot* exactly as you would for *top*, but the chances are that, in rapid speech at least, the plosive is not released (i.e. you keep your mouth closed at the end of the word). The articulation may also be accompanied by, or even replaced by, a glottal stop [ʔ]. Despite these marked differences, somehow we recognise all these sounds as something we call 't' and recognise all t's as different from all letters which are not t's.

Compare the underlined sounds in the following pairs of words. In what ways are they similar? In what ways are they different?

keep–cool
pit–spit
fall–lip
rain–train
bench–chip

Reflection

The following remarks concern features which are likely to vary between different accents, so you should reflect on them carefully to see if they apply to your own pronunciation. The /p/ phoneme in *pit* and *spit* follows the same pattern as /t/ in the previous activity. In the first word it is aspirated, in the second unaspirated. In *keep*, the /k/ is pronounced quite far forward in the mouth, whilst for *cool*, it is formed further back, on the softer part of the palate. The /l/ of *fall* is the so-called 'dark l', which involves arching the back of the tongue as for /u^e/; in *lip* the /l/ is 'clear', with the front of the tongue raised as for /e^e/. The initial sound of *rain* is as described on page 36 whilst in *train* the tongue comes closer to the roof of the mouth to become more like /s^h/. For some, the c^h sounds in *bench* and *chips* are identical, but others pronounce the final sound of bench as /s^h/. All these variations are predictable and occur consistently under the same conditions. Since they make no difference to meaning, for the most part we simply do not notice them and are happy to accept that some markedly different sounds 'sound the same'.

Defining the phoneme

A commonly used definition of the phoneme is to say that it is the smallest unit of sound which is capable of making a difference in meaning. So, the difference between [t] and [d] is phonemic because it is possible to find pairs of words, such as *tip – dip*, which are differentiated only by these sounds. We have just seen that English has a sound (the [t] in *stop*) which is voiceless like [t] and unaspirated like [d], but there are no occasions where this sound could be used to differentiate a word from one with either [t] or [d] in the same position.

Voicing p. 30

Activity 2.15	Observing sounds and articulation ✔

The words *tip–dip* are known as a **minimal pair** as they differ from each other to the smallest possible degree, thereby illustrating the phonemic difference between /t/ and /d/.

Find minimal pairs to illustrate the phonemic difference between:

$$/k/–/g/, /s^h/–/c^h/, /d/–/g/, /r/–/l/$$

Reflection

Members of all these pairs are opposed phonemically. Two sounds belonging to the same phoneme are known as **allophones**. The different [l] sounds in 'light' and 'cool' are allophones because in English no minimal pair can be found using these sounds. This is a feature specific to English (and certain other languages) – there is no 'natural' reason why the so-called dark and clear [l] should belong to the same phoneme.[16] In Russian, for example, they represent two different phonemes. The difference between dark and clear [l] is one of sound. The difference between the /l/ phoneme and other consonants is significant because of each phoneme's role within the phonological system. The range of consonant sounds used by English speakers is potentially infinite; the phonemic principle means that the range of **distinctive sounds** within the **sound system** or **phonology** of English is limited to about 24.

Sometimes the variation between allophones seems quite arbitrary, while sometimes it is easier to explain, as in the following activity.

Activity 2.16	Observing sounds and articulation

16 This fact is important when considering the case of children with English as an additional language – the way they map their phonology onto the English alphabet may well not match the intuitions of a native speaker.

English has a common prefix 'in-' meaning 'not'. Pronounce the following words in your usual way, observing carefully whether the 'n' is articulated in the 'normal' place (just behind the teeth) or elswhere:

infirm

inattentive

intransigent

inconsistent

Prefix p. 65

Reflection

You will almost certainly have found a 'normal' [n] in 'inattentive' and 'intransigent'. Unless you speak in a very 'careful' manner the corresponding sound in 'inconsistent' will have been [nᵍ] and that in 'infirm' possibly an [m] or possibly another nasal consonant, made with the bottom teeth and top lip. In each case the nasal has **assimilated** to the position of a following consonant. With words like '**im**possible' and '**im**probable', spelling catches up with the realities of pronunciation.

Using phonemes, it is possible for the phonology of a language to be described in terms of a relatively small number of *distinctive* sounds (in the case of English, about 40) rather than the thousands of different sounds which may be heard among the speakers of a language. The examples in Activities 2.13 and 2.16 illustrate just a few of the many variations which occur within individual sets of sounds which we recognise as a single phoneme. The phonemic principle is, of course, the basis of our alphabetic writing system.

In this section we have seen that:

▶ The phoneme is the basic unit of the sound system of English.

▶ The phoneme is the smallest speech sound which is capable of making a difference in **meaning**.

▶ The concept of the phoneme is an **abstraction**, grouping a range of related sounds.

▶ The exact articulation of a phoneme may be affected by its **position** in a word and by neighbouring phonemes.

Syllables

A syllable is perceived as a pulse or a beat in a word. If a word of three syllables is set to music then it must have three separate notes assigned to it. Most people, including young children, find the task of identifying the number of syllables within a word very easy.

Using your implicit language knowledge	Activity 2.17

How many syllables do you hear in each of the following words?

job	activity	business	perspicacious	rhythm	university
Lancaster	intuition	symbol	rhythmic	sprints	harmony
Wednesday					

Reflection

This list includes words of one (*job, sprints*) two (*rhythm, symbol, rhythmic, business, Wednesday*), three (*harmony, Lancaster*), four (*activity, perspicacious, intuition*) and five (*university*) syllables. You may have had difficulty deciding over some of the words, and you may well not agree completely with the analysis here.

Defining syllables

Syllables can be accounted for in physiological terms as they can be seen as founded on pulses in the airflow from the lungs – try pronouncing a long [sssss] sound as a series of distinct syllables (ss...ss...ss...ss...) and you should feel this. Usually these breaks are accompanied by some consonantal activity in the mouth, e.g. in saying 'dadadadada' the airflow is interrupted by the consonants, so the lungs are forced to release their air intermittently. If you place your hand under your chin and say the word *greenhouse* you should feel your jaw lower twice, once for each syllable.[17]

It seems that we intuitively identify each syllable as a pulse within each word, since although speakers often differ in their view of where one syllable ends and the next begins, they rarely differ over the actual number within a word.

Syllable structure

We have spent a long time on the 'items' of English phonology – its sound segments and phonemes. Just as important, however, are the rules which govern how these sounds are put together.

English has rules about syllable structure which are based on the categories of vowel and consonant. (The commonest notation system for syllable structure is based simply on the letters C and V.)

It is usual to consider the heart of a syllable to be its vowel, and a syllable may be an **open syllable**, consisting of a vowel alone (*I, owe, are, or* (V))

Vowel p. 31

or of a vowel preceded by one or more consonant (e.g. *pie* (CV), *spy* (CCV), *spry* (CCCV)).

Consonant p. 27

Closed syllables start with a vowel or up to three consonants and end with up to four consonants (e.g. *at* (VC), *plants* (CCVCCC), (*ex*)*empts* (VCCCC)).

While a single syllable may have a large number of consonants (e.g. *splints* (CCCVCCC)) it cannot have more than one vowel, because a second vowel would be perceived as a second 'beat'.

Interestingly, the rules governing how we perceive syllables seem to depend on more than just their sounds or physical articulation.

17 This is not a reliable way to count syllables as some involve greater jaw movement than others – you might want to use your knowledge of vowel positions to discover some more words where jaw movements clearly match syllables.

How many syllables can you hear in each of these words?

(a) *fear, hire, coir*

(b) *skier, higher, sawyer*

Reflection

This is the kind of matter on which both pronunciations and perceptions vary from speaker to speaker. Some people will feel that the words in set (a) have one syllable whilst those in set (b) have two, even though there is no audible difference between their respective vowels (i.e. *hire* and *higher* sound exactly the same). The fact that the set (b) words consist of two smaller meaningful units or **morphemes**, both of which are familiar from other words, is the most likely factor influencing such a perception. Even if you do not share this perception this example does illustrate the dangers of making assumptions about how another speaker's phonology is structured.

Morpheme pp. 63–65

Consonant clusters

We have already looked at some of the rules of English syllable structure, stating, for example, that a syllable may begin with up to three consonants. But can they be *any* three consonants?

Open any book at random and look for words that begin with *three* consonants. Remember that we are interested in *sounds*, so combinations like 'th', 'ph', 'sh' count as a single consonant, 'qu' and 'x' count as two sounds and 'silent letters' are of no interest (e.g. photograph and pneumatic both begin with one consonant while 'quiz' begins with two).

Write down the first ten words that you come to.

What do you notice about the first, second and third letter of each word? Can you make any generalisations based on classes of sounds?

Reflection

Possibilities include: *string, scrape, spring, splay, squash.*

All your words should begin with the letter 's'. All the second sounds should be voiceless plosives ([p], [t], [k]) and the choice for third consonant is restricted to the liquids [l] and [r] except after [k], where [w] is possible (and the words are spelt with a 'q'). There are similar rules governing the composition of all kinds of **consonant clusters**, whatever their length or position in a syllable or word. You may want to investigate some for yourself (the information is useful for crosswords and 'hangman' at least!). It is tempting to think that where clusters are not permitted it is because they present physical difficulties. This is not in fact always the case; you may find it difficult to say *fnack* or *zdock*, but only because of your intuitive obedience to the rules of English phonology. Physically, they are perfectly easy to articulate. (Try it!)

Stops/plosives p. 27
Liquid p. 36

However, phonology is not the only factor in these rules – for example, we have seen that VCCCC syllables are possible, but further investigation shows that they are only possible where the final consonant is an inflexion (as in *exempts*).

Inflexion p. 67

Syllable boundaries

Whilst most people find it easy to identify how many syllables a word contains, the exact location of a syllable boundary is sometimes more difficult to identify. Where, for example, is the syllable boundary in a word like 'western'? – is it wes-tern, we-stern or west-ern?

Activity 2.20	Using your implicit language knowledge ✔

Mark the syllable boundary in each of these **spoken** words:

restrict
only
mistreat
western
bower
waspish
respond

Reflection

Some generalisations are possible. Always split between two vowels (bow-er); clusters which can only be word initial (i.e. not word final) are counted as syllable initial (re-strict); where a cluster may belong to either adjacent vowel it is attached to the stressed syllable (wasp-ish, re-spond); morpheme boundaries should be respected (mis-treat); split between consonants which could not be a cluster within one syllable (on-ly).

These rules apply to spoken words, but the only practical reason most of us have for needing syllable boundaries is found in writing, when breaking and hyphenating (long) words at the end of a line. For this purpose, the obvious rule that digraphs should not be split should be added to the above.

> **In this section we have seen that:**
>
> ▷ **Syllables** are easily perceived as **pulses** or **beats** within words.
>
> ▷ All syllables are based on a **single vowel phoneme**.
>
> ▷ English has **syllable structure rules** based on the deployment of vowels and consonants.
>
> ▷ English phonology specifies the range of acceptable **consonant clusters**.
>
> ▷ **Morphological considerations** have a role to play in syllable structure.

Syllables into words: stress

Stress plays an important role in English phonology. We can hear it very strongly in sentences and it is the major ingredient in the rhythmic patterns of poetry.

The stressed syllables in

Jack and **Jill** went **up** the **hill**.

provide a steady, four-beat pulse.

Where a word is composed of more than one syllable the stress is shared unequally between them. A stressed syllable is not necessarily louder – stress is more closely associated with a distinctive pitch and rhythm, though volume and length may also be factors.

The main stressed syllable is marked in the following words:

a**gain**, ex**plain**, **bi**cycle, repro**duc**tion, **dis**trict, dis**tinc**tion

Using your implicit language knowledge ✔   Activity 2.21

Underline the main syllable with the strongest stress in each of these words:

important	disappear	greenhouse	blackbird
cupboard	eradicate	motorway	caress
explosion	Philadelphia	colour	aboard

Reflection

This is a fairly uncontroversial set which illustrates that stress may fall on any syllable. Some words are stressed differently in different varieties (do you say *tel**e**vision* or *tele**vi**sion*?). Sometimes word and sentence structure play a role – compare the stress patterns of the nouns *__im__port*, *__ex__port* and *__im__plant* with the verbs *im__port__*, *ex__port__* and *im__plant__*; the word *__green__house* is stressed differently from 'green house', where stress on the two separate words is more or less equal. Where a word has more than two syllables there may be a syllable which carries a secondary stress: *eradicate*.

Syllable p. 39

Stress and vowel quality

Within a sentence, difference in stress may cause a difference in vowel quality.

Vowel quality pp. 31–35

Compare the underlined vowels in

I'm not coming from town. I'm going <u>to</u> town. (/tuᵉ town/)

and the more usual

I'm going to town. (/tə town/)

In the first sentence it would be natural to give the vowel the value /uᵉ/. In the second, because it is in an unstressed position, the expected vowel would be 'schwa' /ə/.

In casual speech it is common for unstressed syllables to be all but omitted; we say that people 'swallow' syllables. Listen out for examples of this as it demonstrates how active we are in reconstructing sentences from what we hear.

Vowels within words

The tendency for unstressed vowels to be represented by [ə] is very important in the sound structure of words.

Vowel p. 31

Within words, unstressed syllables very often contain the vowel **schwa** [ə], as in the following examples:

cupboard /ˈkubəd)
caress /kəˈres/
colour /ˈkulə/
aboard /əˈbod/

You'll see straight away that the schwa in each of these words occurs in the unstressed syllable. You'll have noticed also that schwa can be represented by a variety of spelling patterns.

Syllabic consonants

Activity 2.22

Pronounce these words in your usual way. Do you hear a vowel in the final syllable? Can you observe a clear opening of your mouth at this point?

candle   *bottle*   *bottom*   *wooden*

Reflection

You may have been able to identify a clear vowel in one or more of the syllables, but many people will have found final syllables consisting only of the **syllabic consonants** [l], [m] and [n]. Physically this is possible because each of these sounds can be sustained for the length of a syllable.[18]

Read this passage aloud in your usual accent (if you have more than one, choose the one you consider most formal). Then read through it again, underlining all the stressed syllables and circling all the vowels which are pronounced as ə. Cross through the vowel in any syllables containing a syllabic consonant. Be careful to listen to yourself (a tape recording might help) and check each pronunciation as you go. If you can, get someone else to check your script as you read it.

> The door was broken. I wandered in and saw a frightened Marmaduke with another man who was in a state of consternation. Come over here, he stammered. It's important. There's to be a revolution. By tomorrow the Nationalists will have taken charge of the whole community.

Apart from schwa, which vowels can occur in unstressed syllables?

Reflection

Unstressed syllables employ a limited set of vowels which includes ə, o and i. Syllabic consonants occur most frequently in unstressed syllables. Some longer words have a syllable carrying a secondary stress and any of the full vowel set may occur in these. Within sentences, words which do not carry lexical meaning (e.g. prepositions, conjunctions) are often unstressed. Auxiliary verbs are often unstressed to the point where their vowel is lost altogether (e.g. *I have ➤ I've, they are ➤ they're*).[19] In writing the loss of the vowel is marked by an apostrophe and the form is known as a **contraction**.

Preposition p. 78
Conjunction p. 78

In this section we have seen that:

▶ **Stress** is an important feature of English sentences and words.

▶ In words of more than one syllable there is always one syllable which takes the **main stress**; in longer words **secondary stresses** may occur.

▶ Stress affects the way in which **vowels** are pronounced.

---

18 If you speak with an accent where [r] is sounded after vowels (e.g. in 'car') then this may be considered a syllabic consonant in words like 'letter'.

19 None of the above should give the impression that when young children learning to speak hear the vowel [ə] in a word they will know that in some 'ideal' way the vowel has a 'full value'. When they first learn a word like 'tomorrow' for example, they learn the pattern /təmoro/, not any form with a 'full' vowel in the first syllable. When they begin to write, each individual spelling of ə has to be learnt (though, as we'll see later, links with other words can be used to help the learning process).

The English writing system

The English writing system (or **orthography**) is alphabetic. This means that it sets out to represent the phonemes of English by means of a set of letters. The idiosyncrasies of English spelling are famous but we must always be aware that if English spelling appears to be odd it is because we do have some expectation that letters will in fact reflect sounds. Over the years some extreme positions have been taken over the role of letter sound correspondence in the process of reading. Not surprisingly, from extreme positions you can only see part of the picture. Whilst it would be silly to claim that the alphabet is the optimal system for representing the sounds of English it is equally misguided to claim that the mismatch between **graphology**, the system through which words are represented by letters, and **phonology** is so great that correspondences have no part to play in the reading process. In order to understand the complexity of an alphabetic system like English we need to look at some of the difficulties the alphabet has in fully representing the language. There are two kinds of problem, the first being common to all alphabetic systems (though all the examples given will be of English) while the second kind are particular to English.

Problems with alphabetic systems

(i) The sounds we hear and articulate are not always the same as the 'underlying' phonemes.
The **assimilation** you saw in 'inform' and 'impossible' operates widely. Do you say 'handbag' as [handbag] or [hambag]? Is 'plum cake' [plum kaek] or [plunᵍ kaek]? Do you say [tind plumz] or [tim plumz]? If you don't use the second of each pair of pronunciations yourself, do you know somebody who does? Most of us don't in fact make efforts to pronounce each consonant separately and where we do the behaviour is almost certainly based on our knowledge of spelling.[20]

Assimilation p. 39

(ii) Variation within the group of sounds which constitute a phoneme may be quite wide.
The final sound at the end of *bit* may be a glottal stop rather than a [t] and in a sentence like *The bit was missing* may, thanks to assimilation, sound more like a [p] than anything else (try it). Considerable variation arises in English from stress patterns where many vowels are sounded as ə.

Phoneme pp. 36–39.
Stress p. 43

(iii) Segmentation is not nearly so straightforward an operation as it sounds.
In acoustic reality, speech is not a succession of clearly bounded segments. In activity 2.12 you were asked to identify the speech sounds in the word *'ploughing'*. You may have decided that the vowel section of 'ploughing' consists of four sounds – [p l a uᵉ w i nᵍ]. In terms of phonemes this stream of sound can be represented by just two sounds: the diphthong /aᵘ/ and the short vowel /i/, but the boundaries implied by this segmentation cannot be 'heard'; they are imposed on the sounds

20 Victorian phonetician, Henry Sweet (the model for Shaw's Henry Higgins), describes a variety he calls 'Ladies' English', where every consonant is carefully given its 'full' value.

by our implicit knowledge of phonology. The stream of sound and the movements of our mouth are constantly changing.

The word 'plant' offers another example, involving both vowels and consonants this time, of the difficulty in drawing boundaries. The segments of this word can be described according to the conventional features of tongue position, voicing, nasalisation etc. as follows:

Vowel p. 31
Consonant p. 27

Figure 2.3 shows each of the 'segments' as aligned with its distinctive features.

	p		l	a	n	t	
closure	x				x	x	
release		x					x
voicing			x	x	x		
nasalisation					x		
friction							

Figure 2.3

In fact, something like the following is more likely:

	p	l	a	(n)	t
closure	x				x
release		x			
voicing			x	x	
nasalisation			x	x	
friction		x			

Figure 2.4

Here we see some interesting things happening. The [p] is released as the tongue takes its position for [l], producing some friction which might be seen as replacing the voicing which does not begin until the vowel starts. The nasalisation for [n] begins during the vowel and continues until the closure. Given that this is the closure point (tongue just behind the teeth) for [t] there is little *physical* evidence of an [n] at all, since all its features belong either to the preceding or following segment. It is hardly surprising then that young children find sounds like the nasals in /land/ and /lamp/ very hard to hear. Of course, Figure 2.4 represents only one way of pronouncing the word and of course even this representation is an oversimplification. We can describe Figure 2.4 in terms of 'overlap' between the segments, but it would be more accurate to describe Figure 2.3 as a simplification or idealisation of what really happens.

Voicing p. 30
Nasals p. 30

Problems specific to English

(i) Some sounds are represented by a combination of letters.

Opinions differ slightly over the number of phonemes in Standard English. One analysis, that of the National Literacy Strategy, lists 25 consonant phonemes and 20 vowel phonemes. English has a total of 26 letters of which 20 represent consonants, 5 vowels and one ('y') may function as either. Given this fact it is not surprising that some sounds are represented by two letters working together as a **digraph. Consonant digraphs** include 'sh' and 'ph', **vowel digraphs** are numerous and include 'oa' and 'ei'. Sometimes combinations such as 'a-e' (as in 'lake') are known as **split digraphs. Trigraphs** (e.g. in *high* and *witch*) are also possible. The discrepancy between the number of phonemes and the number of letters in English is easily explained: as its name suggests, the Roman alphabet was written for another language altogether – Latin. Sometimes our familiarity with the alphabet blinds us to the phonological facts – many, for example, find it hard to hear 'ng' as a single phoneme (as it is in southern varieties at least). Digraphs and trigraphs should not be confused with strings of letters representing **consonant clusters** such as 'bl', 'cl', 'nd'. These letter strings are often referred to as **blends**.

(ii) Some letters represent more than one sound.

For most of us a phonic basis for reading has some intuitive appeal – for example, even when a letter regularly represents two or more sounds (e.g. 'c' as in 'cat' and 'cede') most of us feel that one sound is its 'most natural' or 'most common'.

Activity 2.24	Analysing language data

Choose a written passage of about 50 words. Look carefully at how the letters represent sounds. Note down some examples of where a letter does not (in your opinion) make its 'most common' sound. How frequently does this happen? Which class of letter is more 'reliable' – vowels or consonants? Are there any letters which seem 100% reliable? Make sure you think about every single letter.

Reflection

You will have been prepared for some inconsistencies – c> [k/s], g> [g/j], for example. Some variations are quite tightly governed by rules, e.g. 'ch' (almost) always says [cʰ], but this doesn't alter the fact that 'c' is not to be depended on to represent /k/. Vowels often depend on a combination of two (or more letters) and appear less consistent than many of the consonants, of which a few (e.g. 'd', 'f') seem very reliable indeed.[21]

21 Though exceptions can be found for many with an otherwise high reliability (e.g. 'h' – hour, honour, 'z' – pizza, 'x' – xylophone, 'k' – knife). It is usually possible to find counter-examples to any generalisations made about English.

(iii) Some sounds are represented by more than one letter.

For each of these phonemes, give some examples of words which spell the sound in different ways:

/k/, /t/, /s^h/, /oe /, /ae /

Reflection

cat and *keep* are obvious spellings of /k/ but did you find examples with 'q' – not just 'quay' but words like '*queen*' too? On the face of it, /t/ appears to be represented only by 't', but the sound can in fact also be represented by 'tt' (hi**tt**ing), or 'tte' (*ciga***rette**) and 'pt' (**pt**armigan). /s^h/ is in *ship, station parachute* and *fuchsia*; /oe/ in *boat, hope, bureau,* dep**o**t;[22] /ae/ in m**a**ke, m**ay**, m**ai**d, and d**u**vet. You may be able to think of other examples for these sounds and of course the same kind of patterns exists for most other phonemes.

Figure 2.5 on page 50, taken from National Literacy Strategy training materials illustrates commonly occurring letter–sound correspondences.

22 You may feel that this and the preceding examples 'don't count' because they are 'foreign'. It it difficult to see where we draw the line between recent imports and 'established' loan words – is 'yacht' foreign? Is 'beauty'? Were you happy to accept 'parachute' because it's a commonly used word with no 'native' synonym? Experienced readers have no difficulty with words like bureau and depot – they can be read by applying the same strategies as we use for more familiar words.

Activity 2.26   Using implicit language knowledge ✔

How many phonemes can you identify in these words?

| cat | mouse | break | window | antiestablishment |
| story | ache | understanding | bough | eye | owe |

Reflection

Did any of these surprise you? Maybe your familiarity with spelling has influenced the way you feel about words, so that 'eye' and 'owe' feel like more than one phoneme to you; or you find it hard to see 'ng' as one phoneme, even if you pronounce it as a single sound. It is important to remember that phonemes exist in their own right, without reference to spelling.

It should now be clear that the alphabetic system cannot always represent English phonology in a way which is either obvious or straightforward.

Letters and phonemes

letters: a b c d e f g h i j k l m n o p q r s t u v w x y z

Some of the 140 (approx) letter combinations illustrated within words:

cat, loo**k**, w**oul**d, p**u**t, p**e**g, br**ea**d, ca**r**t,

fast, p**i**g, want**e**d, b**ur**n, f**ir**st, t**er**m,

h**ear**d, w**or**k, l**o**g, w**a**nt, t**or**n, d**oor**,

w**ar**n, pl**u**g, l**o**ve, h**au**l, l**aw**, ca**ll**, p**ai**n,

d**ay**, g**a**te, st**a**tion, wood**e**n, cir**c**us, sist**er**,

sw**ee**t, h**ea**t, th**ie**f, th**e**se, d**ow**n, sh**ou**t,

tr**ie**d, l**igh**t, m**y**, sh**i**ne, m**i**nd, c**oi**n, b**oy**,

r**oa**d, bl**ow**, b**o**ne, c**o**ld, st**air**s, b**ear**,

h**are**, m**oo**n, bl**ue**, gr**ew**, t**u**ne, f**ear**,

b**eer**, h**ere**, **b**aby, **s**un, mou**s**e, **c**ity,

science, **d**og, **t**ap, **f**ield, **ph**oto, **v**an,

game, **w**as, **h**at, **wh**ere, **judge**, **g**iant,

bar**ge**, **y**es, **c**oo**k**, **qu**ick, mi**x**, **Ch**ris,

zebra, plea**se**, i**s**, **l**amb, **th**en, **m**onkey,

co**mb**, **th**in, **n**ut, **kn**ife, **gn**at, **ch**ip,

wa**tch**, **p**aper, **sh**ip, mi**ss**ion, **ch**ef, **r**abbit,

wrong, trea**s**ure, ri**ng**, si**n**k.

Phonemes: /b/ /d/ /f/ /g/ /h/ /j/ /k/ /l/ /m/

/n/ /p/ /r/ /s/ /t/ /v/ /w/ /wh/ /y/ /z/ /th/

/<u>th</u>/ /ch/ /sh/ /zh/ /ng/ /a/ /e/ /i/ /o/ /u/

/ae/ /ee/ /ie/ /oe/ /ue/ /oo/ /ar/ /ur/ /or/

/au/ /er/ /ow/ /oi/ /air/ /ear/

Figure 2.5

© Crown copyright 1999

> **In this section we have seen that:**
>
> English orthography represents the sounds of English imperfectly because:
>
> ▶ **phonemes** manifest themselves as **different sounds**
>
> ▶ individual **speech sounds are not always easy to isolate** from the stream of sound
>
> ▶ some **phonemes are represented by groups of letters** (digraphs, trigraphs)
>
> ▶ some **letters represent more than one phoneme**
>
> ▶ some **phonemes are represented by a range of letters**.

Regularities in English orthography

Letter/phoneme relations are not as inconsistent as they might appear, however, when other factors are taken into account.

A well-known puzzle is based on the notion that the letters 'ghoti' can spell the word '*fish*' ('gh' as in '*enough*', 'o' as in '*women*' and 'ti' as in '*station*'). Whilst accepting the 'logic' of this argument, most victims can see that it is nonsense, though they may not be able to say why. The reason why it is nonsense is that the sound value of a letter or digraph depends in part upon its position in a word. 'gh' can spell [f], but only at the end of a free morpheme (e.g. *coughing*, *roughage*); 'ti' only says [s^h] in the syllables *tion* and *tious* and 'o' only says [i] in one word. Although a given letter may have a range of possible pronunciations, that range is limited at any given position – many a young or overseas reader may have fallen foul of 'Slough', but no fluent reader would consider reading 'ghost' or 'ghastly' with an /f/.

Activity 2.27

How many ways can you find for spelling each of these phonemes:

(a) at the beginning of a word

(b) at the end of a word

(c) between other phonemes?

/j/, /k/, /r/

Are some possibilities possible but rare? Can you see any patterns influencing what can occur?

Reflection

Although /k/ can be represented by *c, k, ck, ch, cc* and *q* this does not mean that in any context a writer has a choice of six spellings. '*ck*' never occurs in initial position, for example. If you tried very hard you may have found examples in most positions, by including proper names (e.g. *Iraq*) and loanwords (*yak, kayak, loch* (if pronounced 'lock')). However, by excluding rare occurrences and also by taking morphemic structure into account the choices are much more limited, as Figure 2.6 illustrates.[23]

spelling pattern:	initial position	final position	medial position
c	common	tends to be only in 'scholarly' words, e.g. *sac, politic* and words ending in '-ic'	fairly common
k	common (tends to be used in short words)	rare (only in loan words e.g. *yak, kayak*)	common usually at the end of a morpheme and after a long vowel (e.g. *liking, maker*)
ck	never	common (tends to be used in short words)	common usually at the end of a morpheme and after a short vowel (e.g. *sticking, stacker*)
ch	tends to be only in 'scholarly' words, e.g. *chiropodist*	never (unless the pronunciation of /k/ in *loch, Bach* etc. is accepted)	quite rare (between consonants only in *school, scholar* etc., between vowels at the end of a morpheme (e.g. *aching*))
cc	never	never	common in longer words
q	common, but only for words beginning /kw/ (with a few exceptions, e.g. *quay, quoit, Qatar*)	very rare (only in foreign place names, e.g. *Iraq*)	very rare (only in foreign place names and at the end of a morpheme, e.g. *Iraqi*)

Figure 2.6 Distribution of possible spellings for the phoneme/k

An important lesson to take from this kind of information is that reading is much easier when the reader brings to bear their wider knowledge of the language. In other words, the spelling system represents more than just the phonology of the language.

23 You may be aware of factors relating to the history of words which strongly influence spelling patterns. In the section beginning on p. 58 you will be introduced to the most significant historical factors in English spelling. Although many people undoubtedly make use of such knowledge when reading and spelling, it is clearly possible to be an effective reader without such knowledge; factors such as 'vocabulary type' (e.g. 'scientific' words) and word length, however, are accessible to all as the basis for analogy.

Set out like this, however, the rules seem dauntingly complex and hardly any easier to work with than the simple possibility that /k/ may be represented in any one of six ways. If, instead of segments and rules, we think of syllables and patterns, however, a different picture emerges. Whereas the spelling of segments is relatively unreliable, the spelling of syllables is quite consistent.

Syllable p. 39

Syllabic spelling patterns

Using your language knowledge	Activity 2.28

Make a list of as many single syllable words containing the vowel phoneme /iᵉ/ as you can think of.

Investigate the spelling patterns.

Is the choice of vowel letters influenced by the final phoneme? Do word structure and syllable structure play a role?

Reflection

The commonest way of representing this sound is the **split digraph** *i-e* (*mite, pipe*). In open syllables *y* and *igh* (*sky, high*) are also used. *igh* is also used before *t* (*might*), though *ite* is another possibility (*mite*). *ie* is used in some closed monosyllables (*tried, skies*) but only where the final consonant is an inflexion (*-es* or *-ed*) and the 'base' word ends in *y*. The following syllable spellings are therefore quite 'reliable'.

Digraph p. 48
Inflexion p. 67

-ipe, ike, ice, ide, ime, ine, ile, ife, ise,

y, igh

ies (← y+s)

ied (← y+ed)

ite (less reliable but only one possible variant)

ight (less reliable but only one possible variant)

Syllables or segments?

We have already seen that segmenting speech into phoneme-sized pieces does not come automatically – it is a skill which has to be learnt. We have also seen that syllables have a greater intuitive foundation – speakers unfamiliar with alphabetic or syllabic writing systems can identify syllables quite easily.[24] As a unit for describing how the English writing system works, then, the syllable has the advantages of both reliability and intuitive appeal.

Phoneme p. 36
Syllable p. 39

24 It is interesting to note that all the alphabets of the world can be traced back to a single orgin – the idea of segmenting by phonemes seems only to have been had once. On the other hand, there are several independent syllabic systems.

Onset and rime

So far I have made much of the relative difficulty of identifying phonemes and there is evidence for this in children's early attempts at spelling. However, as usual the story is more complex than appears at first sight.

Activity 2.29

Look at the following examples of children's early spellings. The writers have managed to identify some, but not all, phonemes in each case. What factors influence children's ability to isolate phonemes?

ic (like)   *fllawrz* (flowers)
sllee (silly)   *pllat* (plant)
dodr (doctor)   *ces* (kiss)
sad (sand)   *gres* (grass)

Reflection

One thing which is obvious is that children find initial consonant phonemes easiest to identify. Because of this fact, and the fact that children identify syllables with relative ease, some recent research on early reading has concentrated on this aspect of phonological awareness. The terms **onset** and **rime** have been coined to describe two distinct components of the syllable.

The onset of a syllable is the consonant or consonant cluster which occurs at the beginning. In the following words the onset is emphasised: *pin, spin, spring*. The rime is the remaining part of the syllable, i.e. the vowel and any final consonants. Some syllables have no onset, e.g. *in, on, out*.

Although onset and rime are components of the syllable, for practical purposes it makes sense to treat some two-syllable words ending in ∂ or a syllabic consonant as a single unit, e.g. *l/etter, b/ottle*.

The spelling of rimes, especially as applied to commonly occurring words, can be highly reliable. The following 37 rimes are used consistently in spelling almost 500 words.

Thirty-seven rimes that make nearly five hundred words[25]

-ack	-ain	-ake	-ale
-all	-ame	-an	-ank
-ap	-ash	-at	-ate
-aw	-ay	-eat	-ell
-est	-ice	-ick	-ide
-ite	-ill	-in	-ine
-ing	-ink	-ip	-ir
-ock	-oke	-op	-or
-ore	-uck	-ug	-ump
-unk			

25 This list is taken from Wylie and Durrel 1970, reprinted in Dombey and Moustafa 1998.

Long and short vowels

The terms long vowel and short vowel are used often throughout this chapter, but so far we have only defined vowel length in **phonetic** terms – as the duration of a vowel in time. Vowel length also can be viewed in **phonological** and **orthographic terms**.

Vowel p. 31

Phonetic long and short vowels

Several pairs of English vowels are articulated in roughly the same place and differentiated chiefly by their length. We might consider /eᵉ/ to be long /i/, /aʳ/ long /a/, /uᵉ/ long /oᵒ/,/oʳ/ long /o/ and /uʳ/ long /ə/. You might find these pairings surprising, as they do not correspond to the way the sounds are usually spelt.

Phonological long and short vowels

Within the phonology of English there are patterns of vowel alternation which can be accounted for in terms of length. English has pairs like:

state (long 'a') – static (short 'a')
serene (long 'e') – serenity (short 'e')
private (long 'i') – privacy (short 'i')[26]
evoke (long 'o') – evocative (short 'o')

These patterns seem closer to the ones we are familiar with in spelling. (However, note the lack of a long/short 'u' alternation – the closest to this being *profound – profundity*.) Note that some of these long vowels are in fact diphthongs – from the point of view of phonology it makes sense to consider the diphthongs to be long vowels.

Diphthong pp. 34–35

Orthographic long and short vowels

Within spelling rules, /a/, /e/, /i/, /o/ and /u/ count as short vowels. Their corresponding long vowels are to be found in words which use the letters *a, e, i, o, u* in split digraphs: *tape, these, mine, hope, cute*. These alternations are highly predictable in the context of inflected syllables (e.g. *hop – hoping – hoped*). Here is a case where English spelling follows more than just the sounds of speech but reflects patterns of phonology and morphology too.

In this section we have seen that:

▶ Letter/sound correspondences are much more consistent if information on the segment's **position within a word** or syllable is taken into account.

▶ Other information such as **vocabulary type** and **morphological features** can inform how we interpret a particular letter too.

▶ At the level of the **syllable** the orthography represents the sounds of the language in a **surprisingly regular** way.

26 American English has a long 'i' in both words, a usage which is becoming more common in the UK too; this gives us an insight into how historical change leaves us with a system comprising a number of 'partial' systems.

Rules and patterns

Linguists have attempted to describe many features of English in terms of strictly consistent rules; one of the challenges of the task is to make rules cover apparent exceptions and describe the conditions in which they occur. So far as spelling (at least) is concerned it is useful to make a distinction between rigidly applied rules and recognisable patterns.

Rules

Some rules of spelling are quite reliable. One such example concerns adding the inflexion '-ing' to different kinds of word.

Activity 2.30	Investigating language data

Sort these pairs of words into sets which behave similarly. Can you work out rules which would allow you to spell words of the pattern verb + ing correctly every time?

like–liking	*sit–sitting*	*site–siting*	*lick–licking*
see–seeing	*fight–fighting*	*write–writing*	*crack–cracking*
hop–hopping	*stop–stopping*	*grip–gripping*	*move–moving*

Do your rules work for longer words? Do you find these words problematic?

focusing	*confessing*	*targeting*	*regretting*

Reflection

Vowel length is an important consideration here. Where the stem has a short vowel (e.g. *hop*) the final consonant doubles before adding *-ing*. Without this doubling we would read the vowel as long (*hoping*). Words where the vowel (almost always a long vowel[27]) in the final syllable is represented by a split digraph (*bite, hope*) drop the final *e* before adding *-ing*. Most remaining cases are covered by saying that all other verbs simply add '*-ing*'. These rules apply to longer words, where 'vowel' refers to the vowel of the final syllable. Why then do *focusing* and *targeting* have a single 'stem-final' consonant when *confessing* and *regretting* both double theirs? The answer lies in the way each word is stressed. The doubling is only necessary where stress fall on the final syllable.

Long and short vowels p. 55
Consonant p. 27
Verb p. 75
Stress p. 43

Spelling and accent

Some spellings are anomalous for almost all speakers of English. Why, for example, spell pairs like *meet/meat, past/passed, sun/son* differently, when for almost everybody they are **homophones**? The pattern is different for other words, however. For RP speakers (younger ones at least) there is no

Homophones p. 20

27 *love* and *have* are the well-known exceptions.

phoneme corresponding to 'wh' – there is no distinction made with w, so pairs like *witch/which, Wales/whales* and *weather/whether* are homophones too. On the other hand, many Scots speakers do have the *wh* (voiceless [w]) phoneme, so this part of the spelling system reflects their phonology well. Similarly, for speakers in Norwich (this example comes from the work of Peter Trudgill)[28] the spelling of the following pairs:

nose-knows
moan-mown
toe-tow
road-rowed

reflects two distinctive vowel sounds. One of the shortcomings of the Initial Teaching Alphabet, a teaching strategy developed in the 1960s and based on an alphabetic system which set out to represent each phoneme with a single symbol, was that its printed materials only achieved their aim with RP speakers. Speakers with other accents still had problems with symbols which represented several phonemes and phonemes which were represented by more than one symbol. Although the rise of literacy and the mass media have done much to erode the regional dialects of England (at least), the same fate has not befallen regional and social accents[29] whilst RP itself is noticeably changing (listen to old radio recordings if you need convincing). Although we may bemoan the fact that the orthography does not reflect pronunciation consistently, putting the situation to rights would be a trickier job than would appear at first sight.

Variation pp. 12–15
Phoneme pp. 36–39

English spelling – order or chaos?

As you saw with the +'ing' rule, there are some very consistent rules which can guide our spelling. Other examples of rules which cover consistently virtually all relevant cases include:

▶ in initial position, certain letters (b, f, r etc.) always represent the same phoneme

▶ all words must contain a vowel (or 'y')

▶ the plural form of words ending in 'consonant+y' is always spelt '-ies'.

Phoneme pp. 36–39
Vowel pp. 31–35
Consonant pp. 27–31

You can probably think of several more such rules. The phrase 'the exception to prove the rule' was probably coined for English spelling, however, and it is very difficult to find rules which are never broken. The well-known 'rule' 'i before e except after c' is broken many times. Before rejecting it as too unreliable to be useful, we must remember that the 'rule' does work for a large number of words and that many of the exceptions occur in words of very high frequency (*their, eight, height*). The i before e generalisation, then, can be thought of as representing a commonly occurring **pattern** rather than a rule in the sense that the +-*ing* rule is a rule.

Rule pp. 11–12

28 Trudgill, P. (1975) *Accent, Dialect and the School*, London: Edward Arnold.

29 In fact the broadcast media, once strongholds of RP and RADA voices, now seem to offer a daily celebration of Britain's phonological diversity.

English spelling is characterised by a multiplicity of patterns which as readers of English we recognise intuitively, and we are quick to identify spellings which fail to conform. Sometimes manufacturers and advertisers invent product names which do not fit common spelling patterns because they know that as such they will attract the reader's attention; who could fail to stare at 'Häägen Dasz'?[30]

Activity 2.31	Gathering language data

List some brand names which use unconventional spelling to attract attention.

Reflection

One of the earliest examples is the well-known *Kodak*; only a few (imported) words begin with *ko* or end with *ak* (*kohl, koala, yak, kayak* are the only ones that spring to mind). *co-* and *-ack* are what we would expect. The facility to identify non-conforming words is one we use when checking spellings to see if they 'look right'. It offers strong counter-evidence to the view that English spelling is totally irregular, whilst again illustrating the fact that languages do not need to rely on 'logical' or maximally economical systems. English spelling can be seen as polysystematic or simply as 'systematic enough'.

In this section we have seen that:

▶ English does have some consistent **spelling rules**.

▶ English spelling employs a large number of recognisable **patterns**.

▶ English spelling reflects aspects of both derivational and inflexional **morphology**.

▶ English spelling is able to represent a range of regional **accents**.

▶ **English spelling consists of a number of systems** which operate at the same time.

The role of history in English spelling

So far I have explained English spelling in terms of how it operates today; that, after all, is the basis on which most people learn to read and spell. However, having established that our orthography operates according to a number of systems it will be useful to examine the origins of some of this variation. English has developed in the course of more than a millennium and been shaped by a history of invasion, exploration, acculturation, imperialism, industrialisation and technological development.

30 If you are wondering what foreign language the name comes from, you may be surprised to learn that it doesn't! It was invented just to attract attention.

enquire or *inquire*? Which is the correct spelling?

Look both these words up in as many different dictionaries as you can, including an etymological[31] dictionary if you can find one. Does history help account for the two forms?

Reflection

You may have discovered that *enquire* can be found in Old and Middle English and that *inquire* is the Latinised version; that both are generally acceptable in Modern English usage. Some dictionaries might tell you that *inquire* is the standard American English (AE) spelling or that it is policy for *The Sunday Times* to use this form of the spelling. You may have found that some dictionaries draw a distinction between:

enquire – to ask a question

inquire – to investigate

The spelling of particular words can often be explained in historical terms.

Old English

Prior to the Norman Conquest, English was a collection of Germanic dialects now known as Anglo-Saxon or Old English, which were first written down by Roman missionaries. The basis of the written language was the 23-letter Latin alphabet in which there was no distinction between I and J, or U and V, and no W. In addition some symbols from the Celtic runic alphabet were used to represent sounds that did not occur in Latin. Some phonemes were represented by digraphs (e.g. we find 'sc' is used to represent s[h]). Written language was not standardised and words would have been written down in accordance with regional pronunciation.

Dialect p. 12
Phoneme pp. 36–39

Middle English

After the Norman Conquest in 1066 French became the language of government and of the ruling class. During this period English lost a lot of inflexions and gained a lot of French vocabulary. Not surprisingly then, this period sees a convergence of two spelling systems: Old English and French. French scribes working with sounds that were not familiar to them introduced a number of French conventions (e.g. *qu* replaced Old English *cw* in words such as *queen* (*cwen*); *quick* (*cwic*) and *quiver* (*cwifer*)).

Inflexion pp. 67–70

31 Etymology in the study of the history of words – any dictionary which lists a word's origins is an etymological dictionary.

The effects of printing

The introduction of the printing press in the fifteenth century was to be a highly significant event in the development of English spelling as literacy suddenly became widely accessible. Printers needed to decide between alternative spellings and the concept of spelling conventions emerged; the first step towards standardised spelling had been taken.

Many early printers of English texts spoke other first languages, often Dutch, and this shows in some of the patterns adopted. For instance, William Caxton, the first printer of English books, chose to spell *right* with *gh*, probably because this was a common Dutch spelling pattern. Caxton also made the decision to adopt a system which reflected the speech of the London area. However, printing took little account of important changes in pronunciation that were taking place around this time and this resulted in many of the apparent inconsistencies in modern English spelling.

Early Modern English

During the sixteenth century, with the rise in interest in classical texts, it became fashionable to display a knowledge of the etymology of words. In this period some words that had hitherto been spelt phonemically were changed in order to demonstrate their Latin origins (e.g. *debt* from Latin *debitum*; *reign* from Latin *regnum*). The other significant development which dates from this period is English's propensity to borrow words from other languages, often importing spelling patterns at the same time. Sixteenth and seventeenth century borrowings from French, Spanish, Portuguese and Italian (e.g. *mango, emu, potato*) reflected the increase in exploration and overseas trade. Many nautical words (e.g. *yacht, deck*) were introduced from Dutch. In the eighteenth century the revival of interest in French culture was reflected in borrowings related to fashion and manners (e.g. *etiquette* and *vignette*). Musical words (e.g. *concerto, trio*) were borrowed from Italian.

Britain's Imperial and Colonial period also left its mark on the vocabulary and provided some unusual spelling patterns. Words borrowed from Indian languages include: *guru, khaki, catamaran* and *shampoo*.

Activity 2.33   Analysing language data ✔

Many spelling patterns offer clues to the origin of words. For example, words containing the digraph 'ph' (e.g. *philosophy*) or with 'y' between consonants (e.g. *rhythm*) are often derived from Greek roots.

Use the information in the preceding section to help you work out the origins of the following words:

paralysis	*grandeur*	*half*	*legato*	*bungalow*
armadillo	*knight*	*malaise*	*oregano*	*verandah*
phrase	*portico*	*doubt*	*dough*	*chintz*
pandemonium	*llama*			

Recent developments

The following words include elements taken from Latin and Greek which are used with consistent meaning in a number of words.

Isolate these morphemes and try to say what each one means.

telephone	transformation	morphology	interact
transistor	hydrophobia	graphic	haemoglobin
anaemia	aquatic	metamorphosis	international
aquaplane	hydraulic	agoraphobia	telegraph
microphone	micrometer	metre	hypertext

Reflection

Industrialisation in the eighteenth, nineteenth and twentieth centuries and countless advances in all fields of science, technology and medicine have brought further expansion of our vocabulary, often involving the coining of new words. Greek and Latin morphemes (with their scholarly connotations) are frequently pressed into service. *telegraph* and *telephone* begin with a Greek word meaning *far*; *telephone* and *microphone* end with the Greek word for *voice*. Some of these elements have become so familiar that it is often possible to understand a new word the first time you hear it. Although a classical education is not essential for a person to be fully competent in English, familiarity with a set of frequently occurring morphemes can be a real asset.

Morpheme pp. 63–71

A relatively recent change is found in words that once contained vowel ligatures such as the æ in; *encyclopædia*. In modern times, as they are not easy to write and most keyboards do not have keys for them, the letters are usually written separately. In American spelling, ligatures are often reduced to a single letter (the one which best represents the sound), so we find *encyclopedia*, *esthetic*, *phenix* and *medieval*.

This discussion has focused on the spelling of British English, but the emergence of a Standard American spelling (*color* and *behavior* are familiar examples) should be acknowledged. Differences in American English and British English spelling are partly the result of successful spelling reform movements in the USA.

> **In this section we have seen that:**
>
> ▶ English spelling has been **polysystematic** from the start, accommodating regional variation in Old English and French and Germanic patterns in Middle English.
>
> ▶ The introduction of **printing** entailed a degree of standardisation and also established some new spelling patterns.
>
> ▶ English is very receptive to **loan words** and these are often vehicles for new spelling patterns.

A case for spelling reform?

Activity 2.35

In modern times there have been numerous influential advocates of spelling reform, most wanting a system which more accurately reflects the spoken language.

List some possible benefits of spelling reform and then some reasons why it might not be a good idea.

Reflection

The appeal of spelling reform is obvious. Why struggle with polysystematic spelling when a consistent single system (such as ITA) could be introduced? The counter-arguments, however, are numerous. On a practical level, the job of translating all existing texts would be huge and expensive. As English is a world language (maybe soon *the* world language – as Latin was in the Middle Ages) the change would require the consent and co-operation of many nations. Although learning to read might be simpler in some ways, learning a forty-five letter alphabet would be more arduous. It would not be easy always to represent words as they sound, since stress within sentences influences the nature of vowels. One accent would have to be chosen to be represented (and remember that English has many international variants) meaning that the benefits of phonemic regularity would be lost to speakers of all other varieties. Pronunciation changes in time, so that the reformed spelling would, in time, need to be reformed again. Finally, as you will see in the following section, a purely phonemic system would not convey the morphological information which currently aids our comprehension.

Stress pp. 43–45

Morphology: the structure of words

Look at the following list of words. Make marks to separate any smaller units of meaning you can identify within each word.

e.g. fright/en

action	*reaction*	*greenhouse*	*separation*	*friendly*
inhuman	*writer*	*cucumber*	*flies*	*raining*

Reflection

Only *cucumber* is not susceptible to this kind of analysis. Writer, for example, can be divided into an initial morpheme which is a verb – *write* – and a final morpheme *-er* which means something like *person (or thing) that performs the action of the first part of the word*. Write appears with the same meaning in *writing, typewriter* and (with slight modification of pronunciation or spelling) *unwritten*; – *er* appears in *painter, singer* and *typewriter*.

Morphemes may be long (*cucumber, mahogany, leviathan*) or short (*pies* is two morphemes) but each can only carry a single meaning within a word or sentence. Morphemes should not be confused with **syllables** which were discussed earlier. Many words consist of a single morpheme.

Syllable pp. 39–45

Free morphemes

Morphemes which can occur as separate words are known as **free morphemes**.

In the sentence

The mighty ostrich can run free.

each word is a free morpheme. Where a free morpheme is used as part of a larger word (e.g. **freely, ostrich**es) it is sometimes known as the **base**. As a general rule, every word must contain at least one free morpheme, though words like author are problematic – can you see why?

Compound words

It is possible to combine two free morphemes (i.e. two words) to make a new word. These words are known as compounds. '*Greenhouse*' and '*soakaway*' are two examples of **compound** words. The question of whether a word like 'greenhouse' should in fact be treated as two separate words has in the past stimulated some discussion. It becomes clear, however, that the 'compound word' analysis is correct when you consider the stress and intonation patterns involved.

Read these sentences aloud:

I saw a greenhouse.
I saw a green house.
I saw her spitfire.
I saw her spit fire.
I saw a blackbird.
I saw a black bird.

What differences do you notice in how you pronounced the first and the second of each pair of sentences?

Reflection

You probably found that in the first of each pair the penultimate syllable received a fairly heavy stress whilst the final syllable was stressed much less heavily. On the other hand, the final two syllables in the second of each pair received roughly equal stress.

Stress pp. 43–45

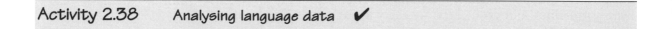

Activity 2.38   Analysing language data   ✔

Mark the internal morpheme boundary in each of these compound words:

armchair	corkscrew	househunt	steamroller
spoilsport	jobshare	lazybones	birthday
letdown	follow-up	tailor-made	stand-in
awayday	getaway	chequebook	eyebrow

Try to identify which word classes are represented in this list.

Word classes pp. 73–79

Reflection

Almost any type of word can be combined with others in this way. English is a language which accepts new words easily, and one mechanism for this is the creation of compound words. In time their compound nature can be forgotten; we probably all think of *lawnmower* in terms of two major elements, but do we still think of a *cupboard* as a table (or board) for putting cups on, or *breakfast* as the breaking of a night-long fast? In describing contemporary English it would be misguided to think of the last two words as anything other than single morphemes, though in practical terms a knowledge of their history may well help us remember how to spell them.

Bound morphemes

Another way of forming words involves adding to the base morphemes which are not capable of occurring in isolation. You probably recognise units like *-ing*, *un-* and *-ous* as elements which recur frequently and which always carry a consistent meaning. Elements like this are known as **bound morphemes**.

| Analysing language data ✔ | Activity 2.39 |

Show the internal **morpheme boundary** in each of these words.

Underline the **base** morpheme of each, then try to say what role each bound morpheme plays. Is there a rule about the order in which bound and free morphemes can occur?

untie	*fixes*	*walking*	*nicely*	*belittle*	*revisit*
booklet	*interlock*	*goodness*	*artful*	*lucky*	*prettify*

Reflection

Bound morphemes can be placed either before or after the base. Those which come before are called **prefixes**, those which come after are **suffixes**. (The collective term **affix** applies to both.) There are two principle types of suffix. Those which are used to convey grammatical information (*fixes, walking*) are called **inflexions**. **Derivational suffixes** have the function of changing the class of a word (e.g from adjective to noun – *goodness*; noun to adjective – *artful*; adjective to adverb – *nicely*). Prefixes (**belittle**, **revisit**) are morphemes which have the power to change the meaning of the base in a consistent way.

Word classes pp. 73–79

Prefixes

The set of English prefixes is not particularly large and their meaning is usually fairly easy to recognise.

| Using your implicit language knowledge | Activity 2.40 |

For each of the following words, underline the prefix and give a suggestion for the meaning added by it.

prepare	*recreate*	*undo*	*abuse*	*belittle*
disappear	*endanger*	*misplace*	*undeniable*	*reaction*
pre-arrange	*forewarn*	*encourage*	*deskilled*	*uninterested*
misuse	*encircle*			

Reflection

Many are associated with verbs and it is not always easy to describe their meaning exactly, even though we do not find them difficult to interpret. *dis-*, *un-* and *in-* all have meanings linked to negating or creating some kind of opposite to the meaning of the base, *re-* usually conveys a sense of 'again' (*repetition*); *be-* (**belittle, befriend**) means something like 'make'; *en-/em-* (**empower, enable, encircle, endanger**) seems to be linked with 'bringing something about'.

Prefixes are not, of course, applied exclusively to verbs; the word itself includes the prefix *pre-* meaning *before* or *in front*. Many adjectives and adverbs use 'negating' prefixes (**unlucky, im**possibly, **dys**functional).

Often history has given us a number prefixes which mean the same thing. *pre-* and *fore-* both refer to something done in advance, the former coming into English from Latin (often via French) and the latter being of native Germanic origin.

As with compound words, prefixes can 'become history'. It may be logical, for example, to see the *pre-* of *prepare* as a prefix, but evidence that people no longer think of it as such comes in the now frequent use of *pre-prepared*.[32]

Derivational suffixes

As you have already seen, derivational suffixes change the class of a word.

Activity 2.41 ✔

Complete this table as fully as you can. For each row, state the word class of the 'base' form. Is it always possible to make an entry in all four columns?

noun	adjective	verb	adverb
dirt	dirty	dirty	dirtily
	beautiful	beautify	
stunner			stunningly
	arguable		
ignition	igneous	ignite	
		produce	
	vibrant		
	happy		
thanks			thankfully
	communicative		
reality			
		testify	

32 *Prepared* itself comes from a Latin root *par-* which has no need of the prefix. How long before *pre-preprepared* makes an appearance?

Using this data and any other words you can think of, make a list of suffixes which can be used to change the class of a word.

Reflection

You will have noticed that certain suffixes recur with the same function. For example *-ise*, *-ate* and *-fy* are used to form verbs while *-ful*, *-ous* and *-ness* can make nouns from adjectives. The base form can be of any word class and the existence of any particular form depends on whether there is a use for it in the language. (The adverbs *igneously* and *testately*, for example, are perfectly plausible forms, but do not exist because they simply would not mean anything.)

The behaviour of derivational suffixes illustrates well the principle that English often follows patterns rather than a single rule. There is no way of predicting (from the word alone),[33] for example, whether a noun takes *-ate* or *-ise* in order to become a verb, though each pattern is sufficiently regular for words like *realise* and *stimulate* to be instantly memorable. Also, whilst some suffixes are clearly 'additional' to a word, in other cases they are not. In *dirty*, for example, the final syllable is a suffix, changing the noun *dirt* into an adjective. The final syllable of *happy* appears similarly to denote adjectival status, but there is no noun *happ*. It seems that we interpret *happy* by **analogy** with *bouncy, dirty* etc. There are many verbs (e.g. *vibrate, create, pulverise, vilify*) which seem to include a suffix but are in fact incomplete without it. The base must be *vibrate, pulverise* etc., but each includes an element signalling that it is a verb. The neat idea that morphology is about ordering morphemes one after another does not always hold water.

History of spelling pp. 58–62

Inflexions

Mark the internal morpheme boundaries in the words in the sentence below. In two-morpheme words, underline the **bound** morpheme.

Tigers run through my father's field – he takes due precautions.

Reflection

The parts you have underlined:

Tigers run through my father's field; he takes due precautions.

are all examples of **inflexions**.

In the case of *takes* this information is purely grammatical – it tells us that the subject of the clause is singular and acts as a link (sometimes called

33 Again, knowledge of a word's history can help.

agreement or **concord**) with the pronoun *he*. Often, however, inflections carry additional information which contributes directly to the way we understand the sentence. The final '*s*' on *Tigers* tells us that the word is **plural** and that, therefore, we are talking about more than one tiger.

Pronoun p. 77
Plural p. 75

English has only a few inflexions, some which attach to verbs and give information on **tense** and the nature of the **subject**, two which attach to nouns to mark **plurality** and **possession** and two which mark **comparative** and **superlative** adjectives. The complete set is shown in the following table:

Tense pp. 104–105
Subject p. 84
Adjective pp. 76–77

Morpheme	Meaning	Word class	Example
-s (-es)	plural	noun	*boots, boxes*
-'s/-s'	possessive	noun	*Henry's hat, the dogs' bowls*
-s (-es)	3rd person singular, present tense	verb	*sings, misses*
-ed	past tense	verb	*painted, listed*
-ed, -en	past participle	verb	*taken, wanted*
-ing	present participle	verb	*taking, paying*
-er	comparative ('more')	adjective	*bigger, faster*
-est	superlative ('most')	adjective	*biggest, fastest*

Activity 2.43

Make these words plural:

   pog   *gook*   *plue*   *blit*

and put these verbs into the past tense:

   brend   *sprine*   *clome*

Reflection

It would be surprising if you came up with anything other than *pogs, gooks, plues, blits, brended, sprined, clomed*. Unlike derivational morphemes, the use of inflexions is very strictly controlled by the rules of sentence grammar or **syntax**. Even here there are a few exceptions, but generally speaking an inflexion can be used with any member of the word class to which it applies, and speakers can intuitively use the rules on new and unfamiliar words. Inflexions do not change the class of a word and they may be added to a word **after** other suffixes. Inflexions are always placed at the end of a word.

Irregular forms

A few (mostly common) nouns and verbs inflect in an irregular way.

Irregular plurals

A few very common words have retained their Old English plural form. Examples include *men, women, children, oxen, mice, lice, geese, teeth* and *feet*. Words ending with the sound /f/ tend to change this to /v/ (*halves, knives, wolves*) when pluralised.[34] Often words of Latin and Greek origin retain their native plural form (*crises, criteria, cacti, vertebrae*) though there is a tendency to revert to the regular when words come into everyday use (e.g. stadiums, forums).[35] This kind of thing is illustrated by the fate of Italian words. We may be unsure whether we say *concerti* or *concertos*, but most would reject *piccoli* in favour of *piccolos*.

Plural p. 75

Irregular verbs

Some verbs have irregular past tense forms. A few are very irregular: '*went*' as the past tense form of '*go*' and *was/were* as forms of '*be*' seem very irregular and can only be accounted for historically.

Tense pp. 104 105

Other irregular forms seem less surprising.

✔   Activity 2.44

Identify the past tense forms of these verbs. Can you make any generalisations about the forms which are possible?

Verb	Past tense 1	Past tense 2
sing	I sang	I have sung
ring	I	I have
swim	I	I have
light	I	I have
hide	I	I have
take	I	I have
read	I	I have
slide	I	I have
wake	I	I have
break	I	I have
have	I	I have
strive	I	I have

Syllable pp. 39–45

34 Thanks to its history, 'roofs' is an exception to the exception though 'rooves' is often heard, demonstrating the power of the tendency to make rules by analogy.

35 With borderline cases there may be a difference between writing and speech. It seems easier to *say* 'styluses' but *write* 'styli', for example. Now that few people below middle age have studied Latin it will be interesting to see how such forms develop.

Reflection

Irregular verbs mostly have only one syllable.[36] Past forms end with *d, t* or *n* but can also end in the final consonant of the 'base' form. Often the change from present to past form is in the vowel. Some verbs follow the same pattern (e.g. *swim–swam–swum, ring–rang–rung*).

Irregular forms, especially in the case of verbs, are adopted almost exclusively by words which are very frequently used. Where irregular forms occur infrequently they tend to be replaced in the course of time by regular ones. Yet again we have evidence that as speakers and language learners we are not necessarily striving to develop the most efficient (or most logical) system, just a system which is manageable and meets our needs.

Hidden morphemes

In some irregular past forms the morpheme meaning 'past' is not visible in its familiar form of *-ed*. In these cases we have to consider the change in the vowel as an alternative manifestation of the 'past' morpheme, so:

Inflexion pp. 67–68

$$climb + \text{past} = climb\textbf{ed}$$

$$come + \text{past} = c\textbf{a}me$$

Morphological/phonological rules

So far we have talked of the regular past tense inflexion as *-ed* (its regular spelling) and discussed some irregular variants of the 'past' morpheme. In reality (and especially in speech), however, even the regular form is not invariant.

Activity 2.45	Using your implicit language knowledge

What is the past tense form of each of the following regular verbs?

climb, jump, land

Listen carefully and see if you can distinguish three different pronunciations for the inflexion.

Reflection

The inflection on *landed* is easily distinguished in speech as it makes an additional syllable. *Climbed* is pronounced as it is written, with a final *d* sound, but if you listened very carefully you would have noticed that the final sound of *jumped* is more like a *t*.

Something similar happens with the verb and noun inflexions which manifest themselves as *-s* (listen to the endings of *climbs* and *jumps* and

36 Hence 'light' < 'lit', but 'highlight' < 'highlighted'.

rushes). The thing to note here is that morphological considerations may have a bearing on the way in which a word is pronounced.

Morphology, phonology and spelling

When it comes to spelling something interesting happens. The underlying <plural> morpheme is represented phonologically by both /t/ and /d/, but in writing by a single suffix -*ed*. The spelling therefore represents the language at the *morphological level*.

Again the pattern for the inflexions spelt -*s* is very similar.

Another way in which spelling reflects morphology is seen when the same morpheme appears in different words.

medicine–medicinal	*sign–signature*
relative–relation	*different–differential*

Despite differences of pronunciation the spelling remains constant – 'one spelling per morpheme' is a useful generalisation for English, putting some phonological inconsistencies into a more favourable context.

> **In this section we have seen that:**
>
> ▶ The **morpheme** is the **smallest meaningful unit** of a language.
>
> ▶ English words may be formed by combining **free** and **bound morphemes**; most words include at least one free morpheme.
>
> ▶ The most common bound morphemes are **prefixes, derivational suffixes** and **inflexions**.
>
> ▶ Morphology plays a role in the **phonology** and **spelling** of English.

3. Understanding English at sentence level

Sentence grammar

By now you should be starting to feel comfortable with the idea of grammar as a set of rules for language. The rules of phonology, which you studied in Chapter 2, are an important part of the grammar of English. Before you embarked on this book, however, it's quite likely that you had quite a different view of grammar: that it is all about nouns and verbs, plurals, tenses, dangling participles and split infinitives and other things with complicated names. Most of the words commonly associated with the term grammar (those in the above list, for example) relate to sentence grammar or syntax, which is the subject of this chapter.

Many people find this aspect of language study bewildering and off-putting, either because they have never studied it and the terms mean nothing to them, or because they have studied it in a way which emphasised the 'naming of parts'. As you work through this chapter there will be, I'm afraid, no escaping the terminology – I need it so that I can explain things clearly and consistently. However, the terminology is not the most important thing; the most important thing is that you gain an insight into the way in which words work together in English. I would advise you not to make learning definitions of terminology your main aim; rather, make sure that you understand how each unit of analysis really works in the context of a sentence. Being able to see which words (and groups of words) 'belong together' is more important than being able to spot a noun from a list. For this reason I would advise you to be sure that you understand each section before moving on to the next one.

Of course, when you can see the relationships within a sentence then you'll understand why different units have different names, the terms will mean something and they won't be hard to remember; and if there are one or two less common ones that you're not sure of, you've always got this book for reference.

Some of the sentences discussed in this chapter have been simply 'made up' for the purpose of illustration. So far as possible however, they have been taken from the texts used in Chapter 4, especially the diary extracts on pages 136–137. It might help you to make sense of some of the sentences if you were to skip forward and read at least these three texts.

As with language rules at any level, as a native speaker you do not need to be taught the rules of English syntax – you learnt most of them in early childhood. However, an explicit knowledge of the rules can help us express ourselves more clearly, particularly in writing, where the possibility of revision gives us a second chance to make sure everything fits together properly. One way in which we make our writing clear is through the use of punctuation to highlight the grammatical structure of a sentence.

In this chapter we shall see:

- how rules of sentence grammar (**syntax**) govern the order of words within sentences;

- the importance of **word classes** to rules of syntax;

- the main features of the eight major word classes of English;

- how **simple sentences** are structured;

- how sentences can be described in terms of **subject** and **predicate** and the different possible elements of the predicate;

- the features of different **sentence types** such as questions and commands;

- how **phrases** and **clauses** are constructed;

- ways of joining clauses to make **complex** and **compound** sentences;

- how **punctuation** aids our comprehension of written English by marking the boundaries of syntactic units.

Syntactic rules

You have already encountered a simple syntactic rule in Chapter 1, when you looked at pivot grammars. Adult syntactic rules work in the same way. Syntactic rules dictate the order of smaller units (words) according to the grammatical category or **word class** they belong to.

Word classes

The names of most of the word classes – noun, verb, adjective etc. – used in describing English will be familiar to you, even if it is difficult to give an exact definition of all of them.

Maybe you are one of those people who have studied formal grammar in the past and found it a sterile pursuit, detached from 'real' English. However, as you have already seen, if a grammar fully reflects the rules of a language it will accord with the intuitions of its speakers.

In the following section you will be investigating your own implicit knowledge or intuition to see if it offers any justification for the use of these categories.

Using your implicit language knowledge   Activity 3.1

Fill in the gaps in the following text. There is no 'correct' answer, so try to list three or four possibilities for each gap.

Robin ran into the room. On the table he saw a _____[1]. It was an unexpected sight and it was obvious to him that it was a very _____[2] example. He walked _____[3] the room, this time going much more _____[4]. He took off his gloves before he _____[5] the _____[6] from the table.

Reflection

You probably came up with a list something like this:

1. *rabbit, clock, teacup...*

2. *old, wonderful, impressive...*

3. *across, into, through...*

4. *slowly, carefully, quickly...*

5. *took, grabbed, lifted...*

6. *object, thing, machine...*

You will probably agree that your list is 'something like this' even if the two lists have few (or even no) words in common.

Gap 1 can be filled by words like '*rabbit, clock, teacup, fish, biscuit*', all of which are **nouns**. It will be equally obvious that words from other classes will not fit:

> *On the table he saw a **wonderful**.* (adjective)

> *On the table he saw a **carefully**.* (adverb)

Old, wonderful and *impressive* clearly also belong to the same class, and are known as **adjectives**. Only adjectives could fit in gap number 2.

Across, into and *through* are all **prepositions**; *slowly, carefully* and *quickly* are all **adverbs**. Gaps 5 and 6 can only be filled by a **verb** (like *took* or *grabbed*) and another **noun** respectively.

Your linguistic intuition is telling you each time that you must choose a word that 'fits'. A word of the 'right kind'. The terminology of *noun, verb* etc. has been developed so that our intuitions in this area can be explained and talked about.

Identifying word classes

Words can be assigned to classes according to a number of criteria. In traditional grammar, word classes are defined in **notional** terms. You may well already think of a noun as 'the name of a person, place or thing', and of a verb as a 'doing word'. These definitions can offer a very useful shortcut to understanding the rules of syntax, but should be treated with caution. It's difficult to see, for example, how the word 'were' in

> *We were a poor family.*

can be seen as a 'doing word' or to insist that 'carefully', in

> *He opened the door carefully.*

is not a 'describing word', when it so obviously describes how he opened the door.

In fact these 'notional' labels appear to be a form of retrospective definition – our intuition tells us that *'was'*, *'cleaned'*, *'opened'*, *'appeared'* etc. belong to the same word class and the term 'doing words' fits most of them quite well, so it sticks.

In Activity 3.1, you were led to choosing words of a particular class by your knowledge of the rules of **distribution**. In other words, you knew that in that particular place, only words of one particular class could appear.

To a lesser extent **morphology** – the internal structure of a word – can give a clue as to its class, e.g. most (but not all) words ending in *'-ly'* are adverbs whilst nouns and verbs often contain identifiable inflections.

Morphology pp. 63–71
Derivational suffixes pp. 66–67
Inflexion pp. 67–68

A word's class can also be defined by its **function** and the function of each of the word classes should become clear in the course of the exploration of sentence, clause and phrase structure which follows. However, in order to make sense of that exploration it is necessary at the outset to have some working definitions.

Noun (N)

family, dishwasher, excellence, blood, Albert

These words are the names of things, which may be concrete or abstract, animate or inanimate.

Most nouns can be marked as plural by the addition of a final *'-s'* (or some closely related variant). Certain suffixes (e.g. as in *happiness, serenity*) are associated with abstract nouns.

Abstract nouns p. 109

Nouns are often preceded by a **determiner** (e.g. **the** *action*, **my** *performance*) or by an **adjective** (e.g. **tired** *eyes*), or by both (e.g. **my first** *lines*).

Determiner p. 78
Adjective pp. 76–77

Verb (V)

started, were, grasping, slip, evaporates

Some verbs really are 'doing words' – they communicate the action executed by the subject of the sentence. Words like *sing, walk* and *write* are known as **action verbs**. However, members of a second class of verb, **stative verbs**, communicate a less active state, e.g. *have, seem*. The verb *'be'* (usually in the form *is, was, were* etc.) has the special function of linking a noun to another noun:

Mars is a planet

or to an adjective:

Mars is red.

Each verb belongs to a whole 'family' of words. This is because this is the only English word class which is extensively **inflected**. Most verbs have different forms for **past** and **present tense** sing–sang, dance–danced with '*-ed*' as a characteristic past tense inflexion. In the present tense most verbs have distinct forms for use with singular and plural subjects:

Tenses pp. 104–105

Water evaporates

Liquids evaporate

Verbs also have a very common form ending in *-ing*: *spinning, grasping, coming.*

The simple regular verb *lift* has the following forms:

lift, lifts, lifted lifting

The highly irregular verb, 'be', has the following forms:

be, am, are, is, was, were, been, being

English makes extensive use of verbs made up of more than one word:

> *was standing*
> *have endeavoured*
> *am running*
> *would escape*
> *would have escaped*
> *would have been going*

These longer structures are referred to as **verb phrases** or as **complex verbs**. As you will see a little later, the term 'verb phrase' can have a different meaning, so as far as possible we will use the latter term in this book.

Certain suffixes (e.g. *clarify, pulverise, vibrate*) are associated with action verbs.

In most simple sentences the verb is the second main constituent, falling after the initial noun (or noun phrase):

Noun phrase pp. 83–84

We **started** off
The two brothers **started** off

Adjective (Adj)

poor, unsuspecting, affordable, dead

Adjectives provide additional descriptive information about nouns.

Certain suffixes and endings (*beautiful, silly, devious*) are characteristic of adjectives.

Adjectives most commonly occur immediately before the noun they describe:

A **little** hut
A **good** deed

or immediately after a linking verb like 'be' or 'seem':

*The hut seemed **little**.*
*The deed was **good**.*

Adverb (Advb)

gently, automatically, well, now

Adverbs provide additional information about a verb or adjective. In traditional terms they **modify** (as opposed to adjectives, which **describe**). They give information about how, where and when an action occurs.

*Please put your trunk in **gently**.*
*Waste can be removed more **easily**.*
*She went to town **yesterday**.*
*I didn't know she'd been **there**.*

Many adverbs are formed from adjectives by the addition of the suffix -*ly*.

Adverbs may be placed in a variety of positions and this mobility sometimes affects the overall meaning of a sentence.

*The bank opens **only** on Wednesday afternoons.*
***Only** the bank opens on Wednesday afternoons.*

Closed and open word classes

Nouns, verbs, adjectives and adverbs belong to 'open' classes. This means that each class contains a large number of words (thousands) and new words can be borrowed and invented. One of the ways in which English is able to create 'new' words is by admitting old words to new classes; for example, nouns can very commonly become verbs (e.g. to *book*, to *pigeon-hole*, to *eyeball*). The remaining word classes are all closed. Each class contains only a small number of words (a few dozen at the most) and cannot easily be added to. This is because their main function is not to convey any information but to express grammatical relationships.

Pronoun (Pn)

I, she, we, me, us, this, those

Pronouns stand instead of nouns, to avoid repetition.

*It was my <u>mother</u>'s idea. **She** wrote the script.*
*I like <u>Jim</u>. **He** makes me smile.*

In terms of distribution they follow the same pattern as nouns except that they cannot be preceded by determiners or adjectives (apart from some odd exceptions like *little me*).

Some of the **personal pronouns** (*I, you, she, he, it, we, they*) have a different form when they function as the object of a sentence.

Object p. 85

Nouns and pronouns are both examples of **nominals**.

Determiner (Det)

the, a, some, this, my

This is a very small class of words which gives some additional information about a noun. If we talk about **the** *door* we are referring to one particular door. If we talk about **a** *door*, it means either that we are referring to a door that we haven't referred to before or that we are talking of an unspecified member of a larger number of doors. *My, your* etc. are known as possessives and are special forms of the pronouns. As such they are both pronouns and determiners.

Another group of words which can be both determiners and pronouns are the **deictics** (pointing words) *this, that, these, those.*

Determiners are found only immediately before a noun or immediately before one or more adjectives which in turn are immediately followed by a noun.

Preposition (Prep)

at, down, from, behind

Prepositions express relationships between **nominals** (nouns, pronouns, noun phrases) and other parts of the sentence. These relationships are often of location or time:

behind the door
before loading the dishes

but may also be of a grammatical nature:

She happened to be run into **by** an SS car.

Prepositions, as the name implies, occur immediately before nominals, including some larger units which function as nominals.

Before loading the dishes

Conjunction (Conj)

and, but, until, although, then, because

Conjunctions are used to join words, phrases and clauses.

They most commonly occur between the elements they are joining:

My hut is very small, **but** there is room for your trunk and myself.

though sometimes they come at the beginning:

Because I wanted to please my mother, I told him she was out.

A few conjunctions come in pairs: *either–or, both–and* etc.

Our knowledge of grammatical structure allows us to identify the class of any unfamiliar words in a sentence. (You may not know what a *donga* is, but you can probably see that the word is a noun.) Read the following sentence and then answer the questions below.

My grundliest prudger smelded brendaciously by the quadgers and brudists.

1 Say which word class each of the words in the above sentence belongs to.

2 For each word, explain why you think it belongs to that class – give as many reasons as you can.

3 Which classes are represented by words which are not invented ones? Why?

In this section we have seen that:

▶ English words belong to **word classes** upon which **syntactic rules** operate.

▶ The class of a word can be identified by the role it plays in the sentence (its **function**), its place in a sentence (**distribution**) and sometimes by its internal structure (**morphology**).

▶ Noun, verb, adjective and adverb are large **open classes** which can admit new members.

▶ Pronoun, determiner, conjunction and preposition are small **closed classes**.

▶ In English only nouns and verbs can be **inflected**.

The concept of sentence

In Chapter 1 you tested your intuitive ability to identify well-formed sentences, and probably you were able to do so without much difficulty. It is more difficult to find a reliable definition to match our intuitions. One well-used definition says that a sentence is a 'complete thought'. It's difficult to see, however, how a string of words like:

a little hut at the edge of the forest

is any less complete in terms of 'thought' than the sentence:

A little hut stood at the edge of the forest.

The other well-used definition – a string of words which starts with a capital letter and ends with a full stop – does not really help us identify sentences.

Giving a capital letter and full stop to a string like:

The man, seeing what situation his friend was in.

does not make it a well-formed sentence. Punctuation is used to mark places where sentences begin and end; well-formed sentences need the right words in the right order.

In Chapter 7 we shall look at the difference between written and spoken sentences and it is important to note here that part of the process of learning to read and write is learning to work in written sentences, rather than simply learning rules to help us punctuate spoken sentences. However, as literacy becomes an integral part of our language competence, written sentence forms become more common in our speech and we acquire their characteristic intonation patterns.

Once we have acquired this knowledge, reading a stretch of language aloud can be a useful check on whether we are dealing with a sentence or not.

| Activity 3.3 | Using your implicit language knowledge |

Try reading the following strings of words aloud:

> a with made man an a elephant friendship
> My grundliest prudger smelded brendaciously by the quadgers and brudists.

Which could you make more sense of?

Which did you find easier to read aloud with natural intonation?

Ask a number of other people to read the two sentences. Do they produce a consistent intonation pattern for either of the two strings?

Reflection

The first string almost certainly tells us about a friendship between an elephant and a man, even though the word order makes it difficult to read aloud with confidence. The second is unintelligible. It is, however, perfectly easy to read aloud with a natural intonation because, despite the originality of its vocabulary, it follows the rules of sentence construction. The intonation patterns of English are very closely linked to units of syntax such as 'clause' and 'phrase' so reading a 'sentence' aloud to see if it 'sounds right' is a better test of grammaticality than looking for sense.

Intonation pp. 88–89

A simple sentence structure

As you will see shortly, there are several distinct sentence types. Many of these can be described by reference to a basic sentence type known as the Simple Active Affirmative Declarative (SAAD) sentence.

The following are all examples of SAAD sentences:

> An elephant made a friendship with a man.
> My hut is very small.
> You have done me a good deed.

In Chapter 1 you looked at pivot grammar, a way of describing young children's two-word 'sentences'.

Pivot grammar pp. 10–11

Adults' simple sentences may also consist of two words:

Doors slam.
Michael ran.
It rained.

Using the same kind of notation as we used for pivot grammar, we can write a rule for a very simple sentence:

A sentence consists of a noun and a verb, in that order.

S = N+V

This rule can be developed into a basis for analysing most English sentences.

In this section we have seen that:

▶ Sentences are defined by their **grammatical structure** rather than their meaning.

▶ In spoken English **intonation** matches sentence structure.

▶ The simplest sentence pattern is **N+V**.

Elements of sentence structure

As we have just seen, simple sentences are composed of ordered elements. Two-word sentences have the simplest possible structure, which can be illustrated on a branching diagram:

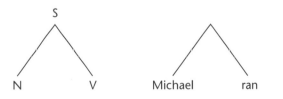

Figure 3.1

If sentences were structured on a word-by-word basis then the corresponding diagram for a longer sentence would be:

Pizza dough is made from flour, yeast, salt and water

Figure 3.2

However, our linguistic intuition tells us that certain parts of the sentence 'belong together' to form cohesive units. In this example, most people would agree that 'Pizza dough', 'is made' and 'flour, yeast, salt and water' constitute the main 'building blocks' of this sentence.

Pizza dough is made from flour, yeast, salt and water

Figure 3.3

A more realistic diagram, reflecting how we feel about the structure

Pizza dough is made from flour, yeast, salt and water

Figure 3.4

| Activity 3.4 | Using your implicit language knowledge ✔ |

would be:

Draw branching diagrams to show your understanding of the structure of the following sentences. Don't worry about 'getting it right' – the important thing is to reflect your own intuition.

Harriet Awdry skated beautifully.
We were a very poor family.
I do just the same.
A spider's body is in two parts.
Large fires of logs burned within an enclosure of wattled hurdles.

Reflection

As you work through the next section you may recognise elements which you have identified in this activity. Although different analyses are possible it is quite likely that you identified strings like *'large fires of logs'* and *'skated beautifully'* as important units. It is elements like this that we will be looking at in the next section.

Expanding elements: noun and verb phrases (NP, VP)

Look at these pairs of sentences:

Set 1	Set 2
Bill fell.	_The boy fell._
Cattle grazed.	_The cows and their calves grazed._
Children played.	_The boys and girls played._

Within each pair, the underlined parts of the sentences perform the same function. (In these examples they refer to the same thing.) You will recognise the single words as **nouns**. The longer strings are **noun phrases (NP)**.

Noun p. 75

Nouns can be **expanded** to form longer and longer noun phrases:

> _a thunderstorm_
> _a heavy thunderstorm_
> _a very heavy thunderstorm_
> _a sudden and very heavy thunderstorm_
> _a sudden and very heavy thunderstorm which worried the elephant_

In terms of their distribution, noun phrases occupy the same place in a sentence as do single nouns. In fact isolated nouns are not the norm, as most are accompanied by a determiner, so a more general rule for sentence structure (especially if we allow an isolated noun to be a kind of noun phrase) would be:

$$S \rightarrow NP+V$$

In the same way, the verb in a simple sentence can be replaced by a more **complex verb**:

> _rained_
> _has rained_
> _has been raining_
> _could have been raining_

or by a **verb phrase** containing other elements:

> _rained torrentially_
> _rained cats and dogs_

Sentences like:

> _Michael/ran._

and

> _The three-year-old boy/ran as fast as he could_ Pronoun

can both be accounted for by the rule: $S \rightarrow NP+VP$.

In each of the following sentences, make a mark to show the boundary between the noun phrase and the verb phrase:

(a) I started to act at the age of three.

(b) My mother/rushed down the three flights of stairs.

(c) The cue to begin my performance/was a ring at the front door.

(d) A spider's body/is in two parts.

(e) My kidnapper and aspiring confidant/came back.

Reflection

You probably found some of these easier than others. The simplest strategy to employ is to mark the break before the main verb. The only sentences which might cause problems then would be (a) and (c) as each has two verbs. In (a), *started to act* is a verb phrase (you could replace it with just *started*) whereas the cohesive unit at the start of (c) is *The cue to begin my performance*, which is a noun phrase.

Subject and predicate

The noun or noun phrase at the beginning of a SAAD sentence is known as its **subject**. (You may have learnt at school that 'subject' can be defined as the 'doer of the action' in a sentence but this only applies to **active** (as opposed to **passive**) sentences with active or **action** (as opposed to **stative**) verbs. As a working definition it is about as useful as the 'doing word' definition of verbs.)

SAAD sentence pp. 80–81

The rest of the sentence is called the **predicate**. When you divided the sentences in activity 3.5 you were separating the subject and the predicate.

Elements of the predicate

The definition 'the rest of the sentence' may seem a little glib and it is worth examining what components the predicate can include.

Underline the noun and verb phrases in the predicates of these sentences:

Rain falls.
Sunday came and went.
An elephant made a friendship with a man.
He gave me some news.
The elephant went to his friend.
We were a very poor family.
My mother rushed down the three flights of stairs.
The spider spins a thread from the centre to a hiding place nearby.
I talk to myself.
My opinions are stupid.
We drove into Chippenham and bought a pair of skates at Benk's.
He brought the prisoner a toothbrush.

Reflection

Some of the predicates consist simply of a verb (*rain **falls***) or two (*Sunday **came and went***) but the remainder include several noun phrases, some of which follow prepositions. We can analyse these predicates using the categories **object**, **complement** and **adverbial**.

Verb p. 75
Noun phrase pp. 83–84
Preposition pp. 78

Object

Objects occur in sentences where the verb expresses some kind of action. It is a noun, pronoun or noun phrase representing the person or thing which is 'acted on'.

In:

*The spider spins **a thread**.*

thread is clearly the object of the verb spin.

In:

*An elephant made a **friendship**.*

things are less concrete, but it is still obvious that the friendship is the thing the elephant made. These words are the **direct objects** of their sentences.

It becomes clear that the verb–object relationship is a grammatical one rather than one based on meaning when in:

Anne feared the SS.

the SS are the object, even though Anne does not *do* anything to them.

Object pronouns

Some English pronouns have a special form when they function as the object of a sentence. This explains why we say:

Pronoun p. 77

I saw him.

but

He saw me.

The complete set of pronouns which change in this way is:

Subject	Object
I	*me*
he	*him*
she	*her*
we	*us*
they	*them*

It is important to note that we know the grammatical role (subject or object) of each word in the sentence because of the place in which it occurs.

Pronouns can be used to support the analysis above which made *the SS* the object of the verb 'fear':

*She feared **them**.* (object pronoun)

is clearly preferable to:

She feared **they.* (subject pronoun)

Word order and function

We know who does the hitting and who gets hurt in:

Lord Royston bumped the skater.

simply by virtue of the word order. The order 'subject–verb–object' (**SVO**) is characteristic of English (and of many, but by no means all, other languages).

Word order can also help us to distinguish between the **direct objects**, which have been the subject of our discussion so far, and **indirect objects**.

Indirect object

In:

He brought the prisoner a toothbrush.

there appear to be two objects: 'the prisoner' and 'a toothbrush'. But what did the man actually bring? It was the toothbrush, so this is the true (or direct) object of the verb 'bring'. The action does, however, have some indirect effect on 'the prisoner' so this NP is the **indirect object** of the verb. An indirect object can usually be substituted by a phrase beginning with *for* or *to*:

*He brought a toothbrush **for the prisoner**.*
*He gave **me** some news. He gave some news **to me**.*
*You have done **me** a good deed. You have done a good deed **for me**.*

In:

I talk to myself.

there is only an indirect object, so the preposition is indispensable.

Subject complement

Not all noun phrases that come after verbs are objects:

Mars is the second smallest planet.

This construction establishes some sort of identity or equivalence between the two noun phrases. (In note form this example could be expressed as 'Mars = second smallest planet'.) The second noun phrase tells us more about the first. Most commonly complements follow the verb 'be' (which in this construction is known as the *copula*) but they also follow verbs like 'appear', 'seem', 'feel' and 'become'. The second noun phrase in this kind of construction is called a **complement**. Compare:

*The Martians were the **peaceful inhabitants**. (complement)*

and

*The Martians killed the **peaceful inhabitants**. (object)*

The complement may also be an adjective or **adjective phrase**:

Adjective pp. 76–77

*The planet was **warm and wet**.*

This kind of complement, where there is some identity with the subject of the sentence, is called a **subject complement**.

Object complement

It is also possible for a sentence to include a complement which links to its object.

	object	*object complement*
Mummy calls	*that sort of thing*	***the art of living**.*

	object	*object complement*
Michael's mother made	*him*	***an actor**.*

Like the subject complement, the object complement can be an adjective or adjective phrase:

	object	*object complement*
Anne's family thought	*her opinions*	***stupid**.*

In the following text, underline three complements and circle three direct objects:

My dear sister Mary. I am afraid that you will go mad when you read this...
poor Thomas is dead. We went along very well till we got within six or seven
hundred miles of California when the Indians attacked us. We had one passenger
with us, two guns and one revolver. As many as twenty of them came down
upon us. The three that shot Tom was hid by the side of the road in the bushes.

Reflection

Afraid, mad and *dead* are examples of complements. *us, two guns* and *one revolver* are direct objects.

Adverbials

The final possible component of the predicate is a word or phrase which functions as an adverb. The role of adverbials is to explain when, where, why or how:

Adverb p. 77

On Monday	adverbial phrase (when)
after the usual ablutions	adverbial phrase (when)
(my kidnapper came) back	adverb (where)

Adverbial phrases commonly begin with prepositions:

*The Irish government had placed a large advertisement **in the local Arabic newspaper**.*
*I was about to be sent back **for all the wrong reasons**.*

Adverbial elements may be placed at different points in the sentence, including initial position.

The relationship between subject and predicate is essential to the sentence and almost all sentence structures can be related back to these two key elements.

Sentence structure and intonation

Intonation is the pitch pattern of a sentence – its 'tune'. Intonation is, of course, not a feature of written English, despite being an important feature of spoken English. Particular sentence structures have their own distinctive intonation patterns.

Compare, for example:

He went to Ware.

with

He went to where?

Most speakers would pronounce the first sentence with a fairly even pitch, rising slightly in the middle and falling at the end and the second with a sharp rise at the end.[37]

In writing, where it is necessary for the sake of clarity, some of the work of intonation is done by **punctuation**.[38] The question mark guides us to read with question intonation. (In fact the symbol itself originates in an early form of musical notation, where it represented a rise in pitch.) Exclamation marks can perform a similar function.

Do you read:

> *Put your trunk in gently.*

and

> *Put your trunk in gently!*

with the same intonation?

It is important not to take this parallel too far. Intonation is always present in speech whilst punctuation is used relatively sparingly. Although intonation patterns extend over groups of words, that doesn't mean that speakers normally pause between these groups. The widely held notion that commas and full stops coincide with pauses in natural speech simply doesn't stand up to scrutiny.

In this section we have seen that:

▸ The N+V sentence structure can be expanded to the structure **subject + predicate**.

▸ The **main verb** of the sentence **inflects** according to the subject.

▸ Noun, verb and adverb and adjectives can be replaced by longer **phrases**.

▸ Word order allows us to identify the components of the predicate. These will always include a **verb** (simple or complex) and one or more of:

– a **nominal** functioning as a **direct object**

– a **nominal** functioning as an **indirect object**

– an **adjective phrase** or **noun phrase** functioning as a **subject complement**

– an **adjective phrase** or noun phrase functioning as an **object complement**

– one or more **adverbial** elements which may be placed before the verb or subject.

▸ Grammatical structures may be marked in speech by associated intonation patterns and in writing by punctuation.

37 If you find it difficult to 'hear' the pitch pattern of a sentence it may help to try whistling it.

38 In the example above the distinctive spellings of *where/Ware* also help to clarify intended meanings.

More sentence types

Sentence types can be classified by the way in which they follow certain structural patterns. These patterns are linked to the **purpose** of the sentence.

Statements

Statements describe or relate events or states of affairs. Structurally, statements follow the form of SAAD sentences (subject + predicate) or **passive** constructions.

SAAD sentences pp. 80–81
Passive pp. 95–97

Minor sentences

A few common spoken utterances function as freestanding sentences. Many examples are mainly interpersonal:

Interpersonal p. 3

Hello.
Goodbye.
Pardon?

Others are responses to questions, requests or commands:

Yes.
Not a hope.
In your dreams.
OK.

The partial sentences given in response to some questions can be considered minor sentences:

Ellipsis p. 118

Where did you find that?
In the river.

Commands

Sentences in which the speaker gives a command or instruction follow the pattern for **imperative** structures.

The most obvious feature of this structure is that that no subject is stated:

Subject p. 84

Infuse one teaspoon of fennel seeds.
Strain through filter paper.

Many commands therefore begin with the verb, or may even be a verb only:

Stop.

though often they will begin with an adverbial element or a negative structure:

Slowly strain through filter paper.
Never strain through filter paper.
Don't strain through filter paper.

The verb has a special form for the **imperative mood** which is the same as the **infinitive**. This is only really noticeable with the verb *be*. Compare:

Infinitive p. 106

*You **are** quiet.*

with

***Be** quiet!*

In writing, statements, minor sentences and commands are all demarcated with an initial capital and a final full stop or, depending on the emphasis required, an exclamation mark.

Exclamations

Exclamations are, in writing, most commonly punctuated by an exclamation mark. A major function of this type of sentence is to express the feelings of the speaker.

What a mess!
What a mess she made of that!

Exclamations do not need to include a verb and may have the emphasised element at the beginning.

Questions

Questions are intended to elicit information. They may be:

▶ **Polar questions**, which anticipate the answers Yes or No:

Does Bill come from Des Moines?

▶ **Wh- questions**, which begin with one of the question words (who, what, where, when, why, which, how) and expect specific information in response:

What did the old man say to the elephant?
Where did the elephant put its trunk?

▶ **Tag questions**, which begin as statements and end with an interrogative 'tag' such as 'didn't he?':

This is the right house for Mrs Caine, isn't it?
You knew I was Irish, didn't you?

A feature of most English question structures is that one part of the verb comes before its subject.

Tag questions are commonly (but not exclusively) used as **rhetorical questions**, which are not intended to elicit information but to emphasise a point. The two tag questions above could be intended rhetorically, as could:

Is this the first time I've told you I'm Irish?

(meaning 'you know very well I'm Irish')

and the polar question:

Does anybody want to live in a slum?

(meaning 'Nobody wants to live in a slum').

> **In this section we have seen that:**
>
> ⟩ There are five major **sentence types**.
>
> ⟩ Each type serves a **specific purpose**.
>
> ⟩ Each type conforms to specific **grammatical patterns**.

Word order and meaning: forming questions

Word order is very important in English. It can help us see what word class a word belongs to and tell us about its function within a sentence. Directly or indirectly this supports the way we understand a speaker or writer's meaning. Not surprisingly then, changing the order of elements in a simple sentence can change its meaning, as when, for example, a subject is exchanged with an object.

Subject p. 84
Object p. 85

You have already seen how questions are formed from statements by changing word order and you are now going to investigate some of the rules by which this happens.

Analysing language data Activity 3.8

Compare these pairs of sentences:

We were a very poor family.	→	*Were we a very poor family?*
Mummy is out.	→	*Is Mummy out?*
A spider's body is in two parts	→	*Is a spider's body in two parts?*

Try to formulate a rule which explains how the declarative sentences on the left have been changed into the questions on the right. What grammatical terms do you have to use?

Reflection

The difference is consistent and based on a predictable change in word order involving the subject and the verb. You might have formed a rule for question formation along the lines of:

$$\text{subject} + \text{verb} (+\text{object/complement})^{39}$$
$$\rightarrow \text{verb} + \text{subject} (+\text{object/complement})$$

or

$$\text{NP} + \text{V} (+\text{NP}) \rightarrow \text{V}+\text{NP} (+\text{NP})$$

The rule above seems to work very well, though problems arise, for example, if the verb is a complex one (i.e. it consists of more than one word):

I am sleeping.	→	*Am sleeping I?
He did steal it.	→	*Did steal he it?
She has given it back.	→	*Has given she it back?
Henry mows the lawn.	→	*Mows Henry the lawn?
Thelma breeds pigeons.	→	*Breeds Thelma pigeons?

Using your implicit language knowledge	Activity 3.9

A

Make yes/no questions out of the following sentences (e.g. 'Have you done me a good deed?' (Yes) rather than 'What have you done for me?' (a good deed)):

> You have done me a good deed.
> I shall return your kindness.
> You will go mad when you read this.
> Dussel has indirectly endangered our lives.
> Lord Royston was coming round suddenly on the outside edge.
> Many different toppings can be added.
> We are cooking a pizza.

B

Now do the same for these sentences:

> Sunday came.
> He seemed excited.
> I talk to myself.
> I do just the same if I have to eat something I don't like.
> She lost her temper and shouted.

How many different rules do you need to account for the two groups of sentences here and the original examples. Can you relate the rules to each other?

---

39 Brackets are used to identify elements which are optional.

Reflection

The verbs in group (A) each consist of two words (have done, shall return etc.). The first word of each pair is called the **auxiliary verb (aux)**. The commonest auxiliaries are *be, have* and *do*, all of which have distinct meanings of their own and can function as **main verbs**. Words like *will, can, shall, must, could, would* etc. cannot be main verbs and are known as **modal auxiliaries**. Where a verb has an auxiliary it is this which changes places with the subject to form a question:

$$NP + aux + V (+NP) \rightarrow aux + NP + V (+NP)$$

In the group (B) sentences there is no auxiliary verb, but an auxiliary appears in the question form:

Sunday came.	→	*Did Sunday come?*
I talk to myself.	→	*Do I talk to myself?*

so the question fits the

$$aux + NP + V (+NP)$$

rule.

It is also possible to add an auxiliary to the affirmative sentences:

*Sunday **did** come.*
*I **do** talk to myself.*

Here we are getting into deep water and I will go no further than to say that one possible analysis is to include sentences like this as an intermediate stage in the process.

Activity 3.10	Analysing language data

Look back at the sentences in activity 3.9.

What do you notice about inflections:

    on modal auxiliaries (*will, shall, can* etc.)?

    on non-modal auxaries (*have, do, be*)?

    on main verbs when accompanied by auxiliaries?

Reflection

Modal auxiliaries are not inflected (though some do have a past tense form, e.g. can–could). Other auxiliaries are fully inflected and it is these which carry the inflections for tense and person rather than the main verb (which may carry a past or present participle inflexion):

Tense pp. 104–105
Participles p. 106

She talk**s**.	→	She **does** talk.
She talk**ed**.	→	She **did** talk.
She **is** talk**ing**.	→	She **has** talk**ed**.

'Wh-' questions are similarly formed by rules, with the 'wh-' word playing a pronominal role standing for the unknown subject or object.

Pronoun p. 77
Subject p. 84
Object p. 85

<u>He</u> stole it	→	**Who** stole it?
He stole <u>it</u>	→	**What** did he steal?

Negative constructions

The behaviour of the verb in negative constructions recalls what happens in questions:

You have done me a good deed.	You have **not** done me a good deed.
I shall return your kindness.	I shall **not** return your kindness.
Lord Royston was coming.	Lord Royston was **not** coming.
Sunday came.	Sunday **did not** come.
I talk to myself.	I **do not** talk to myself.

Again, even where the 'original' sentence doesn't include an auxiliary, the negative form requires one.

Auxiliary p. 94

The role of grammatical rules

Of course, we don't need to know this rule *explicitly* in order to ask questions – we apply it automatically.[40] However, this examination of one relatively straightforward area of English syntax should have illustrated that:

Explicit and implicit knowledge p. 6

▹ syntactic rules (i.e. word order) can express meaning;

▹ the rules of syntax can appear very complex – much more so than most traditional grammatical rules, which take our knowledge of language for granted;

▹ syntactic rules may be related to each other.

Word order and meaning: passive constructions

So far, our examples of statements have been of the kind:

1 *My mother wrote the script.*

40 And I am not, of course, suggesting that you need to memorise the explicit details of rules like these.

English offers an alternative way of structuring this kind of information:

2 *The script was written by my mother.*

The first of these sentences is an **active** construction (the first A in SAAD). The second is known as a **passive** construction.

SAAD sentences pp. 80–81

Sentence 1 has a **subject**, a **verb** and an **object** (SVO). It is tempting to think of these categories in terms of their meaning. *My mother* (subject) performed the action of the verb, *wrote* is the action (verb) and *the script* 'suffered' the action (object). Sentence 2 also has a verb *was written*, and two noun phrases, but although *my mother* is the logical subject of both sentences, the **grammatical subject** of the second sentence is *the script*. A small change in the sentence illustrates why:

SVO structures p. 86
Plural p. 75

*The scripts **were** written by my mother.*

The term, 'subject', therefore, is defined by a grammatical relationship and not by any consideration of meaning.

Passive constructions are formed by using the verb *be* as an **auxiliary** together with the part of the verb known as the **past participle**.

Auxiliary verbs p. 94
Past participle p. 106

Very often the subject of the verb in the active sentence (the agent) is not included in a passive sentence. This can be useful when the agent is not clearly identifiable or where the writer or speaker does not want to reveal 'who did it'.

Activity 3.11	Analysing language data

In each of these sentences no agent is included. Can you say why? Can you suggest an agent for each one?

(a) *While you were out the window was broken.*

(b) *Water is found in all parts of the world.*

(c) *The dough is kneaded for about ten minutes.*

(d) *This work will be completed by Thursday.*

Reflection

Possible answers include (a) the speaker, (b) anybody in the world, (c) and (d) persons unknown. In (b) the phrase *is found* is almost a 'stock item' of the language, more or less synonymous with *exists* and so does not expect an agent. In (c) the writer may not know and the reader probably does not care exactly who kneads the dough. In fact the agent could be a succession of people through the history of pizza making. It is the act which is important, rather than any particular agent, as is probably the case for (d). If the agent in (a) *is* the speaker then the reason for adopting a passive form is obvious!

In this section we have seen that:

▶ Changing **word order** according to consistent rules can change the **purpose** and **meaning** of a sentence.

▶ Other sentence types (questions, passive constructions, negative constructions) can be derived from the Simple Active Affirmative Declarative (SAAD) pattern.

More about phrases

As we have seen, nouns can be expanded to form ever-bigger noun phrases.

Analysing language data   Activity 3.12

Use the knowledge you have gained so far to describe the structure of the subject noun phrase in each of these sentences:

(a) **The building** (*towered over us*).

(b) **The grey building** (*towered over us*).

(c) **The big grey building** (*towered over us*).

(d) **The very big building** (*towered over us*).

(e) **The building that I grew up in** (*towered over us*).

(f) **The building with the plate glass windows** (*towered over us*).

(g) **The building and its immediate neighbours** (*towered over us*).

Reflection

In each of these the noun phrase begins with a determiner (though not all noun phrases do). In (a) – (d) most of the additional elements are adjectives, though *very* is an adverb. (g) has a compound noun phrase – two phrases joined by *and* – whilst (f) includes a **prepositional phrase** which functions as an adjective (this kind of adjective phrase comes *after* the noun it describes). You may have had trouble with (e) as we have not yet looked at **relative clauses**, of which *that I grew up in* is an example.

Preposition p. 78
Relative clauses p. 101

Noun phrases may include words of any class as well as different kinds of **phrase** and **clause**. It is probably easiest to think of phrases as strings of words which can substitute for shorter strings or single words. Identifying the class of word which can be substituted will tell you the kind of phrase you are dealing with.

Clause p. 100

In:

> *I was about to be sent back **for all the wrong reasons.***

the final phrase could be replaced by *erroneously* (or even *cheerfully* as the concern here is grammatical categories, not meaning) and can be seen therefore as adverbial.

Adverbial p. 88

Phrases and prepositions

There are not many instances of phrases standing for prepositions. It may be better to think of strings like *in front of* and *next to* simply as 'compound prepositions'. The structure which traditional grammars call the **prepositional phrase** is simply a type of phrase which *begins with* a preposition. As you have already seen, these can have an adverbial (e.g. *with some degree of anger, as a British subject*), or adjectival (e.g. *with my photograph*) function. The terminology is inconsistent, since all the other names for phrase types (noun phrase, adjective phrase etc.) refer to function. Since prepositional phrases also have a functional name (most usually adverbial phrase) the term is probably best avoided.

Activity 3.13	Checking your knowledge ✔

For each of the sections in the following text find one (or at the most two) words to replace it. Then state what class the word (and therefore the phrase) belongs to.

> *Without making a sound, the old chauffeur was carefully parking the dazzlingly polished vintage Cadillac to the rear of Mrs Evans's colonial mansion.*

Phrase	Substitute word(s)	Class of word/phrase
without making a sound	silently	adverb
the old chauffeur	aged driver	adjective + noun
was carefully parking	was positioning	verb phrase
the dazzlingly polished vintage Cadillac	shiney car	adjective + noun
to the rear of	behind	preposition
Mrs Evans's colonial mansion	the house	determiner + noun

Reflection

Of the eight word classes only pronouns and determiners cannot be expanded at all. Conjunctions and prepositions can consist of longer strings, but these are few and taken from strictly limited sets (e.g. *in addition to, as well as, in front of*). Members of the open word classes (noun, verb, adjective, adverb) can form lengthy phrases.

Word classes pp. 73–79

Punctuation and phrases

As phrases can hardly ever form a sentence on their own, they are hardly ever (except in the case of minor sentences) associated with full stops. In writing they are often demarcated with commas.

In the following examples, adverb and noun phrases are marked off by commas:

Noun phrase pp. 83–84
Adverb phrase p. 88

After the usual ablutions, my kidnapper came back

I had not been on skates since I was last here, five years ago, but the knack soon came back again.

Green, my favourite colour, was on every surface.

There was a distinguished company on the ice. Lady Dangan. Lord and Lady Royston and Lord George Paget, all skating.

This last sentence is also an example of the use of commas to mark off the items in a list.

In a sense, each of these phrases is 'additional' to the basic SV(O) structure and, if deleted, would still leave a grammatical sentence. An initial phrase is marked off by a single comma, while phrases within sentences are marked off by pairs of commas. Paired brackets and dashes perform a similar function:

The unsuspecting third member of the cast, the rent collector, was standing there.

The unsuspecting third member of the cast (the rent collector) was standing there.

The unsuspecting third member of the cast – the rent collector – was standing there.

As with sentence punctuation, commas often reflect intonation patterns and this gives rise to the common belief that commas mark pauses in speech. In fact you usually can pause at a comma, but you'll probably find that in any given sentence you can pause elsewhere too. Commas mark grammatical boundaries.

> **In this section we have seen that:**
>
> ▶ Phrases are distributed within sentences in much the same way as members of the corresponding **word classes**.
>
> ▶ Phrases corresponding to the **open word** classes (noun, verb, adjective, adverb) are very common; those corresponding to **closed classes** (pronoun, determiner, preposition, conjunction) are rare.
>
> ▶ In writing, **punctuation** (in the form of commas) is often used to clarify meaning by **marking phrase boundaries**.

Clauses

If phrases are elements which in some respects resemble words, then clauses resemble sentences.

Phrase pp. 83–84

The sentence:

> *My mother rushed down the stairs and hid behind the door.*

consists of two clauses, the first of which is:

> *My mother rushed down the stairs*

Although in the longer sentence this is a clause, the same string of words can be a sentence in its own right; the simplest sentences consist of single clauses. Like sentences, clauses need a verb of their own. They also need a subject, though this is not always clearly visible.

Sentence pp. 79–81
Verb p. 75
Subject p. 84

Joining clauses: compound and complex sentences

> *This is Rip. Rip can jump. Rip can catch. Rip can run. Run Rip, run…*

In both speech and writing we tend to vary the length of our sentences. In writing especially, a succession of similar sentences can feel very monotonous (even the text above can be expected to burst into *Oh Mother, see how Rip can run* at any moment).

Single-clause sentences can be made longer by adding and expanding phrases:

> *On Monday, after the usual ablutions, my kidnapper and aspiring confidant came back.*

> *The unsuspecting third member of the cast – the rent collector – was standing there.*

Despite their length, each of these sentences is structured around a single main verb and is, therefore, a single clause.

On the other hand, sentences like:

My hut is very small, but there is room for your trunk and myself.

You have done me a good deed and one day I shall return your kindness.

each have two main verbs at the heart of two distinct clauses. A sentence with two clauses joined by a conjunction (usually *or*, *and*, or *but*) and where neither clause can be considered more important than the other is called a **compound sentence**.

Conjunction p. 78

Very often one of the clauses (the **main clause**) carries the main meaning of the sentence whilst another (the **subordinate clause**) provides supporting information:

I answered the door, because my mother told me to.

Clauses paired in this way are often linked by conjunctions which imply their relative importance:

if, because, although ...

If you say I'm not in we won't have to pay the rent.

Relative clauses

A common way of linking clauses within a single sentence is to make the subordinate clause a **relative clause**. These are sometimes called **wh-clauses** because they often begin with the words *which, when, who* etc. (the set we last met as **question words**, but which in these constructions are known as **relative pronouns**):

*I was captured **when** I had been in Beirut for four months.*

*Beirut was a place **where** I could escape from British policy in Ireland.*

They can also begin with 'that':

*I do the same if I have to eat something **that** I can't stand.*

or nothing at all:

I do the same if I have to eat something I can't stand.

One function of relative clauses is to save repeating the subject or object noun phrase:

*I had the honour of being knocked down by **Lord Royston**.*

***Lord Royston** was coming round suddenly on the outside edge.*

→ *I had the honour of being knocked down by Lord Royston, **who** was coming round suddenly on the outside edge.*

Embedded clauses

So far we have looked at ways of ordering clauses one after another. It is, however, possible to order the clauses in the last example differently:

*Lord Royston, **who was coming round suddenly on the outside edge**, knocked me down.*

Here the relative clause is **embedded** inside the main clause. (Note the use of commas to mark off this important structural unit.)

There is no (grammatical) limit on the number of embedded clauses which can be included in a sentence. This makes it possible for unwary speakers and writers to produce excessively long sentences where the subject is quite distant from its verb:

The highest building in London, which is one of the nicest cities that I've ever visited when I've been in Europe, the continent where I do most of my business, which incidentally is selling computers which have previously been used in offices which are being refurbished, is Canary Wharf.

Activity 3.14   Analysing language data   ✔

Sentences containing relative clauses can be broken down to two or more simple clauses:

> ▶ *Hilary,* **who won last year's gold medal,** *broke her own record yesterday.*
>> ➔ *Hilary won last year's gold medal.*
>>
>> and
>>
>> *Hilary broke her own record yesterday.*

> ▶ *Hilary won the prize that Sue won last year.*
>> ➔ *Hilary won the prize.*
>>
>> and
>>
>> *Sue won the prize last year.*

Break each of these complex sentences down into simple clauses:

WWT is a wildlife charity which is unique in promoting wildfowl and wetland conservation.

The three [men] that shot Tom was hid by the side of the road in the bushes

My mother wrote the lines that I was to speak.

From these glands comes a liquid which turns to silk on contact with the air.

Then it makes a series of sticky spirals that run from the centre outwards.

I talk more to myself than to others, which is to be recommended for two reasons.

My kidnapper, who seemed very excited, told me about the advertisement which he had seen in the newspaper.

Reflection

Sometimes the separation can be made without changing the basic word order:

> *My kidnapper seemed very excited.*
>
> *My kidnapper told me about the advertisement.*

though with other constructions some bigger changes are necessary:

> *My mother wrote the lines.*

> *I was to speak the lines.*

Sometimes a relative pronoun can refer back to a whole clause:

> *I talk more to myself than others.*

> *Talking more to myself than others is to be recommended.*

The last sentence contains two relative clauses and can therefore be expressed as three sentences:

> *My kidnapper seemed very excited.*

> *My kidnapper told me about the advertisement.*

> *My kidnapper had seen the advertisement in the newspaper.*

Punctuation and clauses

For the sake of clarity, clauses, like phrases, are often marked off by commas, though there is a well-known convention that '*and*' should not be preceded by a comma. There is one case where the use (or not) of a comma makes a significant difference in meaning.

In:

> *The elephant, who was getting wet, put his trunk into the hut.*

we know that we are talking about one particular elephant and the relative clause just gives us a little more information about him. Its omission would not change the meaning of the rest of the sentence.

Without commas to mark off the relative clause:

> *The elephant who was getting wet put his trunk into the hut.*

the sentence has a different meaning. Here the relative clause restricts the reference of the word 'elephant' – it is now one specific elephant from a larger set.

This kind of clause is known as a **restrictive relative clause**.

In this section we have seen that:

▶ Sentences may consist of one or more **clauses**.

▶ **Compound sentences** may be formed by using conjunctions to join two or more clauses of equal importance.

▶ **Complex sentences** are formed by adding one or more **subordinate clauses** to a **main clause**.

▶ A subordinate clause introduced by a 'wh-' word is called a **relative clause**.

▶ Relative clauses may be **embedded** within a main clause.

▶ In writing, clauses may be demarcated by **commas**, the presence or absence of which may affect the meaning of the sentence.

More about verbs

English verbs have many different forms and the rules which govern their use can be very complex. Speakers use these rules whenever they speak, but most would find it very hard to explain them. However, there are a few features of verbs, explicit knowledge of which can help clearer writing, thinking and editing.

Verb p. 75

Tense and aspect

A major factor determining the form of a particular verb is its tense, often expressed as past, present or future.

Activity 3.15	Using your implicit language knowledge ✔

The following sentences differ only in the use of their verbs. Which are past, which present and which future?

I take paracetamol.

I am taking paracetamol.

I will take paracetamol.

I am going to take paracetamol.

I took paracetamol.

I have taken paracetamol.

I have been taking paracetamol.

I was taking paracetamol.

I had taken paracetamol.

I had been taking paracetamol.

Reflection

You probably found it quite simple to sort these sentences into three categories, but the examples show that there is more than one present tense and half a dozen 'past' tenses? Clearly there are other factors at work, some of which may be linked to the working of nearby verbs.

I took paracetamol.

for example, relates an action which took place in the past but

I had taken paracetamol.

refers to an action further back than the action of another verb:

I declined the offer of a drink because I had taken paracetamol.

Both actions are placed in the past, but the tenses tell us which came first. The verb form using the auxiliary *had* is known as the **pluperfect** form.

Auxiliary p. 94

Using your implicit language knowledge   **Activity 3.16**

The verbs in the following sentences are all in the present tense. Explain the difference in meaning conveyed by the members of each pair.

I drive a car. – I am driving a car.

I drink coffee. – I am drinking coffee.

She paints her toenails. – She is painting her toenails.

Reflection

The second sentence of each pair refers to an action which is taking place *now*. The first refers to a longer period, implicitly extending into the past and the future. The question of the duration of an action or state is the province of the **aspect** of the verb.

Past, present and future tenses may all express different aspects and this accounts for the wide range of verb forms, both simple and complex, available to the speaker of English.

Aspect and tense: adverbs

A sense of aspect (e.g. the duration of an event) and tense may be conveyed by an adverb or adverbial phrase as well as by the verb. For example, in:

I am marrying a girl named Bobbi tomorrow.

The tense is present but the sense is future. Native speakers are quite happy to treat this kind of sentence as a future construction.

Finite and non-finite verb forms

Verbs which are inflected to agree with a subject noun and which express a tense are called **finite verbs**. Almost all the verbs discussed so far have been finite.

Verb p. 75
Inflexion pp. 67–68

Some forms of the verb do not carry so much grammatical information:

Grasping my small hand, my mother rushed down the three flights of stairs.

*Tom fell dead, **shot** at close range.*

*I had come to Lebanon to **work**.*

grasping and *shot* are examples respectively of the **present participle** and **past participle**. The participles are, misleadingly, known as 'past' and 'present' because of the tenses they are most commonly associated with. They cannot by themselves determine tense. The word '*work*' exemplifies the form known as the **infinitive**. Only the verb 'be' has a distinctive infinitive form, which I have used in this sentence as it is usual to refer to verbs by their infinitive form. Otherwise the infinitive has the same form as the uninflected stem of the verb (*go, take, build* etc.). Sometimes the word *to* is considered to be part of the infinitive.

Tense pp. 104–105

Complex verbs contain only one finite element, which is always the first word:

*I **had** been teaching in Beirut.*

You will recognise this part of the verb as the **auxiliary**.

Auxiliary p. 94

The inclusion of a finite element makes the whole complex verb finite. This means that all sentences (apart from minor sentences) contain a finite verb, which is why

£65,000 to build a bus shelter for the village

and

Nothing to learn.

are not considered to be sentences,[41] even though the latter has been given a full stop.

Finite and non-finite clauses

On the other hand, some *clauses* contain a verb which is non-finite:

Clause p. 100

Grasping my small hand, my mother rushed down the three flights of stairs.

*Tom fell dead, **shot at close range**.*

*I had come to Lebanon **to work**.*

Verbal nouns and adjectives

Some words that look like verbs regularly function as members of other word classes.

Verb p. 75

41 Admittedly, given the right context, these might be minor sentences.

For each of the words printed in bold type, say:

(a) which part of the verb it is

(b) which word class it is functioning as.

> He seemed **excited**.
>
> **To argue** would be futile.
>
> Their **arguing** was futile.
>
> It was an **exciting** evening on the ice.
>
> Anne's **talking** annoyed the family.
>
> **Hidden** in the bushes, the attackers shot Tom.
>
> The **talking** elephant promised to repay his friend's **unsolicited** kindness.

Reflection

Past participles can function as adjectives (*excited, hidden, unsolicited*) whilst present participles may function as adjectives (*a talking elephant, an exciting evening*) or as nouns (*Anne's talking, their arguing*). The infinitive may also function as a noun (*to argue*).

In this section we have seen that:

▶ English verbs have many different forms, often complex ones, to express differences of **tense**, **aspect** and **mood**.

▶ Most sentence types must include a **finite verb**.

▶ **Clauses** must contain a verb, but in subordinate clauses this may be non-finite.

▶ Within sentences, certain **verb forms** may function as nouns or adjectives.

More about nouns

There are several categories of noun which have distinctive properties of distribution or form.

Common and proper nouns

Proper nouns are the names of people, places or events; in writing they are marked by the use of an initial capital letter. Confusion often arises from the fact that a particular word may sometimes be written with a capital and sometimes without.

Look at the following sentences and explain the different use of capitalisation for each pair of underlined words.

I took her to the <u>doctor</u>.   We saw <u>Doctor</u> Smith.

What have you got, <u>Mummy</u>?   My <u>mummy</u> has got the measles.

I live in <u>North</u> London.   They went <u>north</u>.

Reflection

The capitalised words refer to particular individuals and places; they are names or parts of names. Where the noun refers to one of a class of people or things it is a **common noun. Proper nouns** refer to people or things which are in some sense unique. Sometimes the line between things which are unique and things which are not seems difficult to draw, so there are some cases where, as writers, we need to know the convention. Why, for example, does *November* deserve a capital when *autumn* does not? Most proper names (mostly of people and places) are not preceded by a determiner (*Peter, Canada, Woking, Everest*) though some do (*the Thames, the High Peak, the Acropolis*).

Determiner p. 78

Singular, plural, countable and mass nouns

We have already seen that nouns are either **singular** (*Paul, screwdriver, apple*) or **plural** (*the Himalayas, screwdrivers, apples*). These are grammatical categories which are linked closely with the concepts of either 'one thing' or 'more than one thing'. As usual, however, there are a few hard cases. Look at the following two sentences:

Oats are grown in this field.

Wheat is grown in this field.

In what sense can *oats* be said to be plural and wheat singular? Only in grammatical terms (oats has a final -*s* and governs a plural verb). In terms of their meaning the words refer to two very similar things.

Singular (common) nouns are usually preceded by a determiner, but wheat is not. This is because *wheat* is a **mass** noun. Other mass nouns include *water, milk, sand* etc. In common-sense terms mass nouns refer to things which are measured rather than counted. Usually they have no plural form (except in constructions like *which of these wheats grows best?*) and behave grammatically as singulars. Nouns which are not mass nouns are known as **count nouns** or **countable nouns**.

Concrete and abstract nouns

Nouns refer to 'things'. Things which can be touched or seen as distinct objects are referred to as **concrete nouns**. **Abstract nouns** refer to ideas which can be thought about and discussed, but not seen or touched as distinct objects. Abstract nouns are often derived from adjectives (*beauty, strength*) or verbs (*direction, introduction*) and have something in common with mass nouns, often appearing in the singular without a determiner.

Animate and inanimate nouns

Animate/inanimate is largely a distinction of meaning – animate nouns refer to beings which are alive. The grammatical significance of this distinction lies in the fact that (with a few possible exceptions, e.g. ships) only animate nouns may be referred to by the pronouns *he* and *she*.

In this section we have seen that:

◗ The category 'noun' can be subdivided into **smaller categories** which usually express a common function or meaning.

◗ Members of particular sub classes may have characteristic features of **distribution** and **form** and may be associated with **rules** for pronoun use, punctuation or grammatical agreement.

More about punctuation

Many syntactic structures are associated in writing with particular items of punctuation and these have been described, in context, in the course of this chapter. This short section summarises the functions of the main punctuation marks.

◗ **Full stop (.):** used to mark the end of most sentences, the only exceptions being questions and exclamations, which end with question marks (?) and exclamation marks (!) respectively.

◗ **Semicolon (;):** these are used to combine two ideas of equal importance in a single sentence.

Sir Christopher Blount and Sir Charles Davers were beheaded; Sir Gilly Merrick and Henry Cuffe were hanged.

You will notice that each half of this sentence is a simple clause and could stand as a sentence in its own right; the use of the semicolon (as in this sentence) rather than a full stop emphasises the close link between the two clauses.

Semicolons are also sometimes used in lists where each item is a phrase or clause, especially where there are commas within each item.

The suppliers were: Smith, Jones and Evans; Spanner and Knutt; Belt and Braces.

- **Comma**: these mark clause and phrase boundaries. One special function is to mark the beginning of a passage of **direct speech**, or its end where the author's sentence continues beyond the speaker's.

> *'When they catch them,' Frog replied.*

- **Speech marks/quotation marks**: these are used to identify a speaker's exact words within a text. Practice over the choice of single quotation marks (or 'single quotes' as they have become known) and double quotation marks ('double quotes') varies, but single quotes are used most commonly nowadays, with double quotes reserved for 'speech within speech'. **Indirect speech**, in which the speaker's exact words are not recorded does not require quotation marks.

> *Frog replied that shrews ate frogs when they caught them.*

The previous paragraph exemplifies another use for quotation marks: to indicate that a word or phrase is being viewed as a subject of discussion or used in some novel or technical way.

- **Apostrophe (')**: apostrophes mark the possessive inflexions (*Bill's hat*). This is an example where the written mode conveys morphological information which is less accessible in speech. For example, the phrase *the girls' hats* is ambiguous in speech but clearly distinguished in writing from the singular form (i.e. one girl) *the girl's hats*. There is no apostrophe in the possessive pronoun *its*.

A second function of apostrophes is to stand for letters which have been 'dropped' in contractions (*don't, I'll* etc.).

- **Colon (:)**: colons usually precede some additional information, often an elaboration of what comes immediately before.

> *There are four groups of instruments: strings, woodwind, brass and percussion.*

> *There are two reasons for this: the ground is too wet and there is no shade.*

- *Capitals*: strictly speaking, capitalisation is not punctuation, but it performs a similar function. Capital letters are used to mark the beginning of sentences, and for titles and proper nouns.

4. Understanding English at text level: the construction of texts

In a sense, all language study is the study of texts. Language data studied at word and sentence level must (if it is in any sense to be considered 'real') come from texts and, conversely, an understanding of features which operate at these two levels contributes to our understanding of whole texts. Texts are where the symbols of language (both spoken and written), meanings (implicit and explicit) and the knowledge and understanding of speakers, listeners, readers and writers all come together.

This chapter begins with a consideration of what we mean by a text and how texts achieve overall coherence, before looking at the formal features of a number of specific text types or *genres*. Chapter 5 examines in detail some of the ways in which *poetic writing* operates. Chapter 6 is concerned with how we read critically, both to determine elements of bias in a text and to make judgements about its quality.

We shall begin, then, by looking at some basic issues concerned with the construction of different kinds of texts.

In this chapter we shall see:

▸ how texts use words and sentences to achieve a unifying meaning or **coherence**;

▸ how texts simultaneously express **information** and take into account the needs and understandings of the **audience** in order to fulfil the writer's **purpose**;

▸ some of the characteristics of **fiction** and **non-fiction** texts;

▸ the features of six commonly used non-fiction text types or **genres**;

▸ how writers may combine the features of several genres to achieve their purpose.

What is a text?

Using your language knowledge   Activity 4.1

Here are some things which are commonly said in connection with texts. Do you think they are appropriate? Can you say why?

Weaving a tissue of lies
Spinning a yarn
Tying up the loose ends
Losing the thread[42]

42 Carter *et al.* (1997) point to these metaphors.

Reflection

Phrases such as these reflect our understanding that just as fabric is woven together from different threads, so in speaking and writing ideas, words and sentences are woven into coherent texts. The word **text** itself comes from the Latin for 'something woven'.

Linguists define the word 'text' as a stretch of connected spoken or written language which is capable of being discussed and analysed as a single entity. More recently the concept of **media texts** – texts constructed not just from words but from images too – has become familiar and film, television, radio and internet texts have shown themselves to be analysable in much the same way as novels or conversations.

Coherence

The main thing that we need from a text is that it should make sense; we expect a text to have a single unifying meaning of some kind. Sometimes we say that we don't know what someone is talking about, or we don't know what a particular written text means. This usually means that we haven't grasped the one overarching meaning which enables us to interpret the words and sentences correctly.

The capacity for a text to convey a consistent meaning is known as its **coherence**. Coherence is achieved as result of several different factors.

In Chapter 1 you saw how ideational, interpersonal and textual features all have a role to play in the construction of an utterance. These concepts are capable of informing our understanding of coherence in terms of the meaning, audience, and structural features of a particular text.

Halliday's classification p. 3

The example of a party election broadcast illustrates how these three elements work together.

> **Ideational factors**. The speaker will have selected some key ideas on the current and possible state of the nation which are intended to convince listeners or viewers to support their particular cause. Though these ideas will be varied (maybe focusing on the economy, the health service and taxation, for example) the overall information content will have been assembled to contribute to a wider (and unifying) argument about the party's fitness to govern. Not all relevant information is contained within the text. The author needs to assume a certain level of **contextual** understanding – in this case essential knowledge will probably include knowledge of the current political climate, details of the electoral and party systems and names of other politicians. To know how much contextual information may be assumed, authors must know their **audience**.

> **Interpersonal factors**. The speaker will seek to convey the key ideas in a way which matches the interests (in both senses of the word) and life experiences of the **audience**. Again, different parts may address different voter groups (e.g. over 60s, young unemployed

men, former voters for another party). Information content and audience factors will both affect the structure of the text.

▶ **Textual factors**. The broadcast will be constructed in a way which conveys the information clearly. Attention will be paid to the overall structure; the speaker will take care, for example, to place statements which arouse the audience's anxieties next to positive information regarding the party's own plans and achievements and all the themes will come together in a final *vote for me* statement. Grammatical structures (e.g. questions, conditional structures, 2nd (you) or 1st (we) person constructions) and vocabulary will be carefully chosen too.

All these elements will be used together in order to meet the author's original **purpose**, in this case to win votes. Ideas are selected according to how likely they are to motivate the audience to support the campaign; text and sentence structures and vocabulary are chosen to reflect these choices. As you will see shortly, a range of conventional forms (or *genres*) has developed to express different purposes.

Word meaning pp. 20–21

Sometimes such broadcasts are dismissed as 'nonsense' because although they are carefully constructed texts they do not make coherent 'sense' to someone whose views are formed by different experiences from the speaker's. The coherence of a text, then, depends not only on how it is woven together, but on its underlying meaning and how the reader or hearer's experience influences the way they read or hear it. A text cannot provide meaning on its own – how it is interpreted always depends to some extent on its context and the reader's relevant knowledge and understanding.

Analysing language data	Activity 4.2

How does the writer of this election leaflet make use of ideational, interpersonal and textual features?

I decided to stand for Mayor of London when I was stuck on a Tube train for the third time in a week.

London's politicians have failed to invest in our public transport. I am determined to put the Tube, our buses and our trains at the heart of my first term as Mayor.

My top three priorities for London are:

▶ Rescuing our Tube, buses and trains with new management and bonds. I will not sell off the Tube.

▶ Reducing crime and the fear of crime with 3,000 more police and 1,000 new Community Safety Constables.

▶ Revitalising London's diverse communities fighting discrimination, bringing more jobs and affordable homes.

As I walk down London's High Streets, people tell me how they have been let down by yesterday's politicians putting themselves and their party before Londoners.

As a businesswoman I bring new management not old politics to London. Please lend me your vote on polling day.

Reflection

The candidate assumes that readers know mayoral elections are to be held in London. Although she and her party doubtless have numerous and complex policies for the capital she restricts herself to three key ideas relating to transport, crime and 'communities'. She shows a high regard for her audience (persuading them of her point of view is, of course, the main purpose of the text): the key ideas are ones she has identified as important concerns for London's voters and she is keen to offer herself as a person voters can identify with – she travels on the tube (and gets stuck) and walks down high streets. She is sensitive to their traditional loyalties and asks only that they *lend* their vote. Great care has been taken over the structure of the text. It is brief, concise and clearly written; most of the sentences consist of single clauses and only two are as long as three clauses. Paragraphs are also short and well spaced, with the three top priorities marked as bullet points. Vocabulary is simple with few adjectives or adverbs. It is a text which has been designed to deliver the candidate's message to people who are not happy with the way London is currently run but who have little time (or inclination) to read political leaflets.

Clause p. 100

Extralinguistic features

Although a reader may be perfectly capable of reading the separate words and sentences of a particular text, it still will not make any sense to them if they are not familiar with the references which the speaker or writer is making to their own knowledge and experience, or to other texts. If you are not from London, for example, you may have missed a reference or two in the last text. Some features of a text lie outside the realm of language.

Activity 4.3	Analysing language data

Do you understand *exactly* what this text means? List any elements which need explaining to you. If you do happen to be fully familiar with the subject matter try to identify those parts which the uninitiated would have difficulties with.

Intended as an aural companion piece to 'ego trip' magazine's entertaining Book of Rap Lists, 'The Big Playback' is a great boon to hard-up and/or lazy old-school hip hop trainspotters. The big draw is surely 'Beat Bop' by Ramelzee Vs K-Rob, an original pressing of which is worth upwards of $1,000.

[*The Big Issue* No. 385]

Reflection

If you are experienced in the world of popular music you may well have understood the message. If not, whilst getting the idea that this *is* about music, from such linguistic clues as '*aural*', '*Rap*' and '*Bop*', the force of this album review may pass you by. This may be because of its **extralinguistic** references to a particular set of cultural experiences. Similarly, wine columns in newspapers or computer manuals can be impenetrable to those who aren't experienced in these areas. Whilst the texts may be perfectly coherent, their meaning is obscured by readers' unfamiliarity with the subject matter.

Using your implicit language knowledge	Activity 4.4

Place the following text types in order of comprehensibility to you (i.e. rank them from 'easiest to understand' to 'hardest to understand'). What factors make a text more comprehensible?

A legal contract for buying a house

A computer manual

A car maintenance handbook

A newspaper report on a football match

An Australian political cartoon

An American high school prospectus

The rules of stoolball

Chaucer's *Canterbury Tales* (in translation)

Reflection

Familiarity is the key to comprehension in almost all cases. This may just seem common sense (and it is) but it does again illustrate the not so obvious point that texts never contain 'all the information'. The reader must supply some of it. Understanding some texts may require specialised vocabulary knowledge (e.g. legal texts) while other texts will confuse by using unfamiliar words in familiar ways (e.g. *drifting* in the car manual will involve the use of a large hammer!).[43] You will probably feel the lack of requisite extralinguistic knowledge most keenly when dealing with Australian politics, though you will probably miss some supporting details and irony in the Chaucer. (All this assumes you do not have expert knowledge in these fields.)

Some extralinguistic factors are intended to aid coherence; for example, the **layout** and **typographical features** of written language: headings, bold print etc. In spoken language **paralinguistic features** such as gesture, emphatic intonation and body language contribute significantly to a speaker's meaning.

Spoken language pp. 168–172

43 Of course, knowledge of specialised word meanings is a kind of linguistic knowledge, but the skills and experience(s) referred to are extralinguistic.

Cohesion

While the term 'coherence' refers to the underlying unity of a text brought about by the meaning it has for its audience, **cohesion** refers to the lexical and structural means used to hold a text together. Coherence is usually easier to see at the level of the whole text whilst cohesion is more visible at sentence level.

Activity 4.5	Analysing language data

The following extract is taken from materials for an Open University distance learning art history course. It forms the opening of a new chapter. Read it through a couple of times then write a short sentence or two about the overall meaning it conveys to you (the passage's coherence). After that, take a little time to note a few things about cohesion. What cohesive devices are used to structure the text? For example, what is the relationship between the opening question and the rest of the piece? How does the writer shape the piece to help the reader?

> How big a part did building and urban renewal play in the fourteenth-century Italian city economy? There are various reasons why it is very hard to answer this question with precision. One is that the surviving evidence makes it difficult to enter into the design process. We have no Italian architectural treatises that can be compared to Cennino Cennini's handbook for painters or to the various manuscripts that have survived elsewhere in Europe, which give an insight into architectural theory. In addition, the buildings that survive have been changed in various ways, by time and fashion. We must therefore assemble a rather diverse assortment of sources to try to assess the impact of building on Italian cities at this time. We know something about how the various building trades were organized professionally and where they obtained their materials. We can deduce something about the skills that were required by extrapolating the evidence from other cultures, to see if it fits the Italian context, and by looking at the buildings and the few drawings that have survived. This should help us to consider with a new eye the buildings of the period that remain and to place them into their social context.

Reflection

The extract starts with a question, which serves to engage the reader in the topic to be discussed. The rest of the paragraph does not in fact answer the question, but discusses the nature of the possible evidence and the difficulties that this presents. You may have noticed a pattern in the construction of the paragraph. After the initial question, there is a statement that there are reasons why it is hard to answer. This is then expanded by listing and explaining two major difficulties: there are no architectural treatises and the buildings themselves have been changed. From this, the writer leads us to his next statement about the diversity of source material needed to assess the impact of building on Italian cities. This statement in its turn is exemplified in three areas: deducing things about skills, comparing them with other cultures and looking at surviving buildings and drawings. A concluding statement asks us to look afresh at the idea of buildings mentioned in the initial question.

Thematic consistency

Organising the information in a text can be done in various ways. Writers choose which bit of information they will start with – and therefore give prominence to – and which items will be left until later. They decide what information – or attitudes of the listener/reader – can be taken as given and which will be likely to be new. These choices are expressed through grammar and vocabulary. In the extract you have been looking at, it is clear that the main aspect of information – the **theme** – is 'building and urban renewal'. The reference in the opening sentence to the economy, which is not taken up in the extract above, suggests that this thematic thread will come later in the piece. The theme of this extract is created through the use of particular grammatical devices and vocabulary choices.

Analysing language data Activity 4.6

Read through the text again and note words and phrases which serve as links in the meaning. For example, notice words which refer the reader back to other ideas (or even to single words), or which link statements together.

Reflection

You may have noted the use of **connectives** such as *in addition* or *therefore*; these are words which link parts of the text together. You might also have picked out words such as *this* and *them*, or a succession of nouns with broadly similar meanings such as *treatises, handbook, manuscript*.

Cohesive devices

The following are the commonest types of cohesive device.

▶ **Connectives**. Different parts of a text are linked together most obviously by **connectives**, words or phrases whose function is to join adjacent sections of text: **conjunctions** such as *but, and, while* and words or phrases such as *secondly* or *however* (which suggest **result**) or linking phrases which are **additive**: *moreover*. Sometimes **temporal** links are used to structure a piece of writing: *previously, meanwhile, later*.

▶ **Reference using pronouns**. Texts make use of a complex system of **reference** back and forth within the text. **Deictics** (e.g. *this, that, these, those*) and **personal pronouns** (e.g. *he, she, it*) are often used to make links between parts of a text. The final sentence of the extract uses both; it opens with the deictic *This*, referring back to *evidence from other cultures* and uses the pronoun *them* towards the end of the sentence to refer back to the buildings of the period. **Comparative** forms such as *other* convey a link between words whilst preserving the distinction between the things they refer to – e.g. *One is well-preserved but the other is in decay*. Reference backward, to ideas already introduced, is a clearly noticeable feature of text cohesion, but reference forward is also used to help the reader get to grips with the structure of a text. In this passage, the writer signals what is to come in the second sentence, using the phrase *various reasons* to refer forward to information which we can expect to read shortly.

Deictics p. 78
Pronouns p. 77

▶ **Substitution**. Synonyms or near synonyms may be used to avoid repetition (e.g. *treatise, manuscript, handbook*), as might shorter or longer words and phrases. The use of comparatives, pronouns and other 'proforms' (e.g. *ones, some*) is a form of substitution.

Synonyms p. 20

▶ **Ellipsis**. Sometimes a section of a sentence or phrase may be omitted altogether. If you were asked *Do you understand what you have just read?*, you might answer *Yes, I do* or *No, I don't* rather than '*I do understand*' or '*I don't understand*'. In the text you have been looking at you might have spotted the use of ellipsis in: *There are various reasons why it is very hard to answer this question with precision. One is that... .* What is the effect of omitting the word *reason* after *One*? In this case, the ellipsis improves the flow of the piece; at another time, the writer might have wanted to retain the word for effect (e.g to achieve a certain rhythm or to place stress on a particular word), to emphasise its importance or for the sake of clarity.

Minor sentences p. 90

▶ **Lexical cohesion**. When making notes on the passage (notice the use of ellipsis here in the omission of *you were*) you probably noted some of the ways in which similar, or even the same, vocabulary can be used to link parts of a text. This is called **lexical cohesion**. As well as noticing words with similar meanings such as *treatises, handbook* and *manuscript* you can't have missed the frequent use of *building* and *buildings* and the author's use of *we* to signal a consistent authorial voice.[44]

Cohesion in spoken language

It is easier to analyse cohesion in written texts than in spoken ones. We can take our time to examine a text; a speech or conversation quickly passes us by. Spoken language, of course, has it own ways of achieving cohesion, which work in different ways from those of written language. We can see it in the way conversations often make use of patterned exchanges. Think of the way you start and finish telephone calls, or take leave of friends. Your mother might recognise the utterance, *Hello, it's me* as a signal to expect the text type *telephone conversation with son/daughter*. The structure of the discourse depends greatly on participants co-operating to develop each conversational theme to bring it to a conclusion and then to move to the next one. Sometimes, as we know, both coherence and cohesion

44 The use of 'we' may also imply that the author is referring to a body of knowledge put together by many academics. The information then has that weight of authority – it's not just the writer who knows these things but 'we' – the academic community of architectural historians.

can be dependent on context, which in the case of a telephone conversation will probably rely largely upon the shared knowledge of the participants.

Extralinguistic knowledge pp. 114–115

Analysing language data   Activity 4.7

Here is a transcript of a complete telephone conversation. It made perfect sense to the speakers; what do you think it is about?

> A Hallo.
>
> B How are things?
>
> A He hasn't come yet.
>
> B Oh. Well, I'll stay around here. I've got plenty to do.
>
> A OK. See you then.

Reflection

You can work out some things from the information this text gives you (e.g. Speaker A is waiting for a man or a boy) and you might guess some others (the two speakers could each be at their respective homes) but you cannot make full sense of the text unless you know that the words *things, he* and *here* refer respectively to the expected arrival of a motor mechanic to repair a car, the mechanic and the speaker's place of work. Both speakers understand the unstated cohesive link between the second and third line and the relationship between the mechanic's not coming and the speaker's staying where s/he is.[45]

All the cohesive devices outlined above, both grammatical and lexical, operate in spoken language at all levels of formality. Reference back – *You know Harry? Well, he's gone and got another dog!* – or forward – *I've got something to tell you* – are both common. As in the telephone example, spoken language depends on knowledge of things outside the text itself, to the extralinguistic features of the context or to knowledge which can be assumed by both speaker and listeners.

> **In this section we have seen that:**
>
> ▌ Texts construct their meaning from **ideational**, **interpersonal** and **textual** components.
>
> ▌ **Textual, linguistic** and **extralinguistic** factors contribute to how a text is understood.
>
> ▌ To qualify as a text a sample of language must be coherent. **Coherence** refers to the unifying structure of the meaning of a text.
>
> ▌ The structural (grammatical and lexical) means by which elements of a text are linked is known as **cohesion**.
>
> ▌ **Written and spoken texts** both have means for ensuring coherence and cohesion.

45 In the case of lines 3 and 4, an explicit link 'in that case I'll stay ...' would have been perfectly possible. B probably opted not to use it because they could count on A's understanding; even if that were not reliable, the interactive nature of oral communication would make the risk acceptable.

Genre

The previous section began with a definition of **text** as a stretch of language which is held together by the threads of ideas expressed (i.e. it is coherent) and the grammatical structures which help to do this (i.e. it is cohesive). Different kinds of text achieve coherence and cohesion in different ways and in recent years **genre theory** has developed to account for these different conventional forms; specific types or categories of text are described in terms of their purpose and their lexical, grammatical and structural features. Each text type (e.g. historical novel, inspection report, riddle) is called a **genre**. Whilst texts can rarely be fitted perfectly into neat categories, it is nonetheless clear that there are numerous cases of texts constructed for similar purposes which include similar formal features.

Coherence pp. 112–114
Cohesion pp. 116–119

Activity 4.8	Analysing language data

You will probably identify the following text very quickly as an African or Asian folk tale. What information leads you to this conclusion?

Once upon a time an elephant made a friendship with a man. One day a heavy thunderstorm broke out, the elephant went to his friend, who had a little hut at the edge of the forest, and said to him: 'My dear good man, will you please let me put my trunk inside your hut to keep it out of this torrential rain?' The man, seeing what situation his friend was in, replied: ' My dear good elephant, my hut is very small, but there is room for your trunk and myself. Please put your trunk in gently.' The elephant thanked his friend, saying: 'You have done me a good deed and one day I shall return your kindness'...

Reflection

The opening *Once upon a time* was probably your first clue, with other clues provided by the setting (the hut, the forest, the thunderstorm) and characters (an unnamed man and a (talking) elephant). Like so many of our feelings and intuitions about language, the reader's impression that this is a folk tale can be accounted for by looking closely at identifiable features.

Activity 4.9	Analysing language data

Answer the following questions about the story in activity 4.8:

▷ Does the narrator use the first (I) or third (he/she/they) person?

▷ Are events sequenced chronologically or in some other way?

▷ What tenses are used?

- ◗ What cohesive devices are used?

- ◗ Are there any aspects of the characters, setting or plot which you consider characteristic of folk tales?

- ◗ What relationship with the reader/ listener is expressed or implied?

Pronouns p. 77
Chronological structure p. 125
Tense pp. 104–105
Cohesion pp. 116–119

Reflection

The narrator puts the story in the third person, thereby establishing some distance between him/herself and the action. Events are recounted in the order in which they happen and the expectation is that they will continue in this way – folktales rarely include flashbacks. Events are recounted in the past tense, with the present tense used for direct speech. The rather stylised forms of speech and the way in which dialogue is used to express key elements of the plot are also characteristic of this genre. Sentences are relatively simple and complex cohesive devices are eschewed in favour of one **temporal connective** (One day) and reference using pronouns and substitution (a man, his friend, him). The frequent repetition of the word *trunk* adds to the impression of simplicity of language. Although we must be dealing with particular individuals in a particular place there is a sense of 'generality' about *a man*, *the forest* etc. We do not expect the character and setting to be developed in the way they would be in a novel or even a 'literary' short story.

Although the narrator does not acknowledge the reader/listener directly, there is an implicit understanding that the structure of the text is familiar (e.g. the listener knows that the second half of the plot will involve the elephant's reciprocating the man's kindness) and that certain conventions are accepted (e.g. that animals and humans can be friends and converse with each other). The storyteller can depend on the listener to supply information s/he would otherwise have to explain.

Activity 4.10

Think about the following folk tales:
Goldilocks and the three bears
The three little pigs
Cinderella*

In what ways are they similar to the elephant story, and to each other?
Would you say they belonged to the same genre?

*If you are unfamiliar with these then choose some other traditional stories.

Reflection

Goldilocks and *The three little pigs* share a number of features, besides animals talking to people. They have an internal structure that groups events in threes (three visits from the wolf, three things 'explored' in the house) which is common to many folk tales and jokes.[46] Tense and person are used similarly and so on. You might feel Cinderella is a bit different, with its grandiose setting, more elaborate plot and its scope for more elaborate language, but you would probably agree the stories involving the elephant, the pigs and the bears have sufficient overlapping features to count as the same genre.

Fiction and non-fiction

Genres may be very narrowly defined (e.g. 'Pizza Hut Menu'), or quite broad categories which include many narrower genres (e.g. 'list').

Probably the most obvious genre distinction is that made between very broad categories of **fiction** and **non-fiction**. These text types can be identified both by their **purpose** and by aspects of their textual and grammatical structures in much the same way that the folk tales were. Most adult readers' knowledge of these features is so well established that distinguishing between genres seems again to be a matter of intuition.

Activity 4.11

The elephant story is an example of a fiction text. Read the following extracts and decide if each is fiction or non-fiction. What formal features are associated with each genre?

(i) 'What are shrews?' asked the child.

'They look something like mice,' said the Frog, 'but they're short-tailed, sharper-nosed and smaller – very little and very bloodthirsty. They eat constantly, and when they have a war they eat even more.' The mouse father's motor having run down*, frog stood him and the child on their feet again. The band of shrews was less than a hundred yards away, and the scout who had signalled with the phosphorescent wood moved off to join them. Frog watched the fox fire bobbing dimly, growing smaller in the distance.

'Their eyesight's very poor,' he said; 'they haven't seen us yet. Perhaps they'll go away, and just as well. They're a commissary company, I think, after rations. That's why the mouse was running so hard. In any case, they don't eat tin.*'

'Do they eat frogs?' asked the child.

'When they catch them,' Frog replied.

The shrews moved into the moonlight, and the child, looking beyond his father's shoulder, saw the little company, spiky with the tiny spears they carried, clustered black against the snow.

*The mouse and his child are a mechanical toy.

46 The most important thing about the Englishman, Irishman and Scotsman is not where they come from but the fact that there are three of them – they are not so much characters as a structural device.

(ii) It is very seldom that mere ordinary people like John and myself secure ancestral homes for the summer.

A colonial mansion, a hereditary estate, I would say a haunted house and reach the height of romantic felicity – but that would be asking too much of fate!

Still, I will proudly declare that there is something queer about it.

Else, why should it be let so cheaply? And why have stood so long untenanted?

John laughs at me, of course, but one expects that.

(iii) Modern circus was started in London in 1768 by Philip Astley and rapidly became the chief form of entertainment throughout much of the world during the nineteenth century. Catherine the Great had invited the English trick rider and impressario Charles Hughes (Astley's rival) to set up a riding school in St Petersburg, and circus quickly spread, eventually producing its own dynastic families – the Durovs, Zapashnys, Kios, Kantemirovs and others – who passed on their skills from one generation to the next.

(iv) Loading the Dishwasher

The dishwasher has a capacity of 12 place settings including serving dishes.

Before loading the dishes, remove the largest scraps of food to avoid blocking the filter.

Very dirty pans or frying pans must be soaked in water before they are placed in the dishwasher, to allow food waste to be removed more easily.

Put pans in the bottom basket.

Reflection

Extracts (i) and (ii) are fiction (short story and children's novel respectively) whilst the other two are examples of non-fiction (*Souvenir Programme* for the UK tour of the Moscow State Circus and the *Installation and Use* booklet for a dishwasher).

Obviously the first question you have to ask is whether the text is 'telling the truth' or 'telling a story' and though you can never be certain without access to relevant external information, it seems fairly unlikely that texts (iii) and (iv) have been invented in order to entertain. You could be forgiven for considering the possibility that (ii) might be non-fiction – autobiography perhaps.[47] Text (i) resembles the folk tale in its grammatical and structural choices: third person, past tense, chronological ordering of events and the use of dialogue to advance the plot. The implied threat of frog-eating shrews anticipates a plot development in much the same way as the elephant's gratitude did. As a more literary text it has more adjectives and the sentences are mostly complex, even in the dialogue. (Note that in both stories the sentence structure and vocabulary of the dialogue differs from those of natural speech in a way which is characteristic of each genre.) There is a greater tendency to provide description and supporting detail and the reader therefore gets to know the characters as individuals, in contrast to the folk tale's *man*.

47 The fact that autobiography depends on the selection and ordering of events has led some recent writers to take the view that all biographies are in fact fictional constructions.

Extract (ii) provides contextual information within the (**chronologically organised**) narrative. In this case the author deliberately adopts a tone of intimacy by employing the first person and the present tense.

Extract (iii) contains a chronologically organised section – a history – but this is within an overall structure which is arranged on other principles. In some ways it resembles the novel extract, but differs in the way in which it gives a great deal of information which is unelaborated and, of course, does not use dialogue. Extract (iv) is the only text here to address the reader deliberately, using the imperative mood (*remove the largest scraps*). However, there is no explicit reference to people at all (though of course the imperative implies the existence of a human agent – the reader is to do the work), with almost all nouns referring to items of equipment.

Imperative pp. 90–91
Noun p. 75

You are doubtless familiar with other texts which resemble these four in their form and purpose and which therefore belong to the same or similar genres.

Distinctive features of fiction texts

The telling of stories, or **narrative**, gives us a recognisable and well-defined body of writing with features which are easily identified by experienced readers and listeners. Our exposure to story-telling from an early age equips us with a body of knowledge and a set of expectations about the way a story is structured. We recognise a story almost as soon as it starts and we expect it, to some extent, to follow a predictable pattern as it develops. Experience of story helps us to recognise the different ways that language can be used to create atmosphere – for example, in describing settings and depicting characters; the knowledge we bring to a story gives us access to the meanings embedded within the text. (Children recognise and anticipate story structures as listeners long before they read for themselves.)

> **Layout.** We may recognise a story simply from how it is set out on the page.

> **Structural elements.** Extract (ii) in Activity 4.11 focuses on an individual and her thoughts about a house, herself and her spouse. This focus, together with the **setting** (the location of the action in place and time), give the orientation of the story – here *a colonial mansion* which is judged *queer*. Another key component of story is the highlighting of an individual's predicament and her response to it: the **complicating** action. Here the teller refers to the prospect of staying in a house *so long untenanted* and to the husband who *laughs at me*. We have come to expect that some exploration of happenings (or **plot**), a focus on **characters** and their problems and the **resolution** of conflict and tension will form the rest of the story. There may then be a **coda** – some comment from the narrator, perhaps, or the reader's inference drawn from the final events, in keeping with the theme(s) underlying the narrative. Extract (ii) exemplifies how readers will want the questions which were raised in

the first sentences to be answered, in order for some kind of resolution of the potential complications to be achieved. Similarly, in extract (i) the sense of threat and travail arouse our interest in the ultimate fate of the toys and the frog.

In terms of textual coherence, fiction often has a recognisable pattern, using a chronological structure (i.e events are ordered in the narrative in the succession in which they occur in 'real' time). Narrative is usually set out in chronological order (the complications of the use of **flashback** notwithstanding).[48] The use of **temporal connectives** is characteristic of chronologically structured texts.

Coherence pp. 112–114
Connectives p. 117

▸ **First and third person narration.** In the first text, the narrator is 'all-seeing' and is able to tell us things about the characters which involve 'knowledge beyond the observable'. The account is, therefore, given in the third person. The woman's narrative in extract (ii) is told in the first person which immediately suggests both the narrator's personal perspective and a relationship with the reader. Whatever kind of narration an author employs, dialogue is usually recorded in its 'original' form, i.e. if a character speaks in the first person the dialogue is recorded in the first person.

Pronoun p. 77
Tense pp. 104–105

▸ **Tense.** Use of the past tense is more usual for narrative, with dialogue (as it would have been spoken) in the present tense. Extract (ii), as we have seen, uses the present tense (with references to past and future) to create a sense of immediacy; occasionally this tense is used to create immediacy of a different kind; jokes, for example, are often told in the present tense.

▸ **Characteristic words and phrases.** Some phrases belong almost exclusively to narrative forms. As well as the obvious *Once upon a time* and *they all lived happily ever after* we often encounter *the next thing to happen was..., Suddenly..., In the middle of the night...* and many others.

▸ **Suspension of disbelief.** Once we recognise a text as a story (and provided we accept its other merits) we do not object to the inclusion of implausible or even impossible elements, such as magic spells, intergalactic travel and talking animals and toys.

Fiction genres

The term *genre* is probably most familiar to you in the context of fiction as it is commonly used to refer to text types such as *myth, legend, fable, thriller, whodunnit, romantic fiction* and *historical novel*. It is easy to see how characteristic use of language, characters and narrative structures are used to meet the author's purpose in each case.

48 This is not to say that many recent writers have not adopted different time structures for their narratives.

The structure of non-fiction texts

You will probably have had little difficulty identifying extracts (iii) and (iv) in Activity 4.11 as non-fiction texts. Extract (iii) emphasises fact-telling. We are given names, dates and a sense of history of the near past as well as of long-standing historical traditions and reputations. The aim of this programme extract is to give readers a context which will enhance their enjoyment of the circus.

Extract (iv) outlines part of a procedure to follow when loading a dishwasher and forms one part of a set of ordered steps for installing, operating and taking care of a purchaser's new product. Its purpose is to support the new owner *to do something real*. This extract is directed primarily at the potential problems resulting from loading the machine with plates which still have food scraps on them. The instructions are given clearly, the reader addressed directly.

The text coherence of non-fiction texts often depends, as these examples show, on accurate and logical sequencing of the content. Time is not, however, the only possible organisational device; the dishwasher text is only partially organised on a chronological basis.

Coherence pp. 112–114
Chronological structure p. 125

Whereas it was quite easy to generalise about the formal and structural features of fiction texts, the differences between the language and organisational features of the latter two texts are obvious. Rather than being a single text type, non-fiction is a category which includes a wide range of text types or genres. In the following section you will investigate the formal and structural features of six established non-fiction genres.

In this section we have seen that:

▶ Writers make **choices** between elements of vocabulary, grammar and text structure to construct texts which achieve different **purposes**.

▶ Recurring text types based on a set of formal features matched to a purpose are called **genres**.

▶ The broad genres of fiction and non-fiction each include a range of more specific (**sub**) genres.

Six non-fiction genres

This section outlines the main characteristics of six commonly occurring non-fiction genres.[49]

49 The detail of genre-specific features in this section comes largely from David Wray and Maureen Lewis's *Developing Children's Non-Fiction Writing* (Scholastic, 1995).

Recount

Read this text and note what you observe about the following features:

▶ the structuring of information within the text

▶ use of special vocabulary

▶ use of tense

▶ use of pronouns

▶ references to people – particular, general or not at all?

▶ references to an audience

▶ use of active and passive verb forms

▶ use of connectives

▶ any other distinctive language features.

> 'My dear sister Mary. I am afraid that you will go mad when you read this…poor Thomas is dead. We started off in July, with plenty of provisions and two yoke oxen. We went along very well till we got within six or seven hundred miles of California when the Indians attacked us. We had one pas-senger with us, two guns, and one revolver; so we ran all the lead…then they gave us the war hoop, and as many as twenty of them came down upon us. The three that shot Tom was hid by the side of the road in the bushes…'

Word pp. 19–23
Tense pp. 104–105
Pronoun p. 77
Active/passive verbs pp. 95–96
Connectives p. 117

Reflection

The purpose of **recounts** is to relate a sequence of events in order to inform or entertain the reader. In terms of structure there is no difference between a fiction and a non-fiction recount – an event in the life of Harry Potter will probably unfold (and therefore be recountable) in much the same way as an event in the life of a real child at boarding school. The recount is probably the simplest way of structuring facts and one used often in the writing of young children (e.g. the *bed to bed* structure which begins *I got up*…and ends at bedtime, outlining all the important events in between).

This letter from an eleven-year-old boy tells a simple story, beginning with a short 'scene-setting' opening or orientation and moving quickly into the main section which concentrates on events and orders them chronologically. We might expect the letter to end with a closing statement or reorientation (e.g. *I pray to God that we reach California before winter*). **Chronological connectives** are used predominantly (until, when, then) and specific participants are referred to – Tom and the writer himself as well as the twenty 'Indians'. The pronouns used (*we, you, they*) reflect this concentration on named (or nameable) individuals. The main narrative is in the **past tense** and all the verbs are in the active voice and most are **action verbs**. All these features are characteristic of the genre known as **recount**. This genre may be found among both fiction and non-fiction texts.

Other features which you may have noted and which help us understand the text more fully include the use of a conventional opening for a letter and the use of the second person to address an identified audience. The latter is not a necessary feature for a recount as the genre includes texts without an easily identified readership (e.g. journals are largely made up of recounts). You learn a little more about the boy from his use of non-standard constructions (*the three that shot Tom was hid..., two yoke oxen*).

Non-Standard English p. 12

Report

Activity 4.13	Analysing language data

Read this text and note what you observe about the following features:

- the structuring of information within the text
- use of special vocabulary
- use of tense
- use of pronouns
- references to people – particular, general or not at all?
- references to an audience
- use of active and passive verb forms
- use of connectives
- any other distinctive language features.

> *Mars is the second smallest planet in the solar system. It is about 228 million kilometres from the Sun. It is the fourth planet away from the Sun. Mars is also known as the Red Planet. It is about half as wide as Earth. Mars has two small rocky moons. There is no water on Mars and it is cold. Scientists think it was once warm and wet as there are dry river beds. It is made of rock and has red, sandy soil.*

Reflection

This example fits into the **report** genre of non-fiction texts. The purpose of reports is to describe things as they are, again to inform the reader.

Reference books often comprise a number of reports. The **present tense** predominates in this kind of writing. This extract clearly provides factual material of the kind found in first-level encyclopaedia texts and is expressed in short sentences with no direct address to the reader. Maps and diagrams of the planet system, and of individual planets, indicating relative size and other qualities are consistently shown in this kind of text. It is organised along **non-chronological** lines with **causal connectives** (*as there are dry river beds*). We do not expect texts like this to make reference to specific individuals unless they happen to be the subject of the report (e.g. an encyclopaedia may have entries on Marie Curie and Beethoven); rather we expect reference to **generic participants** – in this case *scientists*. One strategy writers of such texts employ to avoid naming participants is the use of the **passive voice** (*is known*), though this particular extract, perhaps because it is aimed at a young audience, uses mostly active constructions. Most of these are **complement** structures (*Mars is about 228 million kilometres from the sun, there is no water*) or clauses based on the verb *have* (*Mars has two rocky moons*) in order to tell about the *state* of Mars (i.e. 'what *is*') at a particular time.

As this writer is deliberately writing for a younger audience, the main cohesive device employed is the repeated use of the pronoun *it* to refer back to the subject, 'Mars'. All reference is in the **third person**, with no reference either to the writer (*I*) or the audience (*You*).

This particular text deals with 'key facts' about Mars and therefore the sentences could almost come in any order. However, there is an expectation with more complex reports that facts will be arranged on a logical basis which shows the relationship between the elements of the description. **Logical connectives** such as *therefore* and *consequently* would support this structure. Reports often begin with a **general classification** relating the subject to membership of a wider category (*Mars is the second smallest planet in the solar system*). This may be followed by a more technical classification, but this example moves directly into a fuller **description** of the subject.

It is worth emphasising that the genre terminology used here carries specific and technical meanings. There are many everyday uses of the term *report* (*newspaper report, inspectors' report, auditor's report, school report*) which have a structural pattern of their own but which do not share the formal features of the **report genre** as outlined above.

Procedure

Procedural (or **instruction**) texts tell us how to do something through a clearly stated sequence of actions. Compare the following two texts:

1. Making pizzas

Pizza dough is made from flour, yeast, salt and water. The dough is kneaded for about ten minutes before it is made into a flat, circular shape. It can be thin crust or deep-pan base. It is then baked in an oven.

When the base is cooked, a sauce made from tomatoes is spread over it. Many different toppings can be added: cheese, ham, tuna, sweetcorn, peppers and pineapple. The pizza is then cooked again. It is cut into slices and can be eaten hot or cold.

2. Pizza

Ingredients

dough	sauce	toppings
750g flour	1 450 g can chopped	200 g cheese (grated)
2 tsp salt	tomatoes	100 g ham (optional)
1 sachet yeast	1 tsp oregano	100 g tuna (optional)
450 ml warm water	2 cloves garlic	100 g sweetcorn (optional)

Method

Mix the dough ingredients together in a big bowl, adding the water slowly to make a dough.

Divide the dough into three pieces.

Knead the dough for 10 minutes on a floured board, then press each piece into a thin circular shape.

Cover and leave to rise in a warm place for about half an hour.

Heat the tomatoes, crushed garlic and oregano together in a pan to make the tomato sauce.

When the bases have risen, place them on a greased baking tray and spread the tomato sauce on top.

Cover with grated cheese.

Spread tuna, ham and sweetcorn (as required) on top of the cheese.

Bake in a hot oven (gas mark 7) for 25 minutes.

The first text resembles a report (or an explanation – see below) in some ways, as it increases the reader's knowledge about pizzas without saying exactly how to make one. It also offers examples of how the passive voice may be used to avoid the need to name a general participant (e.g. *It is then baked*).

Passive pp. 95–96

The second text is an example of procedural writing, since its purpose is to guide the reader exactly towards a defined outcome.

Activity 4.14   Analysing language data

Read the text 'Pizza' again carefully and note your observations about the following features:

▶   the structuring of information within the text

- use of special vocabulary
- use of tense
- use of pronouns
- references to people – particular, general or not at all?
- references to an audience
- use of active and passive verb forms
- use of connectives
- any other distinctive language features.

Reflection

The information is structured according to a conventional pattern which will (in this case) be well known to the reader. Ingredients are listed and then the actions the reader needs to take are listed in strict chronological order. Connectives tend to be used rarely as the structure implies 'then...then...then...', but temporal connectives are sometimes found, especially within sentences and where they help convey the exact order in which actions take place.

Other common forms of procedural writing such as safety instructions and instruction manuals follow a similar pattern, often including diagrams to aid understanding of each section. So far as syntactic patterns are concerned, note that much of the text is not written in 'well-formed' sentences. The ingredients are simply listed and unnecessary words are omitted (*Cover* [it/the pizza] *with grated cheese*). Where full sentences are used the main verb of each is in the imperative mood (**Knead** *the dough*, **Cover** *with grated cheese*). Most sentences begin with a verb in this form. Where there is use of the indicative mood, past, present or future tenses may be used (*when they have risen, when they are ready, you will need this later*). Pronoun use is interesting. Where there is any chance of ambiguity, pronouns are avoided and a noun repeated (*...adding the water slowly to make a dough. Divide the **dough** into three pieces*). On the other hand, as noted above, where the sense is clear pronouns may be omitted altogether.

The participant is generally implicit in the use of the imperative (i.e. a second person – *you*), though they can be referred to explicitly, as in the occasional *You will need to do this carefully* or obliquely in reference to operations which are optional or *to taste*.

As procedural writing can cover all manner of activities there is little vocabulary which is specific to the genre as a whole, but particular texts are likely to make use of vocabulary which is specific to the subject matter and often quite technical (*knead, simmer, sauté, icon, drop-down menu, chamfer* etc. etc.).

Explanation

The purpose of explanations can be broadly defined as to describe how things work. The subjects may range through mechanical, natural, social and other processes.

Activity 4.15	Analysing language data

Read the explanation text below and note your observations about the following features:

- the structuring of information within the text
- use of special vocabulary
- use of tense
- use of pronouns
- references to people – particular, general or not at all?
- references to an audience
- use of active and passive verb forms
- use of connectives
- any other distinctive language features.

How Does a Spider Spin its Web?

One distinctive quality which spiders have is the ability to spin webs. This involves some specially developed body parts and a good deal of skill.

A spider's body is in two parts with six silk glands on the end of the back part. From these glands come a liquid which turns to silk on contact with air. As it is produced, the spider holds the silk thread with one leg and can vary the kind of silk. When spinning its web, a garden spider begins with a large, thread square. Then it works from the middle of the edge, putting in about thirty strokes or rays of thread. Then it changes direction again so that it can make a series of sticky spirals from the centre outwards. In order to complete the web the spider spins a thread from the centre to a hiding place nearby.

Webs can be 3m (9.8ft) across or as small as a postage stamp.

Reflection

Explanations have a two-part structure: an **introductory statement** which signals to the reader the subject matter of the explanation, followed by a **series of statements** which explain the subject in detail. The process is explained as a sequence of logical steps.

Since explanations account for processes they are **organised chronologically** and employ **chronological connectives** (*as, then, when*). However, since they provide reasons as well as simply describing the process, they also incorporate **causal connectives** (*so that, in order to*).

Verbs are mostly action verbs in the active voice (*A spider spins... , It works*). The simple present tense is used since the actions described can take place at any time. Explanations have an impersonal tone and rarely make reference to their audience. Participants are general (*a spider* and *the spider*, though singular in form, refer (as does *spiders*) to 'any spider' or 'all spiders') and pronominal reference is usually third person. Vocabulary particular to the subject is expected and may be explained within the body of the text.

Persuasion

Persuasive writing is a genre which is strongly governed by its purpose, which is to win the reader over to the author's point of view.

Analysing language data	Activity 4.16

Read the persuasive text below and note your observations about the following features:

▶ the structuring of information within the text

▶ use of special vocabulary

▶ use of tense

▶ use of pronouns

▶ references to people – particular, general or not at all?

▶ references to an audience

▶ use of active and passive verb forms

▶ use of connectives

▶ any other distinctive language features.

People like you should join the Wildfowl and Wetland Trust.

WWT is a respected wildlife charity which is unique in promoting wildfowl and wetland conservation by bringing people and wildlife together. The trust is a conservation organisation of international standing, providing advice and expertise to governments, industry and individuals in order to protect all wetland wildlife. WWT works to save wildfowl populations and wetland habitats of the UK and the world because trust members know the value and benefits of wetlands for wildlife and people.

WWT works to maintain the diversity of wetland species.

Benefits of WWT membership are numerous. They include free entry to all WWT centres and reduced rates for all events at centres.

You can help WWT with its vital work by becoming a member.

Reflection

The text begins with an opening statement or **thesis** which states the author's position. This is followed by the (in this case two) supporting arguments which are each composed of an initial point followed by an elaboration. The final structural element is a **restatement** of the opening position, which in a longer piece would include a **summary** of the argument.

The present tense is used both because the facts referred to are of an enduring nature and because this also creates a sense of immediacy in the dialogue between author and reader. This duality is reflected in the use of pronouns too: second person to address the audience and third person to relate the arguments. In this particular case, many of the verbs are action verbs which serve to emphasise the active nature of the organisation. Participants are **generic** (*people, industry, individuals*), though there may, as here, be individual reference to the reader (*you*) or even to the writer. The text is **ordered logically** rather than chronologically and therefore uses **causal connectives** (*because, in order to*).

Discussion

Discussion is a genre which is probably familiar to you from your childhood experience of writing essays in history and other subjects. You may also have been taught a formal framework or structure.

Activity 4.17	Analysing language data

Read the discussion text below and note your observations about the following features:

- ◗ the structuring of information within the text
- ◗ use of special vocabulary
- ◗ use of tense
- ◗ use of pronouns
- ◗ references to people – particular, general or not at all?
- ◗ references to an audience
- ◗ use of active and passive verb forms
- ◗ use of connectives
- ◗ any other distinctive language features.

The government has to decide whether to spend more money on public transport or to encourage more and more people to travel by car. People like the freedom their cars give them but other people say they are bad for the environment.

Some people enjoy driving and looking after their cars. Cars are convenient because they let you go where you want whenever you want. That means that you don't have to stick to where the bus or train goes and wait around until one comes. If you've got a car you can always rely on it. Cars create lots of jobs, because people who work in factories, garages, petrol stations and lots of other places owe their jobs to cars.

On the other hand, cars cause a lot of pollution. We are in danger from global warming because cars produce a lot of carbon dioxide. Our towns and cities are congested with traffic and every day lives are lost through road accidents. Also, not everybody has a car and these people suffer because there are not enough buses.

Cars give more freedom to people but it is getting harder and harder to drive around because there are so many cars. If the government made buses and trains cheaper then more people would use them and there would be less congestion and pollution. That decision would make travelling easier for everyone.

Reflection

The structure of this kind of text is very clearly visible. The initial paragraph is a **statement of the issue** followed by a **preview** of the argument. Succeeding sections are **arguments for** and **arguments against**; each of these includes supporting evidence. The final section is **summary** and **conclusion** in the form of a **recommendation**. Organisation is **non-chronological** and **connectives** are **logical** (*On the other hand*) or **causal** (*because*). Reference is to **generic participants** and pronouns generally are third person, although this author has chosen to refer to people in general in the first person – *we*. The simple **present tense** is used (*work, suffer*). Discussion texts often use passive constructions, though this particular text has only two (*are congested, are lost*).

Mixing genres

Analysing language data ✔	Activity 4.18

Search in books, newspapers, on the internet and in any other source of texts to find examples of the six non-fiction genres outlined in this section. Give some general headings for text types within each genre (e.g. for recount you may include 'diaries', for procedural, 'recipes' and so on.)

How easy is it to find 'pure' examples of each genre?

Reflection

Some possible text types are listed on page 200. You probably found it difficult to find 'pure' examples of some genres. It is difficult, for example, when writing a recount not to explain a point or (implicitly or explicitly) argue the pros and/or cons of one component of the narrative. This is not to say that genre theory only works 'in theory' and is irrelevant to real texts. You probably found many texts which fitted one or other genre fairly closely (this is more likely with those genres where we can expect the author consciously to adopt a particular structure, e.g. *discussion* and *procedural*). Moreover, an understanding of how language is used to achieve the purposes of each genre helps us understand how texts achieve their effect when they do take a sudden turn into a different form.

Activity 4.19	Analysing language data

At first sight all three of the following texts appear to be recounts. For each example, say how it differs from the purest form of the genre.

Tuesday, 27 December 1870

After dinner drove into Chippenham with Perch and bought a pair of skates at Benk's for 17/6. Across the fields to the Draycot water and the young Awdry ladies chaffed me about my new skates. I had not been on skates since I was here last, five years ago, and was very awkward for the first ten minutes, but the knack soon came again. There was a distinguished company on the ice, Lady Dangan, Lord and Lady Royston and Lord George Paget all skating... I had the honour of being knocked down by Lord Royston, who was coming round suddenly on the outside edge. Large fire of logs burned within an enclosure of wattled hurdles. Harriet Awdry skated beautifully over a sunken punt. Arthur Law skating, jumped over a chair on its legs.

The Diary (1870–1879) of the Reverend Francis Kilvert

Tuesday, 10 August 1943

Dear Kitty, new idea. I talk more to myself than to the others at mealtimes, which is to be recommended for two reasons. Firstly, because everyone is happy if I don't chatter the whole time, and secondly, I needn't get annoyed about other people's opinions. I don't think my opinions are stupid and the others do; so it's better to keep them to myself. I do just the same if I have to eat something I can't stand. I put my plate in front of me, pretend that it is something delicious, look at it as little as possible and before I know where I am, it is gone... Do you know what Mummy calls that sort of thing? The Art of Living – that's an odd expression... Dussel has indirectly endangered our lives. He actually let Miep bring a forbidden book for him, one that abuses Mussolini and Hitler. On the way she happened to be run into by an SS car. She lost her temper and shouted 'Miserable wretches', and rode on. It is better not to think of what might have happened if she had had to go to their headquarters.

The Diary (1942–1944) of Anne Frank

Sunday came and went. I buoyed myself up thinking of cracks and jokes that my friends in Belfast would make when I returned. I thought also with some degree of anger that I had come to Lebanon to work for a couple of years, had been kidnapped as a British subject, locked up as a British subject, and questioned as a British subject. I had run away to this country to escape the consequences of British policy in Ireland and here I was about to be sent back for all the wrong reasons and only after four months. It angered me and the anger kept away those dark moments which were yet to possess me… . On Monday after the usual ablutions, my kidnapper and aspiring confidant came back. A social visit this time, not to interrogate me this time but to give me some news. He seemed excited, telling me that the Irish Government had placed a large advertisement in the local Arabic newspaper with my photograph and a copy of my passport, appealing to my kidnappers for my release. He laughed. He found it funny. I laughed too, but I laughed out of relief that something was finally confirming my own insistence that I was Irish… One day during those first weeks of my captivity, I was brought a towel and a toothbrush, having asked for them on several occasions. My mind reeled on receiving them, trying to understand what this meant… Each day became another day, unmarked by any difference from the day that preceded it or the day that would come after. Always it began…

An Evil Cradling by Brian Keenan (1992)

Reflection

The Kilvert diary is almost pure recount as it relates a succession of events in strict chronological order. Some sentences omit verbs or pronouns in keeping with a style of writing intended to be read only by the writer.

Verb p. 75
Pronoun p. 77

Anne Frank takes a much less straightforward approach; she uses her diary as an audience and addresses it in the second person (*Kitty*). Only the second half of this extract is really a recount, with the first section, albeit focusing on a recent event, coming closer to an explanation. The connectives, *firstly* and *secondly,* contribute to the logical structure of the piece – they mark out her reasons (rather in the way that bullet points work) and do not imply any ordering, chronological or otherwise. The tense here is present. Even the second section, involving as it does the recounting of events, also has characteristics of persuasive writing with its opening statement (*Dussel has indirectly endangered our lives*), supporting arguments and implicit reiteration of the danger (*It is better not to think what might have happened if…*).

Connectives p. 117
Tense pp. 104–105
Persuasive writing pp. 133–134

Although recounting past events, Brian Keenan's piece is much more crafted than the diary extracts. His basic recount structure is also a vehicle for frequent explanations; like Anne Frank he seems to be using his writing to help himself make sense of the period of his captivity. Keenan himself, in his introduction, goes further than this, describing the work as both 'a therapy and an exploration'.

In this section we have seen that:

- Six commonly occurring non-fiction **genres** can be described in terms of:

    - how information is **organised**

    - devices used for the purpose of **cohesion**

    - characteristic use of **verbs**, **nouns** and **pronouns**

    - reference to specific or generic **participants**

    - characteristic use of **vocabulary**.

- The features of different genres may be employed within a single text to achieve different purposes.

5. Understanding English at text level: poetic and literary devices

One thing which is very obvious from Brian Keenan's account (Activity 4.19) is that he is conscious not just of the facts he is relating and of his feelings about those facts; he is also keenly aware of the language he is using. In composing a sentence like *It angered me and the anger kept away those dark moments that were yet to possess me* he conveys his moods of rage and despair by his use of rhythm, repetition and an image which portrays him as a victim of his later depressions. Almost any kind of writing may make use of poetic devices, so you should remember that although the following section concentrates on the strategies used by poets, these strategies are available for any writer to use.

In this chapter we shall see:

▶ the characteristic features of **poetry**;

▶ how some of these basic features, including **rhyme**, **rhythm** and **metre**, work;

▶ a variety of **poetic devices** which use sound, meaning and associations to achieve their effect;

▶ the features of some common **poetic forms**.

What is poetry?

Exploring your knowledge | Activity 5.1

Which of the following statements most closely reflects what poetry signifies to you?

▶ 'the best words in the best order' (Samuel Taylor Coleridge)

▶ nursery rhymes

▶ bits of stuff

▶ 'a mode of apprehension, not an area of apprehension' (Elizabeth Cook)

▶ felt thought

▶ memorable speech

▶ verse in greetings cards

▶ 'simply the most beautiful, impressive and widely effective mode of saying things' (Matthew Arnold)

▶ difficult to understand

- 'semantic squeeze' (Jerome Bruner)

- 'language used with the greatest inclusiveness and power' (The Bullock Report)

- 'What oft was thought, but ne'er so well express'd' (Alexander Pope)

- words of your favourite song

- 'manifestation of the human spirit and a relief from, or expression of, emotion' (James Reeves)

- flowery and old-fashioned language

Reflection

Poetry is a difficult thing to define, and whatever definition you like the best you are sure to be able to find a work which does not fit the description but which you (or at least someone you know) consider to be a poem. One characteristic of most poetry is its ability to give us access to meanings via a variety of routes. The sound of the words may communicate as much as their meaning for example, and connotations and wider associations may be as important as referential meaning. Some of the distinctive features of the language of poetry are outlined in this section.

The language of poetry

- **Poetry is *patterned* language.** The poet employs patterns of sight, sound and structure in order to express feelings, thoughts and ideas. Patterns might include those of rhyme, rhythm and metre.

- **Poetry is *concentrated* language.** In most poems every word is carefully chosen and there is little redundancy. Unnecessary words are often omitted or reordered (even, sometimes, if this means breaking the rules of syntax). Often words which carry several meanings (both referential and connotative) are employed, sometimes to give a depth or breadth of meaning, at other times to convey enigma and ambiguity. This density of meaning, together with the importance of the sound of a poem, means that it is never possible to skip read a poem – indeed, most poems benefit from being read aloud.

Word meaning pp. 20–21

- **Poetry deals in affective meanings.** Affective meanings relate to personal thoughts, feelings and emotions. Compare the effect of the following two sentences.

(i)   She took the bicycle and locked it in the coalshed.

(ii) She took the boy and locked him in the coalshed.[50]

Most people will not have much of an emotional response to sentence (i). Sentence (ii), however, although almost identical in structure and referential meaning,[51] provokes quite a different reaction. We know that children don't like being locked in dark

50 These examples also serve to illustrate how sentences cannot be meaningful out of the context of a text – who is the women/girl? Who is the boy? There can only be reference when there is something to refer to.

51 Though even referential meaning is changed somewhat. Is the action referred to by 'put' the same in both sentences? Meaning never resides in words out of context.

sheds and that therefore the act was probably committed against the boy's will. Violence or menace is implied, probably followed by misery and despair. These are the affective meanings of the sentence. Affective meanings are often conveyed by association or implication.

Connotative meaning pp. 20–21

▶ **Poetry can be *allusive*.** Poetry often requires its audience to read beyond the literal. **Imagery**, **figurative language** and **symbolism** may be employed by the poet to evoke a personal response from the reader. ✓

Rhythm and metre

Rhythm

The word **rhythm** comes from Greek and literally means 'flow'. We can think of rhythm as the pulse of the language; as you saw in Chapter 2, regular stress is very important to the sound pattern of any English sentence and its appeal in poetry has been linked beyond language to fundamental experiences such as feeling one's own heartbeat or being rocked to sleep as a child. It is certainly possible for poets to match pounding rhythms to excitement or to soothe with a gentle rhythm. Rhythm is more essential to poetry than any other kind of pattern. There are many poems that do not rhyme or contain other sound patterns but rhythm is almost always present; it is an element which contributes to the appeal and memorableness of poetic language.

Analysing language data   **Activity 5.2**

Stress pp. 43–45

The following extracts come from childhood poems remembered by adults. Read them aloud and feel the rhythm of them. Try clapping the rhythm; can you feel the difference between the stressed and unstressed beats?

How does the rhythm match the meaning and mood of each poem?

> Whenever the moon and stars are set
> Whenever the wind is high,
> All night long in the dark and wet
> A man goes riding by.

From *Windy Nights*, Robert Louis Stevenson

> Everyone grumbled. The sky was grey.
> We had nothing to do and nothing to say
> We were nearing the end of a dismal day.
> And there seemed to be nothing beyond
> Then
> ...Daddy fell into the pond!

From *Daddy Fell into the Pond*, Alfred Noyes

On either side the river lie
Long fields of barley and of rye,
That clothe the wold and meet the sky;
And through the field the road runs by
To many towered Camelot;

From *The Lady of Shalott*, Alfred Lord Tennyson

I must go down to the seas again, to the lonely sea and the sky,
And all I ask is a tall ship and a star to steer her by,
And the wheel's kick and the wind's song and the white sail's shaking,
And a grey mist on the sea's face, and a grey dawn breaking.

From *Sea Fever*, John Masefield

Faster than fairies, faster than witches,
Bridges and houses, hedges and ditches;
And charging along like troops in a battle,
All through the meadows the horses and cattle:
All of the sights of the hill and the plain
Fly as thick as driving rain;
And ever again in the wink of an eye,
Painted stations whistle by.

From *From a Railway Carriage*, Robert Louis Stevenson

Reflection

The rhythm of *From a Railway Carriage* mimics the rhythm of the poem's subject, thereby strengthening the image of the train flashing past the scenes from the carriage window.[52] The rhythm of *Windy Nights* reflects a similar sense of urgency. The narrative structure of both *The Lady of Shallott* and *Daddy Fell into the Pond* involve (in very different contexts) a long initial period of inactivity and both poems use rhythm to express a mood of indolence. Masefield begins with a similar languid rhythm as he expresses his longing to go to sea but suddenly breaks into a much more robust pattern to convey the feeling of battling against rough weather.

| Activity 5.3 | Using your language knowledge |

52 This provides an example of interpretation depending on the reader's experience – the poem will only evoke this response in readers who are familiar with (the now rare) trains which produce this particular rhythm.

Think of some verse you remember from your childhood. It may be poetry you chose to (or had to) learn, it may be a playground rhyme or it may be an advertising jingle. If you can, write down a few lines of each type.

How important do you think rhythm has been in helping you remember the words? Do any other features help make it memorable?

Metre

As you saw in Chapter 2 (page 43), English is a language in which speech rhythms are based on stress and on regular intervals between stressed syllables. In poetry, regular patterns have been developed which harness this feature of spoken language. The effect of employing regular combinations of stressed and unstressed syllables is called **metre**. The number of possible patterns is almost endless but in practice most metres conform to a small number of very common patterns.

Iambic metre

In English verse the most common metre is based on a unit (or foot) comprising an unstressed syllable (ˇ) followed by a stressed syllable (/).

A common iambic pattern involves five iambs per line and is known (therefore) as **iambic pentameter**; this metre is illustrated in the following line from *Romeo and Juliet*:

ˇ / ˇ / ˇ / ˇ / ˇ /
Gallop apace you fiery footed steeds.

The common combination of pairs of words like 'the moon' and 'she's gone' where a stressed 'content' word follows an unstressed 'grammatical' word (e.g. the moon) makes English very well suited to iambic metre.[53] However, the tendency to squeeze more than one unstressed syllable in between stresses means that in practice iambs with two (or even more) unstressed syllables feel quite comfortable even if technically they break the rules.

Trochaic metre

/ ˇ (stressed, unstressed)

/ ˇ / ˇ / ˇ /
Jack and Jill went up the hill.

Anapaesti metre

ˇ ˇ / (unstressed, unstressed, stressed)

ˇ ˇ / ˇ ˇ / ˇ ˇ /
There was May, there was June, there was me

ˇ ˇ / ˇ ˇ / ˇ ˇ /
All convened in the garden for tea

Dactylic metre

/ ˇ ˇ (stressed, unstressed unstressed)

/ ˇ ˇ / ˇ ˇ / ˇ ˇ / ˇ ˇ
Dick had a dog, it could sing three part harmony.

53 With one important caveat. Not all varieties of English share these rhythms; many African Caribbean poets adopt the oral structures of their own varieties, rejecting ill-fitting standard English-based patterns.

Mark the stressed and unstressed syllables in this stanza from John Masefield's poem *Cargoes*.

Dirty British coaster with a salt-caked smoke stack,
Butting through the Channel in the mad March days,
With a cargo of Tyne coal,
Road-rail, pig-lead,
Firewood, iron-ware, and cheap tin trays.

Reflection

Masefield effectively conveys the ungainly qualities of the little ship by breaking the rhythm of the lines with additional stresses. Compare this with the regular and flowing rhythm of *From a Railway Carriage* which is intended to convey an impression of unimpeded speed.

Blank verse

Poetry written with rhythm and regular metre but no rhyme is called **blank verse**. Probably the best-known example is Shakespearean blank verse, written in iambic pentameters.

Clap the rhythm of this extract from *Romeo and Juliet*. Can you identify five iambs in each line? How many syllables do you need in the word 'Juliet'?

But soft, what light through yonder window breaks?
It is the east and Juliet is the Sun.

Syllabic patterns

The patterning in some forms of poetry is achieved by exploiting the number of syllables in each line. The Japanese **haiku** form is probably the best-known example of a syllable-based form.

Syllable pp. 39–43

Haikus usually consist of three lines and 17 syllables distributed 5, 7, 5:

A bitter morning: (5)
sparrows sitting together   (7)
without any necks.   (5)

As in the above example, the final line of a haiku often provides a surprise, a contrast or a sudden change of mood.

The waves splash the rocks:
As they go away I jump them
Till the tide goes out.

The sea is pounding:
It is just so strong for us
But is beautiful.

Write your own haiku. You might like to use one of the following as a first or last line. Don't forget the 'surprise' in line three.

A tear drop falling   *The birds fly away*   *An August morning*
A baby crying   *Then there is silence*   *Where is the sunshine?*

Sound-based patterns

A number of common poetic devices are based on repetition or contrast of speech sounds.

Rhyme

Despite the primacy of rhythm, rhyme is possibly the feature most strongly associated with the concept of poetry in the common perception. Possibly this is because rhyme offers a clearly identifiable difference between poetry and everyday speech.

The earliest verses we encounter in childhood usually contain strong rhyming patterns. Rhyme is marked by matching the sounds of accented vowels and subsequent consonants in words. This happens characteristically, but not exclusively, at the end of lines:

Jack and Jill
*Went up the **hill***
To fetch a pail of water.
*Jack fell **down***
*And broke his **crown***
And Jill came tumbling after.

In this well-known nursery rhyme, the rhymes marked in bold are **full** or **exact rhymes**. However, *water* and *after* do not rhyme fully and are called **half rhymes**.

Rhymes which occur at the end of lines, like those in Jack and Jill, are simply called **end rhymes**, but where they occur elsewhere in the line we refer to them as **internal rhymes**:

*The fair breeze **blew**, the white foam **flew**,*
The furrow followed free:

*We were the **first** that ever **burst***
Into that silent sea.

Alliteration, consonance and assonance

Alliteration is another form of sound pattern in which initial consonant phonemes are repeated. When the repeated consonant does not occur in the initial position it is called **consonance**. **Assonance** is the term used to describe repeated use of a vowel phoneme.

Consonant pp. 27–31
Vowel pp. 31–35

Activity 5.7	Using your language knowledge

Identify one example of *alliteration* and one example of *consonance* in this extract from Wilfred Owen's poem, *Anthem for Doomed Youth*. What effect is created by the use of these techniques? What poetic device is illustrated by the title of the poem?

What passing-bells for these who die as cattle?
Only the monstrous anger of the guns.
Only the stuttering rifles' rapid rattle
Can patter out their hasty orisons.

Reflection

rifles' rapid rattle is an example of alliteration. *stuttering, rattle* and *patter* exemplify consonance. *Doomed youth* demonstrates the use of assonance.

Onomatopoeia

Poets may also use *onomatopoeia* – words which attempt to recreate a particular sound or noise. Onomatopoeia is used in all kinds of language and there are many established examples, e.g. *bang, boom, splash, moo, woof, whoosh*. Poets often intensify the effect of onomatopoeia by using alliteration or assonance with it.

Meaning-based devices

Poetry exploits the linguistic resources of both sound and meaning to the full. Poetry has many ways of expressing meanings beyond the literal.

Imagery

Imagery is the term used for writing which represents emotions or ideas through the medium of an immediately apprehensible **image**. As the term suggests, the central image is likely to be a visual one, but imagery is capable of appealing to the auditory and tactile imagination, as well as the visual. Imagery also tends to use associations in a powerful way.

Underline any words or phrases which you think are particularly effective in creating an effective image of the tiger.

The Tyger

Tyger! Tyger! burning bright
In the forests of the night.
What immortal hand or eye
Could frame thy fearful symmetry?

In what distant deeps or skies
Burnt the fire of thine eyes?
On what wings dare he aspire?
What the hand dare seize the fire?

And what shoulder, and what art,
Could twist the sinews of thy heart?
And when thy heart began to beat,
What dread hand? and what dread feet?

What the hammer? What the chain?
In what furnace was thy brain?
What the anvil? What dread grasp
Dare its deadly terrors clasp?

When the stars threw down their spears,
And water'd heaven with their tears,
Did he smile his work to see?
Did he who made the Lamb make thee?

Tyger! Tyger! Burning bright
In the forests of the night.
What immortal hand or eye
Dare frame thy fearful symmetry?

William Blake

Reflection

Blake's tiger is awesome in its appearance and in its power. To convey this feeling of awe, Blake offers images of creation which evoke the terrifying power of the blacksmith's forge. There are several images involving fire (*furnace, fire, burning*) and the smith's equipment (*furnace, anvil, hammer, chain*). Action verbs imply strength or violence (*twist, grasp, clasp*). Blake is using imagery to elicit a response to an industrial scene familiar to readers who would probably never have seen a tiger. By juxtaposing the two he conveys the tiger's terror and strength. This apprehension is intensified by imagery which evokes associations of hell.

Extralinguistic knowledge pp. 114–115

Figurative language

In the traditional sense, *figurative language* is a way of speaking or writing which refers obliquely to the subject in hand or which uses unusually elaborate vocabulary and structures. Figurative language may involve imagery, pattern, comparison or substitution to achieve its effect. Some uses of figurative language have become **idiomatic** or even **clichéd**, e.g. *He was as quiet as a mouse. It was over the top.* In poetic writing we often find concentrated use of figurative language.

- **Kenning**. Kennings are used very regularly in Old Norse and Old English poetry. A kenning is a short phrase which is substituted for a noun:

    seal's field – the sea
    metal storm – battle

Although kennings resemble metaphors, their repeated use (many are 'stock' items) means they often lack the element of surprise or revelation that an effective metaphor brings.

- **Simile.**

    The dog was like a lamb......

This is a figure of speech in which one thing is compared to another. The comparison is explicit and is signalled by use of the words *like* and *as*. Similes which are commonly used in everyday speech no longer grab our attention, e.g. *cool as a cucumber, green as grass*. In poetic writing fresh meanings are created through original use of the simile.

- **Metaphor.**

    ...but the cat was a tiger!

Like the simile, literary metaphor is a figure of speech in which one thing is compared to another, this time implicitly, by substituting a new word for the word referred to. We can think of metaphor as 'imaginative substitution'. Unfortunately, as with kennings, repeated use of metaphors can rob them of their imaginative quality; when we say someone is at the peak of their power, does that always evoke a mental image of a mountain summit? When you first heard of a computer **virus** did the word stimulate thoughts of disease spread by contact? Does it still?

A famous example of a metaphor is found in *Romeo and Juliet*:

    But soft, what light through yonder window breaks?
    *It is the east and **Juliet is the Sun.***

Romeo is saying that Juliet *is* the thing to which she is compared. Successful metaphors often trade on different aspects of the meaning of a word. So, for example, in this case Romeo might mean that as the sun is the brightest object in the sky and the centre of the universe, for him Juliet is the brightest object in his world, the centre of his universe.

◗ **Extended metaphor.**

Sometimes a metaphor may be sustained over a number of lines or even through an entire poem as in the following example (which in fact begins with a simile) written by Stephen Spender:

Word
The word bites like a fish.
Shall I throw it back free
Arrowing to that sea
Where thoughts lash tail and fin?
Or shall I pull it in
To rhyme upon a dish?

◗ **Personification.**

Tho flood waters crept up...

Sometimes poets attribute human qualities to inanimate objects.

Analysing language data   Activity 5.9

Underline words and phrases in the poem that Sylvia Plath uses to personify the mushrooms.

What effect does she achieve through use of this technique?

Mushrooms
Overnight, very
Whitely, discreetly,
Very quietly
Our toes, our noses
Take hold on the loam,
Acquire the air.
Nobody sees us,
stops us, betrays us;
The small grains make room.
Soft fists insist on
Heaving the needles,
The leafy bedding.
Even the paving
Our hammers and rams,
Earless and eyeless,
Perfectly voiceless,
widen the crannies.
Shoulder through holes. We
Diet on water,
On crumbs of shadow
Bland-mannered, asking
little or nothing.
So many of us!
So many of us!

We are shelves, we are
Tables, we are meek,
We are edible,
Nudgers and shovers
in spite of ourselves.
Our kind multiplies:
We shall by morning
Inherit the earth.
Our foot's in the door.

Reflection

Plath makes reference to a number of human body parts and actions which imply human agents. The two come together with chilling effect in '*Our foot's in the door.*'

▶ **Pun**.

> *No one can say that Dennis is not trying.*

A pun is a play on a single word which has more than one meaning. The effect is usually humorous, as another example from *Romeo and Juliet* shows:

> *Ask for me tomorrow and you shall find me a **grave** man.*

As Mercutio utters his dying words, the word *grave* conveys simultaneously the meaning *serious* and another more closely associated with death and burial.

Activity 5.10	Analysing texts ✔

Identify examples of simile, metaphor, pun, personification and kenning in these extracts:

(a) *Ben Battle was a soldier bold*
And used to war's alarms:
But a canon-ball took off his legs,
So he laid down his arms.

(b) *Many-maned scud-thumper, tub*
of male whales, maker of worn wood, shrub-
ruster, sky mocker, rave!
Portly pusher of waves, wind-slave

(c) *Slowly, silently, now the moon*
Walks the night in her silver shoon;
This way, and that, she peers, and sees
Silver fruit upon silver trees;

(d) *The wind was a torrent of darkness among the gusty trees,*
The moon was a ghostly galleon tossed upon cloudy seas,

(e) My love is like a red, red rose
        That's newly sprung in June:
     My love is like the melody
        That's sweetly played in tune.

Symbolism

The inclusion of certain elements in a text can suggest an important element of meaning. For example, references to blood often carry associations of death or violence or alternatively of kinship and nationhood. English folksong uses a host of stock symbols, with much action taking place in the vicinity of significant flowers and herbs. Many symbols are instantly recognisable to members of a particular culture – hearts, red roses and doves, for example, all have meanings which are widely acknowledged.

Some writers develop symbols of their own, which readers recognise when they recur in successive works. Yeats, for example, frequently uses a winding staircase and a tower with consistent significance. Symbols come close in their functioning to metaphors, which also express abstract ideas through concrete images. One difference lies in the fact that the meaning of (a writer's own) symbols is not always made explicit, and this may result in an air of mystery.

The conventional symbolic meaning of the rose has changed more than once since classical times. In Herrick's poem, below, the Renaissance meaning of 'youth' and 'physical beauty' combined with the notion of 'impermanence' or 'transience' is implied:

To the virgins, to make much of time
Gather ye rosebuds while ye may.
Old time is still a-flying:
And this same flower that smiles today
Tomorrow will be dying.

Using your cultural knowledge ✔   Activity 5.11

Think of conventional symbols you might use to represent the following:

peace
love
power
death

Style and voice

In both prose and poetry personal **style** results from an author's characteristic choices of vocabulary, syntactic structures, subject matter, use of imagery and poetic language and other aspects of language. We can analyse and compare writers' styles in terms of these areas, but often the impression a style makes is described in broad terms such as *measured*, *elegant* and *economical*. Metaphorical descriptions such as *turgid*, *breathless* and *smooth* are also used.

The term **voice** is used in two distinct senses. It may refer to the persona adopted by the author of a narrative; the author has to decide between an omniscient narrator and one with a limited point of view – one of the participants in the story, for example. On the other hand, it may have a meaning very close to that of *style*. The use of this particular metaphor emphasises both the relationship between the writer and the audience (as a listener is implied) and the very personal and individual properties of a speaking voice.

In this section we have seen that:

▶ Poetry expresses meaning, including affective meaning, through concise use of carefully chosen **words**, **structures** and **sounds**.

▶ **Sound-based devices** include rhythm, rhyme, alliteration, consonance, assonance and onomatopoeia.

▶ **Meaning-based devices** include imagery, personification, pun, metaphor, simile and symbol.

▶ Writers of both prose and poetry create their **personal voice and style** through their choice of linguistic and literary structures and devices.

Poetic forms

The English poetic repertoire includes a wide range of forms. Before briefly outlining the features of some of these it will be useful to be clear about some terminology.

▶ **Stanza**. The following lines from Blake's poem are arranged in two stanzas:

Tyger! Tyger! burning bright
In the forests of the night.
What immortal hand or eye
Could frame thy fearful symmetry?

In what distant deeps or skies
Burnt the fire of thine eyes?
On what wings dare he aspire?
What the hand dare seize the fire?

A stanza is usually a repeating pattern of lines with recognisable rhyme and rhythm. The unit known as a *verse* is the commonest example.[54]

Rhyme pp. 145–146
Rhythm pp. 141–144

▶ **Rhyme scheme.** Look at the end rhymes in the second stanza of *The Tyger*. The first two rhyme and then the next adopt a different rhyme. This pattern of two rhymes followed by two different rhymes

54 In free verse (page 156) stanzas are not constrained by rules.

is repeated in each stanza and is known as the **rhyme scheme**. It is usual to use an alphabetic system to represent the pattern, so this pattern would be notated as AABB.

In Spender's poem, *Word*, the pattern is more complex:

The word bites like a fish.	A
Shall I throw it back free	B
Arrowing to that sea	B
Where thoughts lash tail and fin?	C
Or shall I pull it in	C
To rhyme upon a dish?	A

▶ **Couplets.** Two successive rhyming lines of poetry (often with the same rhythm) are called **couplets**. Couplets are often used to create a satisfying ending to a poem and Shakespeare often used this device to signal the end of a scene, as this example from Macbeth shows.

> *Away. and mock the time with fairest show:*
> *False face must hide what the false heart doth know.*

The AABB rhyme scheme of *The Tyger* is a pattern of couplets.

Narrative poetry

Narrative poetry is poetry that tells a story. The oldest known poem in English, *Beowulf*, is an example of an **epic** as it tells the story of a heroic figure. Like *Beowulf*, **ballads** belong to the **oral tradition**; originally they were performed and handed on by word of mouth, though since the seventeenth century at least there have been ballads written expressly for publication. Ballads are usually constructed from short regular stanzas.

Oral poetry

Ballads and folk songs are usually available to us because they were 'collected' and published by scholars before they fell out of circulation. Some aspects of the oral tradition are still very much alive, however. **Playground chants** and **skipping rhymes**, both characterised by strong rhyme and rhythm, are passed on and enjoyed by generations of children, whilst parents have a hand in the transmission of **nursery rhymes**. One form of oral poetry which has become popular in Britain in recent years is Rap: an African Caribbean and African American form with strong rhythm and rapid pace. Many verse **riddles** date back to the earliest history of English and probably beyond.

> *The wave. over wave. a weird thing I saw.*
> *thought-wrought. and wonderfully ornate:*
> *a wonder on the wave – water became bone. (Ice)*

Syllable-based forms

Besides the well-known 5–7–5 pattern of the three-line **haiku** there are a number of other syllable-based forms which are sometimes used in English.

Syllable pp. 39–43

- **Tanka** (5, 7, 5, 7, 7) is a form of poetry based on the haiku which arose out of a Japanese courtly tradition. A person receiving a haiku would add two seven-syllable lines and then return to the sender.

- **Renga** is a series of haiku with successive pairs linked by 2 seven-syllable lines. Sometimes each haiku in the sequence is written by a new poet and then passed on to another.

- The **Cinquain** is another form of poetry with a standard syllable pattern invented by American poet, Adelaide Crapsey. It contains five lines of 22 syllables and is more in sympathy with the patterns of spoken English than the Japanese haiku is.

November Night

Listen ...	(2)
With faint dry sound,	(4)
Like steps of passing ghosts,	(6)
The leaves, frost-crisped, break from the trees	(8)
And fall.	(2)

Nonsense poems and comic verse

A surprising number of English poets have produced **nonsense poems**. Often they include invented words which have no conventional meaning, but which are capable of creating a mood, perhaps of silliness:

> On the Ning Nang Nong
> Where the Cows go bong!
> And the Monkeys all say Boo!

Or of menace:

> 'Twas brillig, and the slithy toves
> Did gyre and gimble in the wabe:
> All mimsy were the borogoves,
> And the mome raths outgrabe.

The apparent lack of sense allows an emphasis on the sound of the poem and rhythm is often strong. Nonsense poems are rarely completely devoid of meaning. The poems of Edward Lear, for example, often tell a coherent story which is supported by baffling detail:

> They dined on mince and slices of quince,
> Which they ate with a runcible spoon:

Lear also invented the form of comic verse known as the **limerick**. This has a distinctive rhythm and AABBA rhyme scheme:

> There was a young lady from Riga
> Who smiled as she rode on a Tiger.
> They returned from the ride
> With the lady inside
> And the smile on the face of the Tiger.

A less well-known form, the **Clerihew**, consists of two rhyming couplets. The first line is the name of the (human) subject and the other lines may be of any length:

Sir Christopher Wren
Said, 'I'm going to dine with some men.
If anyone calls,
Say I'm designing St Paul's.'

Ode, elegy, sonnet

These are three consciously 'literary' forms which tend to the use of markedly poetic language.

The **ode** addresses its subject in the second person, as this extract from Keats's *To Autumn* demonstrates.

Who hath not seen thee oft amid thy store?
Sometimes whoever seeks abroad may find
Thee sitting careless on a granary floor,
Thy hair soft-lifted by the winnowing wind;

An **elegy** is a kind of lament, expressing regret at some form of loss, sometimes, but not necessarily, through death.

Seamus Heaney wrote this modern example.

Mid-term Break
I sat all morning in the college sick bay,
Counting bells knelling classes to a close.
At two o' clock our neighbours drove me home.
In the porch I met my father crying –
He had always taken funerals in his stride –
And big Jim Evans saying it was a hard blow.
The baby cooed and laughed and rocked the pram
When I came in, and I was embarrassed
By old men standing up to shake my hand
And tell me they were 'sorry for my trouble'.
At ten o'clock an ambulance arrived
With the corpse, starched and bandaged by nurses.
Next morning I went into the room Snowdrops
And candles soothed the bedside; I saw him
For the first time in six weeks. Paler now,
Wearing a puffy bruise on his left temple,
He lay in the four-foot box as in a cot.
No gaudy scars, the bumper knocked him clear.
A four-foot box, a foot for every year.

The use of *bells knelling* in line two is both a general allusion to death and a (possibly conscious) intertextual reference to Gray's well-known *Elegy Written in a Country Churchyard*.

Unlike odes and elegies, the **sonnet** has a particular form, being composed of fourteen lines. A sonnet may employ any rhyme scheme but a number of conventional patterns do exist. This example follows the pattern of Shakespeare's sonnets, with its iambic pentameter and ABABCDCDEFEFGG rhyme scheme:

Sonnet

Hundreds of people shouting to the world,
Too many speeches to let people breathe,
Too many hopes in vicious flags unfurled.
Eventually for blood they all will seethe
And war and bombs will start to smother us.
And on Death's pillow which will be uplifted
You'll see without regalia or fuss,
How we the nations civilised have drifted
To dust and hell upon this arid plain.
And from this desert new races will grow
And godliness and peace will live again,
Live men not dead machines will reap and sow.
Then they shall learn to love one another
And so to curse the man who hates his brother.

Mathew Festenstein

Free verse

Free verse, a form which has flourished in the twentieth century does not exhibit rhyme or rhythm in a regular way, although all the weapons in the poet's armoury are available to it.

In this poem by Walt Whitman, note the use of alliteration, assonance and repetition as well as occasional use of conventional metre:

When I heard the learn'd astronomer

When I heard the learn'd astronomer,
When the proofs, the figures, were ranged in columns before me,
When I was shown the charts and diagrams, to add, divide and measure them,
When I sitting heard the astronomer where he lectured with much applause
in the lecture-room,
How soon unaccountable I became tired and sick,
Till rising and gliding out I wander'd off by myself,
In the mystical moist night-air, and from time to time,
Looked up in perfect silence at the stars.

In this section we have seen that:

▶ English poetry includes a large number of **conventional forms** which may be defined by factors such as:

- patterns of rhyme

- metrical patterns

- subject matter.

---

6. Understanding English at text level: reading texts critically

The exploration of poetic texts shows that there is more to any piece of writing than appears on the surface. We read between the lines, refer to personal experience, create pictures in our minds, even attempt to engage in a dialogue, discussion or debate with the writer. All of these ways of interacting with texts are important if we are to become analytical or critical readers. As the various persuasive forms of text showed, readers need to be able to weigh up different appeals to their reason or emotions if they are to decide on the importance or value of each text to them. **Critical evaluation** is an essential part of being a reader. Knowledge of the ways texts are structured for different purposes and to create different effects will help. For example, analysis of text can show, amongst other things, how fact and opinion are not always neatly separated in texts. Critical evaluation helps readers to see through the choices a writer makes to appraise the integrity of the work; how much does it owe to the things and events described and how much to the author's personal world view? In other words, the critical reader is one who recognises **bias**.

Persuasive writing pp. 133–134

In this chapter we shall see:

- the difference between **fact and opinion** and the difficulty sometimes experienced in isolating one from the other;

- some of the factors which show a writer's intentional or unintentional **bias**;

- some of the ways in which we decide on the **quality** of a text; how we identify a 'good book'.

Fact and opinion

It is questionable whether there is any such thing as a 'neutral' text – one where there is no bias at all, no reflection of the writer's point of view. If you look back at the different non-fiction texts on pages 126–135, you might decide that the recipe or the instructions were quite neutral; they don't take a particular point of view or try to persuade you of anything. However, the choice of making a pizza might be considered an expression of what counts as 'normal', 'nice' or 'acceptable' as food. The decision to include ham might be considered to have cultural overtones. Any piece of writing constitutes a selection of material; the writer has to decide on one subject, rejecting others, and then choose which details are necessary and which might distract from the purpose of the text. Even if texts do not obviously show any particular bias, it is worth remembering that every text represents a selection of ideas by a writer who has a specific purpose in mind and who shapes that text for an identified readership. The texts in the next activity show that it is sometimes quite difficult to separate factual information from the opinion or bias presented by the writer.

The following extracts from a newspaper, a car brochure, a book about geology, a book about snails and a history book all intend to provide the reader with information. Remembering that it can be tricky to make hard and fast distinctions, try to categorise each as *mainly* fact or opinion.

(a) *Engine type: 16-Valve DOHC with VVTi;*
CO2 mass emission – g/km: S & GS 134; GLS & CDX 137

(Toyota brochure)

(b) *Gordon Brown's budget seems a good one – although we're reserving final judgement till we've seen ALL the fine print.*

(The *Sun*)

(c) *Fog lamps add to your peace of mind and blend perfectly with the front-end styling of your Yaris.*

(Toyota brochure)

(d) *Sir Christopher Blount and Sir Charles Davers were beheaded; Sir Gilly Merrick and Henry Cuffe were hanged.*

(*Elizabeth and Essex*)

(e) *As to their shape, pebbles fall into three groups, but between the first and the second, and between the second and the third, there is an infinite number of gradations.*

(*The Pebbles on the Beach*)

(f) *The Yaris interior is one of the greatest successes of today's spatial designers.*
(Toyota brochure)

(g) *Economy passengers on domestic or Europe-bound flights will pay only £5 airport tax from April next year – half the current rate.*

(The *Sun*)

(h) *Snails are sensitive to cold and hibernate through the entire winter.*

(*Snails*)

Reflection

You will have had little difficulty in classing some extracts, for example (a), (d) and (g), as mainly fact – always assuming, of course, that the facts are verifiable. Extracts (b) and (f), in contrast, seem to be expressions of opinion, (b) actually drawing attention to its status as an interim judgement. Some of the other extracts are harder to categorise. Could the confident classification into three groups, proposed in (e), be an opinion rather than fact?

You may well have had other comments to make about this selection. It is interesting to note, for example, that fact and opinion may use identical sentence structures – what leads us to see (f) as likely to be an opinion and (h) a fact? We probably draw on our wider knowledge of the context: the car brochure will give information, but also aims to persuade us to buy the car it describes. Sometimes knowing who wrote a text is as important to its interpretation as the words themselves.

Writers may consciously mix fact and opinion with the intention of amusing or entertaining. Historical accounts may be 'fictionalised' in order to make them more accessible or memorable to the reader.

Writers by no means always signal the distinction between fact and opinion in non-fiction texts; and sometimes we suspect they are not aware of it themselves.

Language and intention

As you saw earlier in this chapter, our comprehension of language is shaped by its context. As you have also already seen, writers necessarily impose a shape and meaning on their material and this often involves interleaving facts with interpretation and comment.

Analysing language data	Activity 6.2

The following article appeared in the *Sun* newspaper shortly after the March 2000 budget. Read it carefully and then:

◗ list any words or phrases which tell you about the author's (or maybe the editor or proprietor's?) opinions on this news.

HIDDEN TRUTH BEHIND BROWN'S BUDGET 2000

£50 TO FILL A MONDEO

Motorists suffered pain again in the Budget yesterday as the cost of filling a Ford Mondeo's tank rose to £50.

Chancellor Gordon Brown slapped 2p on a litre of petrol – 9p a gallon.

The move means unleaded fuel will now cost around 80p a litre or £3.63 a gallon. And since the hugely popular Mondeo has a 61.5 litre tank, a fill-up leaves only pennies change from a £50 note.

The Tories immediately accused Mr Brown of selling out 'Mondeo Man', a phrase coined by Prime Minister Tony Blair to describe his core supporters in Middle England.

The Chancellor tried to give motorists some comfort by freezing road tax and announcing that excise duty on cars under 1200cc will fall by £55.

But this will not affect the Mondeo because the smallest engine in any of the models is 1300cc.

The fuel rise enraged Mondeo drivers last night. Manchester salesman Jamie Philip, 32, said: 'I need my car for work and do 300 miles a week in it – but this will make me think again. As ever, it's people who can least afford it who'll feel it most.'

Reflection

The main facts to be conveyed were:

- the cost of a litre of unleaded petrol was to rise by 1.89p

- vehicle excise duty would be frozen at its present rate until a specific future date

- the lower vehicle excise duty for smaller cars would be extended to cars up to 1200cc from the same date.

The article sets out to convince by using concrete examples, based on the experiences of people with whom it is easy for readers to identify. The type of car was deliberately chosen, as *Mondeo Man* had become a common shorthand for the 'Middle England' voter. (I can say this with certainty as it is explained midway through the article!)

What may have struck you most forcibly, though, is the way facts have been selected and prioritised to present a certain point of view. It is worth noting that another transport-related fact from the budget – that £280 million would be made available across the country for public transport and congestion spots – has been omitted altogether. The choice of vocabulary – *pain, slapped, feel it most* etc. – is obviously significant.

Connotative meaning pp. 20–21

It is interesting to compare it with other versions of the same events. A regional newspaper, the *Cambridge Evening News*, chose to present the same news with a more positive use of language. Their headline *Drivers 'escape' with 2p fuel rise* was followed with *Motorists this week escaped with a rise in petrol prices of less than 2p a litre.* It quoted government ministers and an approving comment from the AA and concern from Friends of the Earth and included all the other information in some detail. At first sight this piece might appear less biased, but does it change your view if you are told that Cambridge is a city with a severe traffic problem and a large population of cyclists?

Both of these articles, then, can be seen as biased. However, whilst the *Evening News* article may feel 'neutral' to many readers (and, of course, a text will appear neutral if its bias coincides with that of the reader) it is difficult to escape the bias of the *Sun* article.

Bias: unintentional and intentional

Any piece of writing intending to convey information sets out to change the way the reader thinks, even if this is simply at the level of extending their stock of factual knowledge.

Texts will necessarily represent reality in particular ways which reflect the writer's views. Sometimes this will be overt, as in political propaganda and advertising, but often it will be unwitting, with the author's views implicit in the language choices made. Why, for example, did the *Sun* journalist (and Tony Blair before him) choose the example of **Mondeo Man** rather than **Mondeo Woman?** It might be an example of intentional bias: an attempt to portray men as of greater (electoral) importance. On the other hand, it could simply be the journalist and the Prime Minster unwittingly betraying the way they think.

In any event, **gender bias** is a very significant form of bias, both because it can arise from deeply held (but possibly unarticulated) opinions and because the pronoun system (he/she) has a tendency to reflect a particular gender (usually masculine) unless the writer consciously takes avoiding action.

Any writer who hopes to make an impact on readers will take into account their political views, their beliefs and values, in putting together a text which is intended to have a particular effect. We can see this in contemporary brochures for small cars, from which some of the examples above were chosen, where aspects of safety provision, fuel economy and green issues reflect what are seen to be current concerns. Advertisements often draw on this; for example, the Hovis adverts for bread, where values associated with certain regional accents – honesty, tradition, community, wholesomeness – were enlisted to promote a favourable impression.

Connotative meaning pp. 20–21

Analysing language data   Activity 6.3[55]

For each of the following extracts, use these questions to evaluate the extent to which it represents biased writing.

▷ Who is describing or representing what and why?

▷ Is any individual or event being misrepresented or unrepresented?

▷ Who or what is treated as central?

▷ Who or what is treated as marginal?

▷ What meanings are implied rather than openly stated?

▷ What frame of reference is being set up? What values is the reader being invited to share?

1   (From a newspaper report about violence on a housing estate in which eight people were injured)

People living nearby said an incident between members of the two families on Friday had caused bad feeling which turned to violence at lunchtime yesterday. The estate houses a substantial Asian community.

2   (Opening sentences of a report of an incident in 1975 in which police killed 11 black people)

Eleven Africans were shot dead and 15 wounded when Rhodesian police opened fire on a rioting crowd of about 2,000 in the African township of Salisbury this afternoon.[56]

(*The Times*)

55 Adapted from Pope (1998).

56 Graddol *et al.* (1994) describe Trew's (1979) analysis of this and other reports.

Reflection

The first extract conveys an implicit meaning by the juxtaposition of two sentences when in fact the final sentence has little real connection with what precedes it. (Compare *Two men robbed the bank. Both had eaten biscuits.*) In any text we expect cohesion and coherence and, in order to make sense of the report, readers can be expected to make the connecting link themselves – that Asian families were involved in the violence; in this way they take on the responsibility for formulating a meaning that the writer does not wish (perhaps for legal reasons) to state overtly.

Cohesion pp. 116–119
Coherence pp. 112–114

The second extract appears to be a straightforward account of an incident which took place during the struggle for independence in what is now Zimbabwe. By employing a passive structure the writer has been able to bring the victims of the shooting to the beginning of the sentence, thereby de-emphasising the role of the police. Consider this report of the same incident from another daily newspaper:

> *Riot police shot and killed 11 African demonstrators and wounded 15 others here today in the Highfield African township on the outskirts of Salisbury.*

(*Guardian*)

The theme of this sentence is the *Riot police*. Placing this noun phrase first in the sentence makes it clear that it was they who did the killing. In *The Times* report the police are (grammatically) distanced from the action; it is not actually stated that the police killed the victims and although a moment's reflection makes this the most likely interpretation of the facts as reported, the casual reader is not confronted with a (possibly uncomfortable) truth.

Noun phrase pp. 83–84

The extracts could be reduced to almost identical sets of propositions (the only substantive difference between the two being in the choice between *riot* and *demonstration*). The choice of language used to express these propositions, however, makes a significant difference to the impression made on the reader. In Chapter 3 you saw how changing word order can change meanings. Here the changed word order of the passive construction makes a subtle but powerful change to the way the text is interpreted.

As noted in the last paragraph, one person's demonstration can be another person's riot. Choices of vocabulary can be a significant element in expressing a writer's bias as a term often conveys information not just about the thing referred to but also about how the writer views that thing and by implication how the reader is expected to view it. If we take the 'common-sense' line that texts (and especially written texts) contain 'all the information' and that listeners and readers are merely recipients then we are more likely to fall victim to the bias and prejudice of writers.

Connotative meaning pp. 20–21

The following phrases were used in a *Guardian* article to illustrate a biased approach on the part of the British press to reporting the Gulf War.

What techniques have journalists used to convey their point of view?

Terms applied to Allied activity	Terms applied to Iraqi activity
army, navy, air force	war machine
reporting guidelines	censorship
press briefings	propaganda
take out	destroy
suppress	destroy
eliminate	kill
dig in	cower in their foxholes
first strikes	sneak missile
launch pre-emptively	launch without provocation
professional	brainwashed
lion-hearts	paper tigers
cautious	cowardly
young knights of the skies	bastards of Baghdad
loyal	blindly obedient
collateral damage	civilian casualties
planes fail to return from missions	planes are zapped

Reflection

There is in fact cause for comment in the article from which this list was taken. In the process of making a point about biased reporting (presumably none of the examples were drawn from the *Guardian*!) it selects only some of the available material and quotes phrases out of context. It uses layout and headings to emphasise the contrasts. Is this an effective way of stating a case objectively or simply another example of bias?

So far as the vocabulary itself is concerned, you may have noted the strong connotations of some of the words: as you know, words may bring with them meanings from previous usages in other contexts. So, words such as *collateral damage, eliminate, suppress* or *take out* have a neutral, distanced and unemotional feel to them. We might meet them in scientific or other professional discourses. They mask the act of killing. The word *lion-hearts* has quite different but equally positive connotations, the general one of bravery and nobility associated with lions, and the specific one which draws on national pride in its reference to King Richard I. Value-laden adjectives and verbs, such as *sneak* and *cower*, are also used by writers in order to recruit the reader's emotional response. Literary devices of various kinds contribute to the distinctions between the two sides. You will probably have noted alliteration, in *bastards of Baghdad*, and metaphor and assonance in *young knights of the skies*. Figurative uses of language are common ways to influence the reader.

Connotative meaning pp. 20–21
Poetic devices pp. 140–152

The set of guiding questions in Activity 6.3. offers a way of identifying factors which contribute to bias. Choices of vocabulary may amount to **misrepresentation**; for example, in the 'Rhodesia' articles either *riot* or *demonstration* is a biased word. **Unrepresentation**, the selection of information in order not to reveal important and relevant facts to the reader, would be another factor. Absences and silences can misinform readers just as effectively as more obvious devices. However, although there are many and various ways in which writers and speakers can influence their audiences, a critical reader who has developed some awareness of how texts are constructed can read against a text and so resist and challenge aspects of the meanings which are presented.

In this section we have seen that:

▶ Any text constitutes a selection of material and therefore includes an element of **bias**.

▶ **Fact** and **opinion** are not always easy to distinguish.

▶ Bias may be expressed through **choice** of vocabulary and grammatical structures and through the representation, unrepresentation and misrepresentation of particular facts and ideas.

▶ A complete definition of literacy must include the ability to discern the bias within a text.

Evaluating quality

Making judgements about the quality of a text can, on one level, appear very straightforward – we know what we like. But how do we know what we like? Are there rules we unconsciously refer to? And is a subjective measure (what *I* like) adequate?

A body of English literature which is considered to be 'of high quality' often called 'the canon' does exist and is acknowledged explicitly in, for example, the National Curriculum (which refers to 'major writers' and a 'literary heritage') and implicitly in the choices editors of literary periodicals make over which texts to review or publish. But what guidelines do these arbiters of literary quality use? What are the features which make one text better than another? And to what extent can these choices be disentangled from the cultural experience of the reader?

This activity will be more stimulating if you can find one or two other people to do it with.

Spend a few minutes trying to place the following writers in order of quality:

J. K. Rowling

William Shakespeare

Ted Hughes

Roald Dahl

Charlotte Brontë

Charles Dickens

Stephen King

Danielle Steele

Kenneth Grahame

Beatrix Potter

George Orwell

Reflection

You may recall a famous media debate about the relative merits of Keats and Bob Dylan and one pundit's view that the whole thing was like asking 'if a piece of string was better than next Tuesday'. You may well feel that Activity 6.5 is an impossible task; that the authors are too different in language, period and their intended purpose and audience to make any comparison meaningful. You may say that you don't know enough about these authors, or that you haven't read work by some of them, even if you do know their reputation. Indeed some writers have insisted that it is impossible to judge one text as intrinsically 'better' than another. However, if you did try to make comparisons you should have found certain criteria coming to light. Some of the following may have been among them:

▶ **Aesthetic considerations**. Aesthetic factors are concerned with fostering the reader's response at the level of **feeling**, and this is often associated with the concept of 'beauty'. This will be particularly true of poets and authors of poetic prose. Obviously what is regarded as 'beautiful' is highly dependent on cultural and other considerations. Aesthetic considerations are not, of course, confined to the realm of the beautiful; if you like the rhythmic sound of Road Dahl's nonsense verse or the power of Stephen King's images (which even when horrific provoke a response at the level of feeling) you are exercising aesthetic judgements. Of course, you might include illustrations in your consideration too.

Poetic devices pp. 140–152

- **Accuracy of representation**. The poet and the social realist may share the desire to portray aspects of their experience as accurately as possible. Novelists develop characters beyond stereotypes and do extensive background research to make sure all the details match the knowledge of even the most expert reader. These authors work to develop the meaning of their text as fully as they can.

Extralinguistic knowledge pp. 114–115

- **Ideological issues**. Wittingly or unwittingly authors convey their world view through their work. Some works seek actively to convey a moral standpoint, perhaps by revealing events and situations which the author considers to be morally wrong. It might be dangerous to consider this factor in isolation; is the leader writer of *Socialist Worker* as good a writer as Dickens or Orwell?

- **Effect on the audience**. You might rate highly the authors of books which have changed your way of thinking or, like Dickens, the perceptions of a wider public. You may feel that some books are able to extend imaginative, linguistic or empirical horizons.

- **Complexity**. Some books have many layers of meaning. This can make a book accessible to a variety of readers or can add to the power of a narrative and make a book worth reading more than once. Often books use references (expressed or implied) to other texts (intertextual references) or to the experiences of the reader in order to deepen or broaden their meaning.

- **Popularity and durability**. This is perhaps the only democratic criterion and it has a certain scientific appeal; large-scale data collection is associated with reliable results. However, the effects of availability, advertising, fashion and so on should not be overlooked. Moreover, the popularity of authors can wane suddenly, so perhaps an enduring popularity is a better guide. This is obviously linked to the concept of **literary heritage** (the so-called 'classics' of English literature), though in this, popularity with the wider public does not appear to be a criterion for membership of the canon.

All of these (among others) can be considered legitimate bases for judgement, and if you did Activity 6.5. with a partner you were probably able to agree on criteria even if you couldn't agree over the authors. Interestingly, few if any of the criteria can escape the charge of subjectivity and so far as membership of the canon is concerned, much appears to depend on the views and aesthetic sensibilities of those in positions of power and influence.

Audience and purpose

Several of the criteria outlined can be linked to a text's purpose and the response it evokes in its audience. These might offer reliable touchstones for both fiction and non-fiction texts. If a set of instructions is fully intelligible to its intended readers and results in the intended outcome then it is successful. Similarly, a biography might be judged on its accuracy, comprehensiveness and 'readability', qualities striven for by the author and sought by the reader.

The National Curriculum for teaching English in secondary schools lists the following as 'major writers' of fiction published since 1914. For all those whose work you are familiar with, try to decide their strengths in terms of the above criteria.

E. M. Forster

William Golding

Graham Greene

Aldous Huxley

James Joyce

D. H. Lawrence

Katherine Mansfield

George Orwell

Muriel Spark

William Trevor

Evelyn Waugh

In this section we have seen that:

- It is possible to describe some grounds on which the **quality of texts** can be judged, but most rely to some extent on **subjective judgement**.

- The **literary heritage** view is influential and rests on the judgement of people (editors, curriculum authors etc.) with the power to influence the reading public.

7. Spoken and written English in action

This final chapter focuses on what we do when we read, write, speak and listen. It begins with a closer look at how spoken language works and then outlines the kinds of behaviour we adopt when we read and write.

In this chapter we shall see:

▷ how and why **spoken English** differs from **written English**;

▷ that the **process of reading** calls on all aspects of our competence as language users (as well as our extralinguistic knowledge) and involves far more than decoding to sound, letter by letter;

▷ that it is more accurate to think of **written language** as a distinct mode of language, rather than as the written representation of spoken language;

▷ how written texts are developed and refined through a process of **planning**, **drafting** and **revision**;

▷ how **handwriting**, like most other forms of language, may be adapted to suit different purposes.

Spoken and written English

Whilst the texts I have used so far to illustrate the workings of the English language have tended to be written ones, from time to time the opportunity to contrast speech and writing has been taken. In this section, we shall look at some of the important differences between spoken and written English.

Activity 7.1	Analysing language data

Read these two Standard English texts. The first is a spoken text and the second written. Identify the differences between the two in terms of:

(a) organisation

(b) sentence structure

(c) vocabulary.

(i) *But it it it it it'll still be Wells Fargo but I mean one must distinguish the two things one must distinguish … producing a sort of Wells Fargo … er … or I Love Lucy which people watch in long huts in Borneo and saying well it's a pity they can't do you know a kind of Coronation Street of Long Hut in Borneo for a … for a… on themselves and the … which is one form of manipulation and I don't know whether it's perhaps even more insidious than the political but the other one is a*

---

deliberate use of saying we will take this medium and we will put the message into people's heads that we want them to have ... after all the man producing Wells Fargo if suddenly nobody was very interested would be quite happy to do something else as long as it was sold

(ii) *How big a part did building and urban renewal play in the fourteenth-century Italian city economy? There are various reasons why it is very hard to answer this question with precision. One is that the surviving evidence makes it difficult to enter into the design process. We have no Italian architectural treatises that can be compared to Cennino Cennini's handbook for painters or to the various manuscripts that have survived elsewhere in Europe, which give an insight into architectural theory.*

Reflection

The differences are plain to see and since by now you are used to analysing texts according to their formal features, you should have found the description of these differences to be a fairly straightforward task.

(a) **Organisation.** In the spoken text we see an argument which seems to be formulated as it goes along, with diversions and asides loosely linked to the main ideas (we have, of course, to remember that there would be very few difficulties in following this in its original broadcast version, where intonation and pauses would be an integral part of the text).

The actual content – the argument – in this extract seems to take up a lot of space; the written extract, in contrast, is much more tightly organised. An initial question is followed by a response listing and explaining reasons why it is difficult to answer (the text continues with further reasons after this extract). There are references back and forward to aid cohesion: *this question, One is that... .*

Intonation pp. 88–89

(b) **Sentence structure.** This is perhaps an unfair heading as some structures are peculiar to spoken Standard English. Informal speech is not in fact organised in sentences in the way that written language is, but rather in chunks of meaning with looser connections. This is observable in nearly all speakers, however educated, in informal contexts – in fact, we notice as an exception the occasional person who is able to produce fully cohesive text in complex sentence forms in spontaneous speech. They are often labelled as people who 'speak like a book'. In the spoken text, phrases and clauses are often linked by 'and' or juxtaposed without obvious connectives. There are hesitations, changes of direction, repetitions and fillers such as *er, um.* Phrases demonstrating the speaker's attitude and relationship with the audience, such as *I mean* or *you know,* are used throughout. In contrast, example (ii) tends to use complex sentences, with clauses and phrases carefully linked by words such as *that, which* and *why.* The writer's attitude to his readers is shown in less overt ways; for example, in the choice of an initial question which involves them in the argument to come.

Complex sentence pp. 100–104
Connectives p. 117

(c) **Vocabulary**. This is an area in which we can often see marked differences between spoken and written English. Leaving aside the area of technical or subject-specific vocabulary, we can see that the content of example (ii) is much more concisely expressed than that of example (i). This **lexical density** is achieved by packing content words, particularly noun phrases, closely together; here we have phrases such as *building and urban renewal, the fourteenth-century Italian city economy, Italian architectural treatises*. Nominalisations such as *renewal*, where the function of a verb phrase (*have been renewed*) has been taken over by a noun, are characteristic of the formal written English this text exemplifies. We are able to understand this kind of writing because, where it is very dense, as readers we are able to pause and reread in order to take it in. Spoken language is different; you may well have had the experience of hearing lecturers read out their written lectures and will remember the difficulty you sometimes had in following the argument.

Noun phrases pp. 83–84
Noun p. 75

For all these reasons, it is very easy to spot when a speaker (on the radio, say) is reading from a script.

Dialogue and discussion

Even the spoken text in activity 5.1 has something in common with written language in that it is a fairly lengthy pronouncement by a single individual. It is more common for speech to be conducted by two or more people taking turns in contributing to the construction of the text which is their conversation. If the speakers don't know each other well, then time must be spent at the outset in establishing a common understanding of the subject. As the conversation develops, words will be supported by intonation, gesture and facial expressions. Nods and stock locutions (*yes, right, I see, really?* etc.) help to support the speaker of the moment and to move the conversation along. Often the immediate physical context or reference to shared experience or knowledge has a role to play.

A principal difference between written and spoken English is that writing can function without a supporting context. This gives writing the advantage of being transmissible over long distances and durable through time. On the other hand, this lack of physical and social context means that writing needs to make its meaning much more explicit; the writer is limited in the extent to which they can make assumptions about the reader's knowledge and is not available to answer questions if the reader doesn't understand.

Because writing does not have to be delivered immediately the writer has time to shape a text more carefully; a progression of ideas can be carefully set out, and the organising features of **layout** such as paragraphs, headings and all the resources of print styling – capitals, bold print, different fonts etc. – can be employed. The reader also has more time for the comprehension of a complex or dense written text than would be available to a listener.

Similarities between spoken and written modes

We have been focusing on the differences between speech and writing. It is important, however, to remember that there is an overlap between them. Both modes can, for example, vary in the degree of formality they display. Spoken language can range from a formal lecture to monosyllabic grunts over the breakfast table; written language from a scribbled label to *War and Peace*. The preceding argument about the lack of interaction between 'producers' and 'receivers' is an oversimplification too.

Register p. 12

Using your language knowledge

Activity 7.2

Which of these language events involves the highest degree of interaction between 'producer'? Which involves the least? Rank the whole list in order from most to least interactive.

using a dictionary
passing notes in a classroom
hearing the six o'clock news
joining a phone-in programme
writing a shopping list
writing a letter of condolence
leaving a message on an ansaphone
telling the children it's time to get up
following recorded messages to try to find out the time of a film

Reflection

You could add your own examples to this. Note how written and spoken language examples are not exclusively at one end or the other, and that higher levels of formality, e.g. the letter of condolence, do not necessarily coincide with low levels of interaction.

You may be one of the growing number who regularly use email for business and personal communication. If you are, you will doubtless have been fascinated to watch the development of an entirely new genre. What is particularly interesting is the way in which emails are tending to combine features associated with both speech and writing.

Analysing language data

Activity 7.3

What features of spoken and written English are evident in the following example of a complete email?

great .. jane's not in today but i can phone her …
meeting the woodworm man today, so fingers crossed.. . the builders are
great so far, even hoovered before i got home last night
see you tonight
love sally

Reflection

The text sounds more like speech than writing. You will have noticed the lack of full stops and the use of '...' This writer can assume shared knowledge with the reader, so the references to *Jane* and the *woodworm* man do not need to be made explicit. The message is not designed to preserve its meaning over time. Nor is it written in the complete sentences characteristic of much written English, and capital letters are not used.

On the other hand, vestiges of the writer's repertoire are to be seen in a sort of paragraphing (new topics start on a new line) and the final signing off (*love Sally*).

Speaking and writing: the same language?

In Chapter 2 you saw how in order to learn to read and write children need to master the correspondences between letters and sounds which in turn enables them to reconstruct words. You may have felt that this implied that reading is a process of 'building up' from these small units, and that the larger units of phrases, sentences, paragraphs etc. would 'look after themselves'. In Chapter 4, on the other hand, you saw how the language of written genres can be quite different from that of speech, and it follows therefore that learning to write entails the acquisition of structures and vocabulary which do not naturally occur in the speech of the learner. You will see, later in this chapter, that learners thrive on familiar language which helps them predict the occurrence of words.

When you consider the differences between speech and writing it is clear that it would be quite wrong to consider writing merely to be transcribed speech. The model which most closely corresponds to reality then is not:

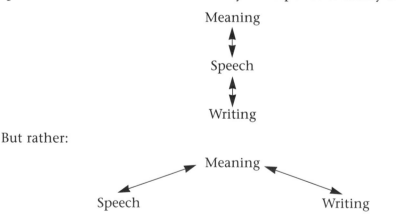

But rather:

To be fully literate it is necessary to be fully competent in the use of **written language**.

As usual with language, there is a complication. As we learn written language, its forms start to make their way into our speech and are particularly useful on formal occasions such as meetings and when giving speeches and presentations. One of the benefits of being highly literate is that it increases your chances of being orally articulate.

> Communication through **speech** is supported by such factors as **context, shared experience, gesture** and **listeners' supportive responses.**

> Communication through **writing** largely lacks these means of support but has the advantage of being able to address a (large) **distant audience** and of **preserving information** through time.

> Written language and spoken language are **different language modes**; writing is not transcribed speech.

The reading process

As you have just seen, reading involves much more than the translation of written symbols, item by item, into sounds which can then be combined successively into words and sentences. Being a proficient reader involves skills at all levels of language.

Phonic and graphic cues

✔   Activity 7.4

This poem attempts to represent a particular variety of spoken English (a 'low status' US variety in fact). How easy do you find it to read? What causes you difficulties? Does it help to read it aloud?

ygUDuh

     ydoan
     yunnuhstan

     ydoan o
     yunnuhstan dem
     yguduh ged

     yunnuhstan dem doidee
     yguduh ged riduh
     ydoan o nudn
LISN bud LISN

       dem
       gud
       am

       lidl yelluh bas
       tuds weer goin

duhSIVILEYEzum

E.E. Cummings

Reflection

Although this poem prioritises the representation of the sound of speech (even going further than conventional orthography by representing emphasis), I'm sure you will agree that it is not, at first sight, easy to make sense of. The pattern of broken sentences, the ignoring of word boundaries and the representation of a (probably) unfamiliar accent take away a number of support systems which we usually depend on. If you found the task got easier as it went on that was probably because (a) you were beginning to make sense of it and (b) you were able to reuse some of the units (words?) you learnt earlier in the text. Although information gained by applying **graphic knowledge** (knowledge about the shapes of letters and words) and **phonic knowledge** (knowledge about letter/sound correspondences) is very important to readers, other language knowledge is vital too. Reading is a linguistic process in the same way that listening is, and as such, it depends on the operation of a number of systems of **cues**.

Sentence pp. 79–81
Accent pp. 13–14

Syntactic cues

Activity 3.2 in Chapter 3 shows how we naturally **predict** the class of a written word according to its position in the sentence and to the way in which that position fits into the syntactic pattern. Even experienced readers can be expected to make the occasional slip when reading aloud, but it is extremely rare to produce a word from the wrong class – an adjective instead of a noun, say.

Syntax pp. 72–79

Activity 7.5	Analysing language data

Account for this reading error, made by a nine-year-old relatively new to English.

The book said:

> Sally spent all day sitting on the <u>jetty</u>.

Emily read:

> Sally spent all day sitting on the <u>jelly</u>.

Reflection

Emily was obviously using her graphic knowledge in paying heed to the individual letters of the word and to its overall shape and length. She also called on her phonic knowledge, for the most part accurately. Although, given this information, she failed to identify the word correctly, she was obviously using her **syntactic knowledge** to guide her to opting for a **noun**. Probably because *jetty* was an unknown word to her, Emily did not, however, produce a sentence which made sense, especially in the context of the book's large illustration.

Noun p. 75

Semantic cues

When we are reading we impose syntactic patterns on texts as we proceed. It's a process rather like the annoying habit some people have of finishing your sentences for you. It seems that the 'receptive' modes of language – listening and reading – are not so passive in their nature as one might expect. As we listen or read we actively construct the structure of the sentence alongside the speaker or the text. Syntactic cues provide important information to enable us to do this and as more information becomes available we are able to revise our predictions. Syntactic cues have an important contribution to make to the reading process. In the example in Activity 7.5, Emily correctly chose a noun, but if she had used **semantic cues** these would have guided her more precisely – she needed to choose a noun which would *make sense* in the context of that sentence, as of course *jelly* would have.

Semantic cues also occur in the wider context, beyond the sentence in question.

Analysing language data	Activity 7.6

Why is this headline ambiguous? What would resolve its ambiguity?

JONES AND EVANS ROW AGAIN

Reflection

It is, of course, impossible to tell whether the verb here means *quarrel* or *propel a boat*; *row* is a homograph – a spelling which represents two different words. If we were to read the headline in *Watersports Weekly* (a winning pair to reunite) or *Showbiz News* (an on–off celebrity relationship) we should know at once which was intended. Sometimes the same kind of information is contained within the text:

As soon as he had found the correct set, Roger introduced himself to the director.

As soon as he had found the correct set, Roger switched it on and found the channel he wanted.

Here the words are **homonyms**: both **homographs** (same spelling) and **homophones** (same sound). Notice that in each case it is necessary for the reader to read ahead in order to make sense. Although reading is predominantly a left to right activity, when we need to we are able to skip back and forth in this way.

Read the following passage. Do you need to hesitate or correct yourself anywhere? What reading strategies are you using?

Imran knew Yasmin was upset when he saw tears had appeared in her favourite dress. After a minute but meaningful pause she walked across to the dog and took a lead pencil from the box on the table.

Reflection

Again, you had to use semantic cues to interpret the homographs *tear*, *minute* and *lead* correctly, though earlier semantic cues probably led you astray.

The searchlights model

When we read, and particularly when we encounter unfamiliar words, we use our skill in interpreting phonic, graphic, syntactic and semantic cues. Where one of these cuing systems cannot be relied upon on its own then one or more of the others is brought to bear. You saw in Chapter 2 that letter combinations with more than one possible sound occur frequently. In these cases, cues from grammar, context and meaning play an important role in reducing uncertainty to the point where the word can be confidently identified.

Letter/sound correspondences pp. 46–51

Sometimes a *searchlights* metaphor is used to describe the way in which the cuing systems work. We shine syntactic, semantic, graphic and phonic 'lights' onto a word and each illuminates a different aspect. By using the information from all four we see the whole picture. For example, given the following:

Rosalind put the egg into the p_t.

put would be a reasonable guess on grapho-phonic grounds, *pet* would indicate additional use of syntactic information whilst semantic considerations might tell us that *pot* is the most likely word.

In the case of reading the full sentence:

Rosalind put the egg into the pot.

it would be possible to read *pot* using grapho-phonic cues alone, as there is no possible alternative pronunciation. The grapho-phonic system is, in fact, the only one which can be reliably used on its own, and this fact makes it possible to read words out of context (e.g. from lists) and to build up a stock of **sight words** – words which the reader recognises immediately and does not need to process in smaller parts.

However, even when relying mainly on one cuing system, we use the others to check our interpretation. I expect that when you read the sentence:

Rosalind put the egg into the pet.

your automatic use of semantic cues will cause you to look carefully at the final word, just to be sure.

Reading at word, sentence and text level

Most of this discussion has been about operating as a reader at word and sentence level. However, as we have seen, both here and in Chapter 4, our wider **extralinguistic** knowledge is often essential if we are fully to make sense of a text. Our familiarity with the structural and other aspects of a genre also aid our comprehension, and this facility can be of particular value to children learning to read. Given all this it becomes clear that comprehension of a text depends almost as much on what a reader brings to it in terms of structural and contextual knowledge as it does on what the text itself contains. Of course, our ability to interpret words and sentences is only of any value if we are able through this to make sense of the whole text – to apprehend the author's intentions and see its overall **coherence**.

Extralinguistic knowledge pp. 114–115
Genre p. 120
Coherence pp. 112–114

Inferential reading

Activity 7.8

What extralinguistic knowledge do you need in order to understand this text?

What information which is not explicitly stated can you infer? What clues are there?

> *The Russians watched the Polish resistance fighters try and beat the Nazis in Warsaw towards the end of the conflict and although the Russians were the allies they sat for 63 days watching the brave revolt rage on until inevitably it was quashed by the Germans. German retribution was fierce – Warsaw was literally razed to the ground street by street.*

Reflection

You need to know that Warsaw is the Polish capital (and therefore that the Poles had more right to be there than the Germans) and that the words *Nazis* and *Germans* refer (in this context) to the same people. If you knew that the Nazis occupied Poland during the Second World War, it would make your comprehension easier, but this fact you could have inferred, since the native *Polish resistance fighters* were *quashed by the Germans*. The author also wants readers to **infer** that the Russian army behaved badly. We are told that *although the Russians were the allies they sat... watching the brave revolt*, with the clear implication that they should have intervened on the resistance fighters' behalf. **Inference** is an essential skill for the proficient reader and without it we can only, in most cases, make partial sense of a text. Because it deals with meaning derived from whole sections of a text (i.e. the highest level of analysis) inferential reading is called a **higher order skill**.

Different texts, different ways of reading

One of the things you might have inferred from this discussion of reading is that readers always read a whole text and that they begin at the top left-hand corner and continue reading until they get to the end. This is an appropriate way to read a novel (though even then readers often look back to remind themselves of details they have forgotten or missed, and of course there are people who can't resist skipping on to the end) and some other text types, but it is by no means the way we read all texts.

Activity 7.9	Exploring your language behaviour

How do you go about reading each of the following? What skills and knowledge do you need in order to be able to use each genre effectively?

a telephone book
a dictionary
a recipe book
film reviews in your local cinema guide
a bank statement
a letter following a job interview
a Sunday newspaper
an encyclopaedia
an internet search
a history of the Second World War
a coffee table book
an election leaflet
a gardening book

Reflection

You are quite unlikely to read any of these examples from beginning to end. You might possibly read the history book *in toto*, either for entertainment or as a prelude to deeper study of the period, but you might alternatively use it as source material for an essay, on some wider aspect of European history, for example. If you are using it as a **reference book** you will need to know how to use the **index** and the **contents page** to locate the information you are after. Once you have found the pages indicated you need to decide quickly whether it meets your needs. You can do this by **skimming**: reading quickly through the whole page or section in order to get a general idea of what it is about. Once you have decided that you wish to use the section you will use your skill of **scanning**: again reading quickly, this time locating particular parts of the text where the specific information you need is to be found. Like inference, skimming and scanning are higher order skills.

You will skim the film reviews in order to gain an impression of whether each film is one you want to see and the letter from the potential employer to see if the gist is favourable or unfavourable.

You will probably scan the bank statement to locate the 'bottom line' and discover your current financial situation and of course scanning is the conventional way of using dictionaries and telephone books. Here the layout of the text helps you, with headwords and names printed in bold type. You will also need to know how **alphabetical order** works and of course know the alphabet.

Using encyclopaedia-type books requires special skills. You need to know how to select an appropriate searchword – if you want to know about fifteenth-century Italian architecture do you look under Italy, buildings, cathedrals, the Renaissance or the fifteenth century? In most cases, the trick is to be specific enough to find an article which is sufficiently relevant but not so specific that the article doesn't exist. Internet searching is similar but also depends on an ability to identify words which do not trigger links to irrelevant sites.

Activity 7.10   Using your language knowledge

Look back at the text types in Activity 7.9. Decide on the extent to which you use the separate skills of skimming and scanning in each.

Reflection

Most of the skills described in this section are probably ones you take for granted and in some cases acquired for yourself through your own literacy practices. They are examined here partly for the purpose of demonstrating that what we call literacy, especially when you consider the skills involved in **critical reading**, is a much more complex matter than simply decoding letters to ascertain the sound of words.

In this section we have seen that:

▶ Reading is an active process of **constructing meaning**, not a passive process of reception.

▶ When we read we co-ordinate information gained from graphic, phonic, syntactic and semantic **cuing systems**.

▶ The **knowledge and experience** we bring to a text is crucial to our understanding of it.

▶ Competent readers are able to use the **higher order skills** of skimming, scanning and inference.

▶ Competent readers have **additional skills** such as the ability to use alphabetical order, indexes and contents pages.

The writing process

What makes a good writer? What skills do they need? What must they be able to do?

Make a list reflecting your own views on this subject and then ask some other people, including, if possible, one or two school-age children.

Reflection

It depends on how you ask the question, but adults often answer it in literary terms. The ability to use poetic language perhaps, or to structure a novel so that it holds the reader's attention to the last. These people prize a writer's ability to **compose** text well. Children, on the other hand, very often home in on aspects of their writing – spelling, handwriting and punctuation, for example – which they feel are most highly valued by their teachers. They are concentrating on the writer's ability to **transcribe** their compositions.

Dialogue with text

We have already discussed how writing differs from speech in that it has to operate with much less information by way of supporting context (both physical and linguistic) and without the aid of a conversational partner. It seems obvious to think of writing as a one-way process. We compose our text and then somehow make it available to the intended audience. We write, they read. But is this what really happens? Do you not glance through even the 'hastily scribbled note' before you send it? And if there's something you don't like about it do you not change it?

As we read our work, or sections of it, 'in progress' the text implies questions (how to resolve two inconsistent assertions, how to explain a detail which has been missed, which sentence to delete in order to avoid repetition) which give the process of composition some resemblance to dialogue.

One of the great powers of writing is that it gives us a second chance to get things right, though, as in the case of the following writer, this benefit is not always fully understood.

At school, we always wrote in exercise books and crossing out was frowned on. When I was told to do a 'rough copy', I considered it almost as a punishment for not being able to 'get it right first time'. I though that good writers never made mistakes when they were writing.

Getting my first word processor changed my life. The 'delete' key (not to mention cutting and pasting) meant that I could change things as much as I wanted and nobody need ever know. Now I was worrying less about the state of my first draft and spending much longer on making the changes that let me say exactly what I wanted to.

How well does this experience accord with your own? Do you still try to get a piece of writing 'right first time' or have you learnt to use the **drafting** process (with or without the aid of a computer) to shape your text to your intended meaning? Incidentally, did you notice the difference in connotation between *rough copy* and *first draft*?

Exploring your language behaviour	Activity 7.12

Which of these would you redraft? Which only need a first draft?

a letter to a friend
a letter of application
a shopping list
a short poem
a note cancelling the milk
a short story

Reflection

Some of these I would expect you to redraft. A letter of application you would almost certainly rework, moving similar points together, adding supporting evidence and finding just the right words to show your experience in the best light. Almost any professional writer will tell you that they redraft many times. (Roald Dahl claimed nine drafts per book, though Enid Blyton claimed to write as the ideas came into her head, never changing a word!) Some writers also put their near final drafts away for weeks or even months so that they can come to them fresh for a final revision. Poets, of course, write more drafts than anybody. Even the shopping list may undergo some redrafting – last minute additions or the deletion of things you find you already have.

The writing process has been described many times, using different terms, but over the main elements there is a surprising degree of agreement. These elements can be ordered as **pre-writing**, **writing** and **rewriting**.

The pre-writing stage

The writer begins by deciding what to write and the form in which it is to be written. At some point they may well outline these ideas on paper in the form of a **plan**, which again will reflect both the content and the structure of the text. Knowledge of text structures dictated by genre will be important in drawing up a plan. Note that planning is not the very first thing a writer does; there has to be some thinking done first. Writers vary in the amount of detail they put into their plans. If there is a lot of detail, then some gaps and inconsistencies of thought may be ironed out at this stage. In any event, it is quite likely that the final text will not match the plan exactly.

Genre p. 120

The writing stage

This is also known as the **drafting** stage. Drafting is simply the process of getting ideas down onto paper (or screen) and as we have already seen, involves two sets of skills:

▶ **compositional skills**: basically a matter of choosing the right words and putting them in the right order in order to express the intended ideas;

▶ **transcriptional skills**: the skills involved in translating the words and sentences in the writer's head into marks on the page. Transcriptional skills include handwriting, spelling and punctuation.

As a draft progresses the writer may elaborate or modify the original plan as the developing text clarifies thought and suggests other ways of arranging the material. Sometimes even the original intention changes; for example, in writing a discussion the writer realises that the opportunity for reflection afforded by the writing process has changed their mind about the virtues of the conflicting viewpoints.

Discussion pp. 134–135

In any event, the value of the **first draft** is paramount; it is the clay from which the *final draft* is fashioned.

The rewriting stage

Experienced writers tend not to spend too much time on an initial draft; they know that the real work goes into modifying and developing their text through successive **draft stages**. Writers working on manuscripts and typescripts usually mark **additions**, **deletions** and **translations** (movement of blocks of text) onto their scripts until the point comes where the original script becomes difficult to read fluently. Then they write or type a fresh draft, incorporating all the stages before making further changes. All these activities are known collectively as **redrafting** and there is no limit to the number of draft stages a text may go through. Word processing means that the process of redrafting is now very much easier than it was only a few years ago.

As soon as a draft is complete the writer can begin to **revise** it. In revising a text the writer must ask a number of questions:

▶ Does the draft make sense?

▶ Does it say what I wanted it to?

▶ Is the text properly structured?

▶ Does it always obey the rules and conventions of Standard English?

Standard English pp. 12–18

When revising it is essential to take into account the needs of the audience. The writer must take account of those things which need to be made explicit to the reader and this is one reason why some writers choose to leave a draft and return to it fresh after a day or two.

At the revision stage, it is useful to make the distinction between **reviewing**, **editing** and **proofreading**.

- **Reviewing** can only be done by the author. It is the process of checking that the intended meaning has been conveyed and may involve the writer in making substantial changes.

- **Editing** can be done by somebody else (by the time you read it this book will have received attention from an editor) and involves revising the text in order to ensure that overall and at sentence level it obeys the conventions of English and makes sense. Editors also check for consistency of both style and content.

- **Proofreading** is a term which originates in printing. A **proof** is a sample page, printed for the purpose of checking quality. Proofreaders concentrate on finding errors at the lowest level, such as in spelling and punctuation.

Except where they are carried out by different people, the separation of these processes is somewhat artificial and the dividing lines somewhat arbitrarily drawn. The National Curriculum, for example, speaks only of *revising* (making changes and improvements) and *proofreading* (checking for errors of spelling, punctuation, repetition or omission). The National Curriculum also treats **presentation** ('the preparation of a neat, correct and clear final copy') as a separate stage and considers ensuing **discussion and evaluation** to be part of the writing process.

A dynamic process

Writing is a **dynamic** process. It has been convenient in this section to consider writing as something done in discrete stages, but a moment's reflection tells us that this is far from the truth. We revise as soon as we've written our first few lines. We proofread as we go. The original plan may be returned to and modified, in some cases many times over. In a way the procedure outlined here (plan, draft, revise etc.) is best thought of as a guide or discipline for the writer. There's nothing to stop them undertaking any aspects of revision at any time and, of course, revision implies the need occasionally to change the plan or do more drafting.

Because writing is a dynamic process for arranging the raw material of our thoughts, it is more than likely that our thoughts will change in the process. The essay is a traditional tool of education because it forces the writer to marshal arguments, back them up with evidence and thereby confront any gaps or inconsistencies in their thought. At a simpler level, people find that note-taking helps them remember facts and that rewriting their notes in a better-organised fashion is even more effective. Any kind of writing has the power to extend and clarify thought; it is a means of understanding and of learning.

Handwriting

Maybe the children you interviewed for Activity 7.11 thought that writing meant the act of putting conventional and legible marks onto a page. As adults we usually consider handwriting to be an activity distinct from (though often essential to) the main business of composing texts. Whereas the aspects of writing we have considered so far can be seen as *linguistic* activity, handwriting is predominantly a *motor* activity in the same way as tongue and lip movements in speech are. Learning to write involves learning to make fine movements of the fingers, hand and arm consistently and easily. The pinnacle of handwriting skill, **calligraphy**, can be done without reference to language at all; not everyone who produces a (visually) beautiful Latin text understands every word of it.

The letters can be analysed into certain basic shapes such as **ascenders** (strokes going up above the main body of a letter) and **descenders** (strokes going down). We learn to form letters conventionally, first when **printing** (writing letters separately) and then in **cursive** (joined) **script**. Conventional formation is an aid both to producing letters of good appearance and to achieving the most efficient movements across the page.

When producing a text for an audience we need to present it in a form which is easily legible. When we need to impress, well-formed letters of consistent size and inclination can make a difference; we are judged on our handwriting in much the same way as we are judged by the way in which we speak. Readers commonly conclude that the untidy of hand are untidy of thought. The science of graphology purports to link handwriting styles to personality types.

When writing for ourselves (e.g. in lecture notes), we don't need to impress but we do need to be legible. We also need to write quickly, so a balance needs to be struck between these two conflicting demands. Like many other aspects of writing, the style of handwriting we adopt needs to meet the purpose of the text.

In this section we have seen that:

- The process of writing can be seen as one of **pre-writing**, **writing** and **rewriting**.

- **Redrafting** enables writers to develop and clarify their thoughts to a high degree of refinement.

- Writing is a **dynamic process** where skills of planning, drafting, revision and proofreading are continually being applied.

- **Handwriting** is a motor skill which writers apply differently to suit different purposes.

Afterword

You probably feel you've come to the end of a long journey through the intricacies of the English language. It has involved you in a lot of work, but it will have been worthwhile if it has increased your willingness and capacity to get to grips with language and the ways in which it operates. There are bound to have been parts which you found challenging, but I hope there have also been parts (maybe even the same parts) which you found enjoyable. I hope you feel that your skill as a reader, writer, speaker, listener and above all teacher has developed as a result of your efforts.

There is a story of a centipede who was asked how it was that it managed to walk efficiently with so many legs. The sad ending is that not only could it not explain, but the act of trying left it unable to walk! There is a danger with books about language structure that readers will come away with the impression that analysis is all. They may be able to take a poem to pieces, but in pieces it is no longer a poem. As I said at the beginning, texts function as wholes notwithstanding the fact that they comprise a whole array of constituent parts; I hope you will not lose sight of that fact no matter how advanced your ability to analyse language becomes.

When you approach any text it is important to keep in mind your purpose as a reader. Is it to acquire information? Are you looking for a text to use in teaching about adjectives? Do you need to make a formal assessment of it for the purposes of the National Curriculum? Do you simply want to enjoy reading it? You should find that your newly acquired knowledge about language will help you, whatever your intention.

Assessing your knowledge

This final activity is an opportunity to check what you have learnt about how English is used at word, sentence and text level. Remember, the goal of this book is not to enable you to identify a set of nameable language features but to develop your ability to understand and explain (using necessary terminology) how a text has been constructed and how it works its effect on its audience. It is most important, therefore, that in answering you are satisfied that your response makes sense to you. Read the text carefully, answer the questions as fully as you can, and then check your answers on pages 202–204.

OLD WESTMINSTER – 1,000 Years of History

2:45 pm Westminster Underground exit 4 (Circle, District & Jubilee lines)

This is the cornerstone, the seminal London Walk. Miss it and you've missed London. For Old Westminster is London at its grandest: the place where kings and queens are crowned, where they lived, and often were buried. It's the forge of the national destiny, the place where the heart of the Empire beat, the Mecca of politicians through the ages. The past here is cast in stone and we take it all in: ancient Westminster Hall, the Houses of Parliament, the Jewel Tower, and Westminster Abbey. And to see it with a great guide is to have that past suddenly rise to the surface … like seeing a photographic print come up in a darkroom. It doesn't get any better than this. And a bonus: we also go off the beaten track, exploring picturesque eighteeenth-century back streets that are almost equally rich in history – but without the tourists! We end at the Cabinet War Rooms, the fortified bunker that housed Winston Churchill's centre of operations during the war. You'll get a handsome discount on the price of admission if you want to visit the War Rooms.

Guided by Graham.

N.B. Never part with your money or set off with anyone until you're absolutely certain you're with Graham. He is a distinguished looking gentleman with a jolly face. He is clean shaven and has short, neatly trimmed hair. He will be holding up copies of this leaflet. Please note, Graham never ever starts the walk before 2:45 pm.

1. What genre does this text belong to? What structural evidence can you find?

2. Who is its intended audience? How do you know?

3. What evidence of bias can you find? Is it restricted to the writer's attitude to Graham and his walk or can you find other forms of bias?

4. What do you notice about the vocabulary choices the author makes?

5. What features of a different genre does the final paragraph display?

6. How are presentation and layout used to support the meaning of the text?

7. As a reader, what particular knowledge do you need in order to understand this text fully? What is this kind of knowledge called?

8. What pronouns has the author used? Can you explain why these were chosen? (And can you explain why I used a passive construction in the last sentence?)

9. How does the choice of adjectives and adverbs contribute to the writer's purposes?

10. What cohesive devices are used?

11. Find some examples of the way the writer uses literary or poetic devices? To what purpose are they put?

12. What speech-like features can you find in the text? Why do you think they are used?

13. Find examples of:

    (a) a simple sentence

    (b) a compound sentence

    (c) a complex sentence.

14. Find two punctuation marks which mark off sentences.

15. Name the different functions performed in the text by commas.

16. Name two different ways in which apostrophes are used in the text.

17. How many different kinds of noun can you find? List them and give an example for each.

18. Find two adjectives and two adverbs in the text.

19. Find one example each of an action verb in past, present and future tenses.

20. Find two passive constructions and explain why the writer has chosen to use them.

21. List any compound nouns you can find.

22. How many phonemes are there in the words:

    photographic

    Churchill's

    Mark the boundaries between them. Mark the primary stress on each word (and secondary stress if there is one). How is the second vowel in *photographic* pronounced?

23. Describe the morphemic structure of: *picturesque*; *crowned*; *queens*.

24. What is the word class of each of the following underlined words?

    off <u>the</u> <u>beaten</u> track;
    to have that <u>past</u> <u>suddenly</u> <u>rise</u> <u>to</u> the <u>surface</u>
    <u>*back*</u> *streets*

    Why is it necessary to the question to place these words in context?

25. List the auxiliary verbs in the text. Write each in its 'full' form.

26. For each of the following strings of words, say what grammatical unit it represents and give evidence for your decisions:

   the forge of the national destiny
   that housed Winston Churchill's centre of operations during the war
   without the tourists

27. How many syllables are in the word *politicians*? How many morphemes?

28. Mark the onset/rime boundary in these words:

   crowned
   this
   track

29. Describe the elements of the predicate in 'Old Westminster is London at its grandest'.

Bibliography

Carter, R. (1997) *Investigating English Discourse*, London and New York: Routledge.

Carter, R., Goddard, A., Reah, D., Sanger, K. and Bowring, M. (1997) *Working with Texts*, London and New York: Routledge.

Crystal, D. (1995) *The Cambridge Encyclopaedia of the English Language*, Cambridge: Cambridge University Press.

Department for Education and Employment (1998) *The National Literacy Strategy: Literacy Training pack*, London: HMSO.

Department for Education and Employment (1998) *The National Literacy Strategy: Framework for Teaching*, London: HMSO.

Department for Education and Employment (1999) *The National Literacy Strategy: Training Module 4: Phonics Y1*, London: HMSO.

Department for Education and Employment (1999) *The National Literacy Strategy: Training Module 5: Spelling Key Stage 2*, London: HMSO.

Department for Education and Employment (1999) *The National Curriculum Handbook for Primary Teachers in England Key Stages 1 and 2*, London: HMSO.

Department for Education and Employment (1999) *The National Curriculum: Handbook for Secondary Teaching in England Key Stages 3 and 4*, London: HMSO.

Dombey, H. and Moustafa, M. (1998) *Whole to Part Phonics: How Children Learn to Read and Spell*, London: Centre for Language in Primary Education: Language Matters.

Graddol, D., Cheshire, J. and Swann, J. (1994) *Describing Language*, 2nd edn., Buckingham, Philadelphia: The Open University Press.

Graves, D. (1983) *Writing: Teachers and Children at Work*, Portsmouth, NH: Heinemann.

Halliday, M. A. K. (1975) *Learning How to Mean: Explorations in the Development of Language*, London: Arnold.

Halliday, M. A. K. (1985) *An Introduction to Functional Grammar*, London: Arnold.

Huddleston, R. (1984) *Introduction to the Grammar of English*, Cambridge: Cambridge University Press.

Leech, G., Deuchar, M. and Hoogenraad, R. (1982) *English Grammar for Today*, London: Macmillan.

Lewis, M. and Wray, D. (1995) *Developing Children's Non-Fiction Writing*, Leamington Spa: Scholastic.

Maybin, J. and Mercer, N. (1996) *Using English: From Conversation to Canon*, London and New York: The Open University and Routledge.

Miller, R. and Greenberg, R. (1981) *Poetry: an Introduction*, London: Macmillan.

Pope, R. (1998) *The English Studies Book*, London and New York: Routledge.

Quirk, R., Greenbaum, S., Leech, G. and Svartvik, J. (1971) *A Grammar of Contemporary English*, London: Longman.

Russell, S. (1993) *Grammar, Structure and Style*, Oxford: Oxford University Press.

Trew, A. A. (1979) Theory and ideology at work, in R. Fowler, R. Hodge, G. Kress and A. A. Trew (eds) *Language and Control*, London: Routledge and Kegan Paul.

Wells, J. C. and Colson, G. (1971) *Practical Phonetics*, London: Pitman.

Answers to activities

Suggested responses to activities with relatively 'closed' outcomes (signalled by the symbol ✔ in the text) are given here. In some cases the solutions given are the only possible correct ones (e.g. there is only one standard past participle of the word 'swim'). Often, however, there are several possible answers, in which case only one is given. If you find your answer does not match the one given, work back and decide whether your own is just as good. If you're not sure (or if you're sure you were wrong) then that's probably a sign that you need to go over a section again (or you might possibly talk it through with a friend). If you can see why the answer given here could be correct then your understanding is probably sound.

Word level activities

Activity 2.15

e.g. card-guard. ship-chip. cod-cog. lorry-lolly

Activity 2.20

re/strict. on/ly. mis/treat. west/ern. bow/er. wasp/ish. re/spond

Activity 2.21

impor*tant*	disapp*ear*	*green*house	*black*bird
*cup*board	erad*i*cate	*motor*way	car*ess*
exp*los*ion	Phila*del*phia	*col*our	ab*oard*

Activity 2.26

c/a/t (3). m/ou/se (3). owe (1). b/r/ea/k (4). w/i/n/d/ow (5). a/n/t/i/e/s/t/a/b/l/i/sh/m/e/n/t (16). s/t/o/r/y (5). a/che (2). u/n/d/er/s/t/a/n/d/i/ng (11). b/ough (2). eye (1)

Activity 2.33

Germanic	half. knight. dough
Greek	paralysis. pandemonium
Italian	legato. oregano. portico

French	grandeur, malaise, phrase
Indian	bungalow, verandah, chintz
Spanish	armadillo, llama
Latin	doubt (via French)

Activity 2.34

tele	far
phone	voice
trans/meta	across (sometimes with the meaning 'change')
phobia	fear
an	not
aem/haem	blood
aqua/hydr	water
micro	small
meter/metre	measure
hyper	above
graph	write/draw
form/morph	form/shape
logy	study (Greek 'word')
inter	between

Activity 2.36

act/ion	re/act/ion	green/house	separat/ion	friend/ly
in/human	writ/er	cucumber	fli/es	rain/ing

Activity 2.38

arm/chair	cork/screw	house/hunt	steam/roller
spoil/sport	job/share	lazy/bones	birth/day
let/down	follow/up	tailor/made	stand/in
away/day	get/away	cheque/book	eye/brow

Activity 2.39

un/tie	creates an antonym
fix/es	verb inflexion: third person singular, present tense
walk/ing	verb inflexion: present participle
nice/ly	changes adjective into adverb
be/little	changes adjective into verb

re/visit	adds meaning of 'again'	
book/let	diminutive: a 'small book'	
inter/lock	adds meaning of 'between'	
good/ness	changes adjective into noun	
art/ful	changes noun into adjective	
luck/y	changes noun into adjective	
pretti/fy	changes adjective into verb	

noun	adjective	verb	adverb
dirt	dirty	dirty	dirtily
beauty	beautiful	beautify	beautifully
stunner	stunning	stun	stunningly
argument	arguable	argue	arguably
ignition	igneous	ignite	
product	productive	produce	productively
vibration	vibrant	vibrate	vibrantly
happiness	happy		happily
thanks	thankful	thank	thankfully
communication	communicative	communicate	communicatively
reality	real	realise	really
testament	testate	testify	

Some other answers are possible, e.g. *stunned* (adj)

sing	I sang	I have sung
ring	I rang	I have rung
swim	I swam	I have swum
light	I lit	I have lit
hide	I hid	I have hidden
take	I took	I have taken
read	I read	I have read
slide	I slid	I have slid
wake	I woke	I have woken
break	I broke	I have broken
have	I had	I have had
strive	I strove	I have striven

Sentence level activities

My	*determiner/possessive pronoun* **Position**: at start of noun phrase
grundliest	*adjective* (*superlative*) **Position**: before noun, after determiner **Morphology**: '-est' superlative suffix
prudger	*noun* **Position**: after determiner + adjective **Morphology**: '-er' suffix
smelded	*verb* (*past tense*) **Position**: after initial NP **Morphology**: '-ed' inflexion
brendaciously	*adverb* **Morphology**: '-ly' suffix '-ious' adjectival suffix
by	*preposition* **Position**: before NP
the	*determiner* (*definite article*) **Position**: at start of NP
quadgers	*noun* (*plural*) **Position**: after determiner **Morphology**: '-er' suffix, '-s' inflexion
and	*conjunction* **Position**: between nouns
brudists	*noun* (*plural*) **Position**: linked to noun by conjunction **Morphology**: '-ist' suffix, '-s' inflexion

3. preposition, determiner, conjunction (pronoun); closed classes

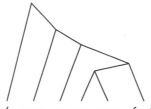

Harriet Awdry skated beautifully.

We were a very poor family.

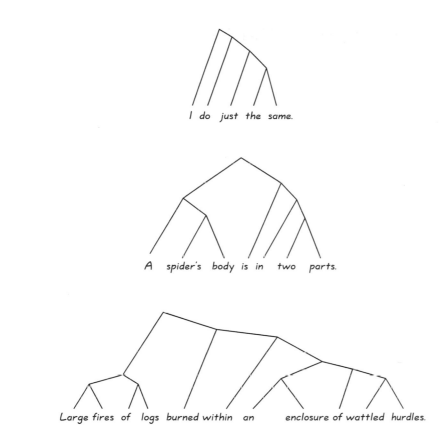

I do just the same.

A spider's body is in two parts.

Large fires of logs burned within an enclosure of wattled hurdles.

I /started to act at the age of three.

My mother/ rushed down the three flights of stairs.

The cue to begin my performance/ was a ring at the front door.

A spider's body/ is in two parts.

My kidnapper and aspiring confidant/ came back.

    VP

Rain _falls_.

       VP

Sunday _came and went_.

```
              VP        NP          NP
An elephant made a friendship with a man.

    VP NP    NP
He gave me some news.

                   VP          NP
The elephant went to his friend.

    VP           NP
We were a very poor family.

                 VP                    NP
My mother rushed down the three flights of stairs.

            VP     NP           NP              NP
The spider spins a thread from the centre to a hiding place nearby.

  VP    NP
I talk to myself.

                   VP
My opinions are stupid.

    VP          NP           VP        NP          NP
We drove into Chippenham and bought a pair of skates at Benk's.

    VP       NP          NP
He brought the prisoner a toothbrush.
```

Activity 3.13

without making a sound	silently, adverb
the old chauffeur	Henry, noun
was carefully parking	parked, verb
the dazzlingly polished vintage Cadillac	the car, noun
to the rear of	behind, preposition
Mrs Evans's colonial mansion	the house, noun

Many other substitute words are appropriate, provided they belong to the correct word class.

Activity 3.14

WWT is a wildlife charity.
WWT is unique in promoting wildfowl and wetland conservation.

The three [Indians] shot Tom.
The three [Indians] was hid by the side of the road in the bushes.

My mother wrote the lines.
I was to speak the lines.

From these glands comes a liquid.
The liquid turns to silk on contact with the air.

Then it makes a series of sticky spirals.
The spirals run from the centre outwards.

I talk more to myself than to others.
Talking to myself is to be recommended for two reasons.

My kidnapper seemed very excited.
My kidnapper told me about the advertisement.
He had seen the advertisement in the newspaper.

Activity 3.15

I take paracetamol. (present)

I am taking paracetamol. (present)

I will take paracetamol. (future)

I am going to take paracetamol. (future)

I took paracetamol. (past)

I have taken paracetamol. (past)

I have been taking paracetamol. (past)

I was taking paracetamol. (past)

I had taken paracetamol. (past)

I had been taking paracetamol. (past)

Activity 3.17

excited	past participle, adjective
to argue	infinitive, noun
arguing	present participle, noun
exciting	present participle, adjective
talking	present participle, noun
hidden	past participle, adjective
talking	present participle, adjective
unsolicited	past participle, adjective

Text level activities

Recount: diary, some magazine articles (e.g. personal stories), witness accounts, simple stories (fables, jokes, folk tales)

Report: encyclopaedia entries, articles in reference books, entries in guidebooks

Procedure: appliance instructions, assembly instructions, recipes, repair manuals, craft books

Explanation: articles in reference books (especially technological or referring to social institutions), 'how it works' articles, textbooks

Persuasion: all kinds of advertising, political leaflets etc., job applications, newspaper articles (especially editorials)

Discussion: essays, enquiry reports

Activity 5.4

/ ⌣ ⌣ ⌣ / ⌣ ⌣ ⌣ / / / /
Dirty British coaster with a salt-caked smoke stack.

/ ⌣ ⌣ ⌣ / ⌣ ⌣ ⌣ / / /
Butting through the Channel in the mad March days.

⌣ ⌣ / ⌣ ⌣ / /
With a cargo of Tyne coal,

/ / / /
Road-rail, pig-lead,

/ / /⌣ / ⌣ / / /
Firewood, iron-ware, and cheap tin trays.

Activity 5.5

⌣ / ⌣ / ⌣ / ⌣ / ⌣ /
But soft, what light through yonder window breaks?

⌣ / ⌣ / ⌣ / ⌣ / ⌣ /
It is the east and Juliet is the Sun.

simile:	*like a red, red rose; like the melody*
metaphor:	*The wind was a torrent of darkness; The moon was a ghostly galleon*
pun:	*he laid down his arms*
personification:	*the moon walks the night; she peers*
kenning:	*wind-slave; maker of worn wood etc.*

peace:	olive branch, dove
love:	heart
power:	lion, crown
death:	cross, gravestone, skull, bell

you've got to

you don't

you understand

you don't know

you understand them

you've got to get

you understand them dirty

you've got to get rid of

you don't know nothing

listen but listen

them

God-

damn

little yellow bas-

tards we're going

to civilise them

Assessing your knowledge

Answers to the final assessment activity

1. Persuasive writing. The main body of the text is structured as: opening statement followed by three main points, which are elaborated. There is no summary, however; readers are left to draw their own conclusion.

2. Visitors to London. We recognise the layout and distinctive style of a text for a leaflet or guidebook entry and also the references to famous landmarks.

3. Exaggerated positive descriptions of the walk (*seminal, cornerstone, great guide, it doesn't get any better than this etc.*). Similar descriptions of the locations using words with strongly positive connotations (e.g. *heart, forge*). Also implicit support for concepts of empire and monarchy.

4. References only to 'important ' people – politicians, kings and queens, Winston Churchill. Use of words with strong positive (and glorious/grandiose) associations, often used as metaphors (e.g. Mecca, heart, destiny, handsome).

5. It resembles procedural writing, beginning, as it does, with an imperative structure. It prescribes correct actions and provides supporting information.

6. We recognise the convention that a subheading indicating place and time signals that the text describes an organised event. Experienced readers will head straight for the main block of text, where they know the information which will inform their choice is located, and probably only skim the last paragraph.

7. Extralinguistic knowledge of London sights and place names, of the conventions of tourism and of tourist literature. It helps to know that London is the capital of Britain and that Britain was once at the centre of a vast empire. We also need to know about the Second World War and Churchill's role in it and that British history includes a long-lived monarchy and an established democracy.

8. Use of *we* implies the reader's participation. The audience is directly addressed as *you. It* is used comparatively rarely – note the repetition of *past* in preference to using a more mundane pronoun. My use of the passive is to avoid a third person pronoun (*he/she*) as I don't know the gender of the author.

9. Adverbs are hardly used, probably for the sake of economy – getting the message over in the minimum number of words. Adjectives are not numerous (probably for the same reason) and when used often add to the grandiose tone (*national, ancient, great, fortified*).

10. Connectives: *for, and* (*and* is used at the start of a sentence to emphasise the special qualities of a *great guide* and later to

emphasise the great number of interesting sights to see). Cohesive ties: use of the pronoun *it*, different noun phrases referring back to Westminster – *the forge of national destiny, the Mecca of politicians*.

11. Metaphor: *Mecca, heart*. Simile: *like seeing a photographic print*. Rhythm and repetition of structure (pattern): *Miss it and you've missed London; the forge of national destiny, the place where the heart of the empire beat, the Mecca of politicians through the ages* (each consists of a noun phrase followed by a supporting phrase or clause). Rhyme: *the past here is cast*.

12. *And a bonus... But without the tourists... You'll*. These are probably used to suggest familiarity with the audience and perhaps also that the whole text exemplifies Graham's rhetorical style. The use of 'never ever' to emphasise the change of topic and maybe assert the 'real world' nature of the problem of bogus guides.

13. (a) *It doesn't get any better than this.*

    (b) <u>*The past here is cast in stone*</u> and <u>*we take it all in*</u>. Two simple clauses joined by the conjunction *and*.

    (c) Almost all the sentences are complex, e.g. <u>*You'll get a handsome discount on the price of admission*</u> if you want to <u>*visit the*</u> War Rooms. Two simple clauses with the subordinate clause introduced by *if*.

14. Full stops, exclamation mark.

15. Marking off phrases (*This is the cornerstone, the seminal London walk*). Marking off clauses (*...,where they lived, and often were buried*). Separating items in a list (*Westminster Hall, the Houses of Parliament, the Jewel Tower...*).

16. Possession (*Churchill's bunker*). Contractions (*doesn't, you're*).

17. Common (*kings, queens*), proper (*Graham*), mass (*stone*), countable (*heart*), abstract (*destiny*), animate (*politicians*), inanimate (*streets*).

18. Adjectives: *seminal, better*. Adverbs: *suddenly, often*.

19. Past: *housed*. Present: *go*. Future: *(wi)ll get*.

20. *Kings and queens are crowned* (not important who crowns them – maybe the author doesn't know). *The past is cast in stone* (a metaphor emphasisng the 'stone-like' nature of the relics of the past, so nobody actually did any casting – something difficult to do with stone!).

21. *darkroom, cornerstone*.

22. [2]*ph/o/t/o*[1]*/g/r/a/ph/i/c* (10); <u>*Ch/ur*</u>/ch/i/ll/'s (6).

    The second vowel in *photographic* is usually pronounced [ə] (schwa).

23. *pictur(e)* noun, free morpheme

    esque derivational suffix changing a noun to an adjective, bound morpheme *crown* verb

ed past tense inflexion

queen noun

s plural inflexion

24. *the* determiner; *beaten* adjective/ past participle

    past noun; *suddenly* adverb; *rise* verb; *to* preposition; *surface* noun

    back adjective;

    Grammatical context determines word class – e.g. back could be an adverb (*She went back*) or a noun (*He scratched my back*).

25. *'ve/have, are, were, does(n't), 're/are*

26. *the forge of the national destiny*: Noun phrase – it begins with a determiner and its main focus is a noun (*forge*). The unit functions as a noun in the text and occupies the position after the verb 'is'; it therefore functions as complement.

    that housed Winston Churchill's centre of operations during the war: Relative clause – the place of the subject of the verb *housed* is taken by 'that', a relative pronoun.

    without the tourists: Adjectival phrase – supplies additional information about a NP (eighteenth-century back streets) (could be called a prepositional phrase because it begins with a preposition).

27. 4 syllables: *po/li/ti/cians*; 3 morphemes: *politic/ian/s*.

28. *cr/owned, th/is, tr/ack*.

29. *is*: simple verb (copula) present tense; *London*: proper noun; *at its grandest*: adjectival phrase; *London at its grandest* is a noun phrase.

Index